I0474896

About the Author

Dave Whitney, who has been nominated for the Pulitzer Prize three times, has spent seven decades studying the difference and similarities between the cultures and economies of Japan and the United States.

Beginning with Pearl Harbor Day followed by a tour with military intelligence in Japan in the 1950s, through an International Press Institute fellowship to study and tour in Japan in 1981, and following a tour of Japanese industry as leader of a Rotary International group in 1993, Dave Whitney has traced the evolution of modern relationships between two of the world's leading economies and most diverse cultures and takes a glimpse at what lies ahead following Japan's historically devastating 2011 earthquake and tsunami.

A lifelong journalist and essayist he is currently a contributing editor to *www.suddenlysenior.com*.

FOREWORD

Gaman (がまん) is a Japanese word that best describes the Nipponese people. It is defined as a combination of endurance, patience, perseverance, self-control, self-denial, and tolerance unique to the ethnocentricity of the Japanese.

When the great earthquake/tsunami hit Japan in the spring of 2011 I immediately contact a dear friend in Japan, first to see if he needed any assistance in recovering from the disaster and second to discuss how the Japanese would face the problems that had been thrust on them as a society.

We agreed the word *gaman* best described how the Japanese would eventually recover, just as they have recovered from the many disasters they have faced in the seventy years I have been immersed in watching this unique island nation develop.

My interest in the Japanese dates back to one of my first memories as a child – Pearl Harbor Day. After graduating from Missouri Military Academy and attending Westminster College in Fulton, Mo., where Winston Churchill made his famous "Iron Curtain" speech, I spent nearly three years in Japan as an intelligence analyst for the U.S. Army Security Agency.

My first ride, from the Port of Yokohama to the U.S. Army
Security Agency, Pacific, headquarters in Tokyo in 1956, took me
through parts of the Kanto Plain surrounding Japan's capital city that
were still barren from the devastation of World War II. Along the
route I also saw acres and acres of reconditioned U.S. Army vehicles
that had been turned over to the Japanese following the Korean War
in which they had served as our rear guard supplier for our troops
engaged on the Korean peninsular.

As a journalist I returned to Japan in 1981 on a fellowship from the International Press Institute to study the golden years in the growth of the Japanese economy, years in which the Japanese achieved unparalleled phenomenal economic growth into the world's second largest economy. From this visit I filed a group of stories for the Florida Times-Union in Jacksonville, Fla., where I served as Business & Economics Editor.

I returned to Japan in 1993 as a Group Study Exchange Leader for Rotary International and once again toured Japanese businesses and industries at a time when it was becoming evident that the much-touted "Bubble" was beginning to leak. From that experience I wrote a book – *The Ephemeral Bliss of the Free Fall* – examining the evolution of the Japanese culture and economy from my first exposure to it.

The Japanese economy did burst and the country has been treading economically for more than a decade at this writing. Being hit by one of the largest earthquakes and tsunamis ever recorded has added to the economic pains facing this nation.

Will the Japanese recover? Eventually because *gaman* will again prevail.

This book is a compilation of my writings over the years. It begins with my recollection of Pearl Harbor Day from my book

Growing Up Sunbury and contains the series of newspaper columns written in 1981 followed by the text of my book *The Ephemeral Bliss of the Free Fall* written in 1993. It concludes with a column written for *SuddenlySenior.com* shortly after the 2011 earthquake that points out one of the many complex problems the Japanese face in bringing their nation back together.

--Dave Whitney

A STOLEN CHILDHOOD

While we didn't really know it at the time World War II literally stole the childhood many of us would have otherwise had.

I was five years old when the Japanese attacked Pearl Harbor. I had no idea what a "Jap" was or where Pearl Harbor was located.

All I remember is that I had apparently been to Sunday school and had returned to my grandparents' house on Cherry Street in Sunbury. I was kneeling on an old couch for which my grandmother had hand-pearled a beautiful needlepoint design for the upholstery. I was looking out the front window watching Mid Perfect, a blind man who lived across the street, come out his front door and settle, with his cane guiding him, into his favorite rocking chair the bottom of which he had caned in his blindness, his primary means of making a living.

Mid Perfect was one of those wonders of my early childhood. Being blind he never turned on a light in his house. He made a living hand-caning chairs and other furniture and when someone would take me across the street and let me watch him, something I could do by the hour or until it became too dark to see what he was doing. Usually by that time someone had come to retrieve me. I never got into any trouble, which was a near impossibility for me at that age, when I was in Mr. Perfect's house. If I made even the slightest move from the stool or chair on which I sat watching him, he would start talking to me – often explaining just how he was doing the caning in front of him – and I was instantly entranced.

The sky was blue with puffy white clouds floating serenely across it on Dec. 7, 1941, and all I wanted to do was go outside and play.

My grandmother, Pearle Green Whitney (or Pearl Greene Whitney at times), came into the room daubing a tear from her eyes hidden beneath her pinch-nose spectacles.

"The Japanese have bombed Pearl Harbor," she said with a stutter from a mouth that never spoke an inappropriate word nor spoke other than the perfect King's English.

"Your Uncle Walt is stationed at Pearl Harbor!"

It was a most confusing situation for me. I wanted to go out and play. I could not sort out just who my Uncle Walt might be.

I was all of five years old, with a new stepmother, and a set of grandparents who had helped raise me after my mother died from staph infection contacted when she gave birth to me.

My young life, spotted only with vague random memories, was confusing enough without the addition of more relatives with whom I could not quickly relate.

Uncle Walt Bodenman was my real mother's – Ruth Marie Bodenman's – brother. He was a career sailor. He had been assigned to Pearl Harbor but, as it was learned a few days after the Japanese attack, had shipped out for the States just days before the Japanese struck.

While I must have known him it was difficult to recall just who Uncle Walt was at that point. The Bodenmans had come to the U.S. from Switzerland in 1914 aboard the Listutania a few trips before she was sunk helping catapult the U.S. into World War I.

The Bodenman family – headed by my grandfather John, or Johannes, passed through Ellis Island and headed for Kansas but on arrival found the Reform Church he was to have become minister of had disbanded. He placed his children with other Swiss familes and worked the wheat fields until he found a church in Saskatchewan, Canada, where he once again gathered his family back together and resumed preaching.

From Canada the Bodenmans immigrated to the U.S. a second time settling first in Menlo, S.D., and then eventually in Wischek, N.D., where Grandpa Bodenman lived out his life ministering to German Reform churches.

My dad, Hoyt Whitney, met my mother when she was a nurse in a Dakota hospital to which he had been taken after a truck accident. He married her and brought her back to Sunbury where they raised my brother, Jim, who was two years older than me until her death six weeks after I was born.

It took me many years to sort out the Bodenmans so it is no mystery that I was puzzled about Uncle Walt on Pearl Harbor Day compounded by a total lack of knowledge of anything Japanese.

The latter I would remedy over the years by serving three years in Japan in the 1950s in Military Intelligence, returning on a fellowship from the International Press Institute in 1982 to study the

Japanese economy and again in 1993 as a Group Study Exchange Leader for Rotary International and eventually publishing a book – *The Ephemeral Bliss of the Free Fall* – tracing my half century of observing the evolution of the relationship between Japan and the U.S.

But regardless of my lack of knowledge of the Japanese on Pearl Harbor Day and my more complete understanding of Nippon today, Dec. 7, 1941, was one of the major turning points in my life.

Up until that day I had lived a happy life under the protection of my grandparents, father and a relatively new stepmother, Laura Crawford.

It had not been many days since my father remarried and a strange, new lady came to my grandparents' house on Cherry Street, took me by the hand and walked me up the street to the corner, turned left and then walked several more blocks up Columbus Street until we stood in front of a big, two-story white house where she informed me, "This is our new home."

To this day I remember every crack in the sidewalk along Columbus Street, especially past the cemetery where I knew my real Mom, "Mother Ruth," rested in peace.

Eventually I learned to call Laura "Mom" but always held some reservation about her sudden appearance in my life, extracting me from the comfort of my grandmother and my grandparents' home and replacing a mother whom I had been told about but never recalled seeing, feeling or hearing.

Nonetheless we were living on Columbus Street on Dec. 7, 1941, and my parents had apparently taken me to Sunday School and then gone somewhere to visit friends and had my grandfather pick me up. That's the most logical reason I can recall that left me on his couch peering out the window at Mr. Perfect's house when my grandmother came in tearfully saying the Japanese had attacked Pearl Harbor.

The rest of that particular day is lost somewhere in memory but it triggered a style of living over the next few years that taught me to question everything, practice frugality, join in the team work of fighting a war, and how to live with a new family in a new home in a fashion to which I was totally unaccustomed.

The first thing I remember changing was the automobiles. My granddad's splendid old Packard disappeared and whatever my father had been driving was traded in on a 1941 apple green Plymouth two-door sedan. An "A" sticker appeared on the window that meant we were allocated something like five gallons of gas a week. Granddad, dad and others in the family used that one car for business for the duration of the war. Mostly we walked everywhere. There were no more long rides in the country until well after the war.

My father, who was 33 at the time, was too old for the draft but he insisted on enlisting in the Army. I remember whispered conversations between him and "Gramp" – the name I called my grandfather – that often got quite vigorous, especially after a few shots of whiskey around one or the other's kitchen table. I don't believe my grandfather was overjoyed with my father's enlistment but nonetheless Dad joined up and was assigned to the Military Police as a cook and ended up at Fort Custer outside Kellogg, Mich., where the MPs guarded a large Prisoner of War camp. The German prisoners worked in the many cereal factories in Kellogg displacing American men who were being called up for war.

Dad owned an insurance agency, appropriately named Whitney Insurance Agency, in Sunbury. I suppose much of my grandfather's concern over my father enlisting in the Army was about who would run the insurance business. My grandfather had been a partner in it at one time but politics had become his business prior to the war when he was elected to the Ohio House of Representatives and then to the Ohio Senate.

My stepmother, Laura, was a nurse and had been working in hospitals in Columbus before marrying my dad. She stepped up to the plate and took over the reins at the insurance agency and dad went off to war.

One of my earliest memories of adventure – my life has been a continuous series of adventures – was visiting my father at Fort Custer. It was memorable because it was my first train ride. We boarded the train in Columbus and rode to Detroit where we had to change trains for Kellogg.

I'm sure it was my stepmother who was with me but my mind keeps telling me it was my grandmother who was holding my hand as we walked from the platform where we detrained into the great marble hall of the Detroit station. I was simply awed by the magnitude and the beauty of all the marble and the rows upon rows of long wooden benches where other passengers waited for their trains.

At Fort Custer I can remember visiting Dad in the big mess hall where he worked and the German prisoners who wore big "PW" letters on the back of their shirts. They lived in wooden buildings, some so new they had only tar paper for an outer covering.

Back in Sunbury I found myself living in a household of people I didn't really know. Of course, I knew my brother, Jim, but recall only that we spent sparse hours together probably because there were many people in town who had stepped in to help raise us after our mother's death.

The principal occupants of our house on Columbus Street during much of the war were Laura, her mother Ethel McCurdy Crawford, Jim and I. "Grandma Crawford" as we called her was a mystery to me from the start. In my young mind I already had a grandmother and that was sufficient.

Besides that Grandma Crawford was so unlike my grandmother, whom we called "Gaga" (pronounced Gah-gee), that I could not reconcile the two of them in my mind. Gaga was the most proper of people, raised and educated by Episcopal nuns in Colorado, she was the epitome of propriety. She wore white gloves to Sunday dinner served on the best bone China and you did not dare pick up a piece of chicken. Everything was to be eaten with knife and fork and the knife and fork was to always be placed in the proper position.

My grandfather had false teeth and liked to drink his after dinner coffee out of his saucer after pouring some from out of his cup to cool. He called his false teeth his "China Clippers" and would run the top ones out of his tongue and make a face at us while he sipped coffee from his saucer. It made us laugh but it made Gaga cringe and snivel.

On the other hand, Grandma Crawford was all business. She washed dishes after every meal, baked bread on Tuesdays, did the laundry on Mondays, canned vegetables in season, cleaned house constantly, and read her Bible. She, and my mother, were members of the Church of Christ, a fundamental sect that did not allow musical instruments in its churches.

The Crawfords had come from Wingett Run, a town smaller than Sunbury, down in the southwest hill country of Ohio near

Marietta. The McCurdys had run the country store in Wingett Run and my dad, when he would get upset with Laura would accuse her of not having any shoes until she was 18. He always stopped short of calling her a "hillbilly" which was the usual nickname for those from the hills who had migrated north to the rolling country of Central Ohio.

Mostly I remember Grandma Crawford's wonderful homemade breads and her constant "Titch, titch, titch!"

I learned to live with all of it, but when they turned their back on me I was tempted to scoot out the door and run down the street to Gaga's house where they often found me enjoying one of her famous cherry pies or the special angel food cakes she work bake me.

The cherry pies predated the war. The cherries came from the big trees in Gramp's backyard. They were delicious big, red Bing cherries. My grandmother would make a delightful crust with lard and butter, pack it with her special blend of cherries and sugar, top it off with another piece of pie crust, bake it and then set it in the kitchen window to cool.

Before the war I remember men – apparently attracted by the smell of the homemade pies cooling in the windows – coming to the back door, knocking and then standing there hat in hand to ask my grandmother if she had any odd jobs they could do.

In many ways The Great Depression was still alive and well in Sunbury and my grandmother always found some odd job the men could perform before she sat them down on the back door stoop and served them a full home-cooked meal on a china plate with the proper silverware, a tall glass of ice tea laced with a leaf from her wintergreen plant near the door, and a cloth napkin. I never remember a single man who did not finish that big meal and earn a piece of Gaga's homemade cherry pie.

There was no way of telling at my age whether we were rich or poor during the war. We always ate well. We had gardens and raised chickens and rabbits to supplement our table fare.

I remember rationing. I had a ration book just as did everyone else in the family. With the coupons from it we could buy necessary food items from the local grocery store, usually Blakley's Red & White on the northeast corner of the town square.

On one trip to the store with a ration coupon to pick up something for Mom, I dallied along the way as was my style, and when I got to the store I could not find the coupon. I was terrified. I had visions of being tortured for having lost the coupon, as were some prisoners of the Japanese I had seen in a war poster. I found myself standing in front of the candy dish at the cash register in the store wondering what to do. I must have been trembling with fear because one of the grocers came over and asked me what was wrong.

I reluctantly told him Mom had sent me to the store for something but I could not find the coupon she had given me. He gave me a little lecture on the importance of not losing our coupons and then went and got the item Mom had wanted. With it he brought another package, neatly wrapped in the white paper they used to wrap meats.

"Here's a little extra liver I had. Give it to your mother," he said sending me on my way. Money was no object to me since they simply wrote down what you owed on a card kept in a box near the cash register and Mom, or Dad when he was home, would settle up with the grocery store at some future date.

Things like the "little extra liver," an occasional beef heart and other odd-and-end cuts of meat were kept for the store's steady customers and given out as favors apparently when someone needed a little cheering up for one reason or another.

The gardens were glorious affairs. They were where I first saw a seed put in the ground and later a plant sprout through the soil and still later bear fruit or vegetable. It is a process with which I am still fascinated – one that led to my love of the outdoors and the wonders of the natural world, a love that flourishes yet today.

One way or another I worked in gardens from the beginning of World War II until I left Sunbury for good a decade later. If it had not been for the vegetable gardens – called "Victory Gardens" – during the war many people would have gone hungry. Not in Sunbury, though.

I know we were patriotic before Pearl Harbor but I don't recall any talk about isolationism in those days most likely because I was too young to understand any of it.

But we did have parades on Memorial Day, the Fourth of July and Labor Day, which was accompanied by the town's annual Ox Roast. I can still taste that wonderful beef after they dug it out of the pit where it had cooked slowly for a day and a night.

I loved parades. It meant the whole town turned out around the square, bands played, veterans marched, and there was always more food than one could eat. One of my favorite pictures comes from a Sunbury calendar produced by the local historical society. On one page is a photo of a youth band being conducted by a woman on a stand sitting on the brick pavement of the street around the town square, the old Town Hall in the background.

And there I am, off to the far right, tooting away on a Kazoo in my little sailor's hat, short pants and high-top shoes. I'm the only one not in line, standing just a step further away than the rest and at a slight angle to the rank and file. If you've ever studied body language this photo is enough to convince you, and me, that I have probably been a little off-center most of my life.

It had to be taken on July 4, 1941, before the war started. My brother is standing next to me standing a good head taller approaching the ripe old age of 7 compared to my 4-3/4 years. I have no idea who shot that photo. It might have been my Uncle Bill Whitney who owned and published *The Sunbury News*.

The two largest recollections that I have of World War II are the scrap heaps and the newspaper routes.

The scrap heaps grew on the school grounds a block east of our house on Columbus Street so it was simple to visit them regularly. There were several heaps and bins. The heaps were divided by metal types – brass, aluminum and iron and steel. There were paper bins for newspapers, magazines and cardboard boxes and bins for old radios and appliances.

As they grew they became literal gold mines for a curious young boy of my ilk. I could spend hours climbing them and picking through the old pots and pans, brass bedposts, and old farm machinery. I could spend hours on my own trying to figure out how such things were made and how they worked. When possible, I would take them apart. It was like having a huge Erector Set in reverse. Rather than building something, I could spend forever taking it apart to see how it worked. I am sure my parents were relieved that I practiced my dismantling on the scrap heaps rather than on their house.

Every stray piece of metal or paper we found went to those scrap heaps. They were just one of the town's many ways of contributing to the war effort.

The fact the country was at war was brought home constantly in many ways. I can remember lying in my bed in the upstairs bedroom on Columbus Street and watching the Air Raid Warden in his World War I helmet with its Civil Defense emblem painted on the side. He would walk the street and when the occasional air raid siren would blow he would check the windows on the homes to make sure they were properly blacked out. Air Raid Wardens were those men from the town who were too old to be conscripted for the war.

Most of all I remember newspapers and newspaper routes during World War II. They were my first windows to the world.

Five years old is a bit young for one to have a newspaper route but my brother had gotten one and one of my best friends, Tom Lenhart, had gotten one. I think Jim had a *Columbus Dispatch* afternoon route and Tom had the *Morning Journal* route in town.

The *Columbus Citizen* was the other daily newspaper distributed in town and it had the least subscribers.

Somehow I ended up with the *Citizen* route. Tom and Jim had bikes and delivered their more numerous papers by rolling them up, riding down the street and throwing them hopefully on their subscriber's front porches. I walked the *Citizen* route, big canvas paper bag over my shoulder, and put each of my subscriber's newspapers neatly inside their front screen door with the exception of Mrs. Schnediker's. Mrs. Schnediker was an invalid who lived alone in a house out East Cherry Street. She asked me to just come in her back door every day and hand her the paper as she sat in her chair looking out her window down the hill towards the town's football field and playground.

If her helper had been there that day before I arrived, there would be a plate of cookies and a glass of iced tea and sometimes milk for me. I relished those days, especially after walking a couple of miles making my newspaper deliveries.

But often I dallied too long there and customers on out my paper route would be irritated because they got the papers late not to mention Mom who would be upset because I failed to make it home before dark on short winter evenings. When Dad was home he sometimes would come looking for me in the car and I would get a good dressing down for my having wandered a bit off track on my route.

I've always had that problem. When I see something that grabs my interest I am prone to stop and explore it. My wife, Marie Taylor-Whitney tells people to this day, "David cannot go anywhere in a straight line!"\

I'm afraid it's true.

Back in the 1940s the *Columbus Dispatch* had the only Sunday newspaper and it came in two or three sections thrown off the truck from Columbus in front of Main's Drug Store on the Sunbury town square. I would help my brother with that one, stuffing the sections together and loading his bike for his runs. I think he paid me a few pennies of his collections each week for the help.

I learned early on that newspapering was all about collecting the money. Whether I collected for everyone's subscription each week or not, I was expected to turn in the proper amount for each paper the truck had dropped for me or have a newspaper with the front page banner torn off to turn in for a no-charge.

My main goal was saving for a bike of my own.

I saved money I made on my newspaper route and did errands for anyone who would pay me a penny. Especially I remember mowing yards. There was a shortage of men in town during the war and what seemed like an abundance of yards.

Of course gasoline mowers were out of the question with rationing being as it were. Push mowers were the thing and the ladies whose lawns I mowed always waited to ask me to mow until the last minute as the grass got taller and taller, stretching every quarter they paid me as far as it would go.

Saving for the bike was important but paying for the war was equally so. As soon as I entered the first grade I began plunking down my nickel or dime a week for Savings Stamps that would be pasted in a book until a total of $18.75 was reached. The book was then turned in for a $25 War, or Victory, Bond as it was called at various times during the world conflict.

It took me what seemed forever to save up $15 with which I was determined to buy a bike. Bikes, like everything else during the war, were scarce.

I remember Dad was around at the time and I don't know if he was home on leave from Michigan or if it was after he was medically discharged for having taken a fall on maneuvers and damaging his neck and spine just before his outfit was due to ship out for Europe. Nonetheless he shopped around for a bike for me and found one up in Condit, a small settlement a few miles east of Sunbury.

Riding in the old, green Plymouth up to Condit with him had to be one of the longest rides I have ever taken. I was so anxious to get that bike I could not sit still.

When we arrived at the man's house he met us and took us out to his shed where the bike was stored. He went in to get it and rolled it out the door. My heart sank. It was a girl's bike!

I had dreams of a shiny, newer Flyer and all he could produce was a beat-up girl's bike.

It took some convincing on Dad's part to get me to cough over my $15 for a girl's bike. He won mainly on the point that we had been looking for a bike for some time and this was the first one we found available. After all, there was a war going on.

I sulked all the way back to Sunbury hoping that by some miracle that old, blue girl's bike in the truck of the Plymouth would be transformed to a handsome boy's Flyer by the time we got home.

It was not to be. I was stuck with that girl's bike and all the ribbing that came with it from the rest of the guys until well after the war ended. It carried a lot of newspapers and gave me enough spare time on my route to read every column Ernie Pyle wrote. They were published only in the Scripps-Howard newspaper that I carried.

I must have started reading at a fairly young age because I was only an 8 going on a 9-year-old at war's end. I remember delivering the "Extra" editions when the atomic bombs were dropped on Japan and finally the "VJ-Day Extra" in August 1945. By then my girl's bike was brightly decorated with small American flags and I could shout "Extra" with the best of them. I peddled from one end of Sunbury to the other with the VJ-Day extra excited that the war was finally over.

Shortly before VJ-Day an event - almost of A-Bomb magnitude - occurred at our house on Columbus Street. On July 17, 1945, my sister Brenda Jane Whitney arrived just one day after the Trinity Test of the world's first atomic bomb. She was the first member of our family to have been born in the Atomic Age. Dad nicknamed her "Pookey."

My grandmother, Gaga, was a member of The Progress Club and a Worthy Matron of the Eastern Star. Along with my Aunt Marion they conspired to build a library for Sunbury and got the job done with the aid of a friend, Dillie Burrer. Gaga took me to Story Hour one or two afternoons a week and by the time I got to the first grade in Sunbury Elementary School "Run, Dick, Run" was a piece of cake.

It was that early reading exposure that made a life-long book worm out of me and enabled me to read all of those Ernie Pyle columns. I was such a Pyle fan that when I was stationed on Okinawa in the 1950s I had the opportunity to travel to Ie Shima where he was killed and visit the memorial to him. I wrote a small historical booklet for the American Legion Post on Okinawa on Pyle and on the 25th anniversary of his death, when I was a writer/photographer for The Associated Press wrote a recollection of his life and his work, complete with photos I had taken of the Ie Shima memorial, for the wire service. In 1982, after delivering a lecture at the East-West Institute in Hawaii on my return from Japan I had the opportunity to visit Pyle's grave in the Punch Bowl Cemetery in Hawaii. Ernie Pyle's writing was the compelling force in my choosing writing, and especially essay writing, as the basis of a lifetime career.

The war honed my reading skills but also taught me some of the great sadnesses of life. I remember one street on my paper route in Sunbury where a beautiful young woman lived whose equally young husband was killed in the war.

For some reason I did not know how to react to that so I always rode my bike on the other side of the street when I passed her house. I always felt she was somehow tainted by the loss of her husband.

And then there was Charles Reese who came home with one arm missing the result of crashing a plane he was piloting on the deck of an aircraft carrier in the Pacific. I was always fascinated by how he could swing a golf club, mow his yard and do other things with only one arm.

Next door to us in the house on Columbus Street lived Lloyd Brake and his family that included a daughter name Jane who had married a young Navy pilot – a "Flying Chief" – named Neil Pruden. I was always aware of the anxiety the war thrust upon that family as they followed the war through the Pacific where Neil was flying combat. He came home unscratched and made a career of the Navy.

And then there was my Uncle Bill McKinney, married to Laura's younger sister Betty. Bill flew Lockheed P-38 Lightnings over Germany. He flew cover for early morning photo missions taking off in the dark from a base in Italy so his squadron could arrive over Germany at daybreak. When the war in Germany ended, Bill was brought back to the States and was retraining in the new Northrop P-61 Black Widow, America's first night fighter and one of the most sophisticated planes of its day. Bill was slated for the Pacific War when Japan surrendered.

I can remember throughout the war of visits by Aunt Betty, less than a handful of years out of high school, to our house where Grandma "Titch, titch, titch"ed and Mom "Well, I just don't know"ed as Betty talked on nervously in her high-pitched voice, always concerned about Bill's absence.

The exploits of Neil and Bill, with some reservations about how Chuck Reese lost his arm, germinated in me the desire to fly airplanes.

One afternoon I was lounging on an old slide in our backyard engrossed in a book from the library called Eight Hours to Solo when Mom walked by. She wanted to know what I was reading and I showed her the book about flying Piper Cubs.

"You're never going to do that! I won't stand for it!" She admonished me. So I postponed it for a dozen years before qualifying for my Private Pilot's License and hopping around from news story to news story in single-engine aircraft.

While I was only five years old when the Japanese bombed Pearl Harbor, and definitely an innocent young boy, I was not yet ten years old when the war ended and felt like a young man. I had learned something about business, sacrifice, love and hate.

I still remember the posters on the wall of the farm store on the northwest corner of Cherry and Columbus streets in Sunbury.

"Loose Lips Sink Ships" was one.

Another encouraged us to "Buy War Bonds."

Another, the message of which I have long forgotten, showed large swastikas overshadowing the continental U.S.

And there was a little ditty we all sang as we went about our war work:

"Whistle while you work.

Hitler is a jerk.

Mussolini is a meany.

And the Japs are worse!"

I would spend a good portion of my life trying to unravel that one.

Florida Times-Union, Sept. 29, 1981

RETURNING VISITORS TO NEW TOKYO SHOULD BE READY FOR CULTURE SHOCK

TOKYO, Japan - This is a column for people over 40 - those people who visited Tokyo dressed in olive drab, in Navy and Air Force blue, the people sent to the city as members of the U.S. armed forces during the occupation of Japan after World War II and during the Korean conflict.

A word of caution before you read any further: Be ready for some cultural shock. They have rebuilt this burg. It's more like an American city today than the Oriental communities you remember.

With the exception of the signs, written in Japanese characters, you wouldn't be able to tell this city from London or Los Angeles. Even many of the Japanese signs are slowly being replaced with ones written in English, or with dual Japanese-English signs.

It's easier than ever to get around on subways and trains with the dual-language signs. Many of the people speak English to give you good directions when you need help.

Forget about taxicabs, though. They still jam the city streets, but the 70-yen cab is gone. Minimum charge today is 430 yen, and the Japanese have learned how to build a time element into their cab meters. When you get stuck in traffic, which is the case most of the time, the meter keeps ticking. You can pay an arm and a leg to cab it across town today.

The money will confuse you, also. It is no longer pegged to a constant exchange rate with the dollar. The old 360-yen-to-the-dollar rate is gone. Just this week, the rate fluctuated from 227 to 234 yen to the dollar. And, the yen doesn't buy as much even though the stores are stuffed with goods today.

That big bottle of Kirin Beer you used to get for 100 yen is now 400 to 600 yen, depending on the bar you stop in. If you stop where there is a little conversation, it can cost you as much as 1,500 yen. A bowl of soba, that great old noodle soup with the king-sized vegetable slices in it that used to sell for 20 yen in the shops along the street will now cost you 600 yen.

Don't expect any breaks on cameras and electronics. With the exception of a couple of discount, tax-free stores in Shinjuku that specialize in selling to tourists, there is generally no break in prices over what the same goods will sell for in the U.S. Even at the discount shops, the most you can save is 10 to 15 percent.

Shinjuku is a good example of what has happened to Tokyo in the past 25 years. It now has skyscrapers 50 stories high. The city is no longer a city of two-story wooden buildings. It is concrete and steel reaching for the sky. The construction goes on day and night. The old bamboo scaffolding used in building has been replaced by steel and machinery.

The streets have been rebuilt, and all sewage has gone underground. In fact, the individual shopkeepers from the Ginza to Yokohama scrub the sidewalks in front of their shops every morning. The city is unusually clean for those of us who remember the days when you had to step over the rubble and raw sewage here.

Even the air is clean. No longer do people cook and eat with their little charcoal fires. The 8.5 million people of Tokyo proper now can walk the streets without their face masks. The government has spent billions enforcing clean-air regulations, and they have worked.

Shimbashi Alley still exists for those of you who remember the R & R days from Korea, but the Ko Sisters have disappeared, or at best have gone underground. Shimbashi is now a relatively high-priced shopping district, not far from the skyscrapers that house the bureaucracy of national government, and the Japanese Diet.

If you came to Tokyo today for a night out, or a little R & R from the front, you wouldn't know the place. The people, including those girls in kimonos who used to charm the GIs out of their paychecks, now dress completely Western. It's a shock to see an urban cowboy in the midst of Tokyo Station, or a Brooks Brothers suit at the baseball game. Calvin Klein designer jeans have sent the kimono packing in modern Japan.

For your money, you would do just as well to take that night out on the town in Atlanta, New York, Seattle or St. Louis.

With the exception of the signs, you could hardly tell the difference today.

JAPANESE MILITARY APPEARS
READY TO DEFEND OWN ISLANDS

YOKOSUKA, Japan - The first thing that hits your eye when you come aboard the joint U.S.-Japanese naval base in Yokosuka is the large contingent of ships flying the flag of the Rising Sun.

According to figures obtained from the U.S. Seventh Fleet Command in Yokosuka and the Japanese Maritime Self-Defense Force, the Japanese now have more destroyers and submarines assigned to Yokosuka than do the Americans.

Twenty-five years ago when I served with military intelligence in this area, the Japanese had just been given the green light to begin rebuilding their military, which was struck from existence after World War II.

The Korean War brought about the beginning of what is now ranked as the seventh-largest military power in the world. U.S. commitments in Korea siphoned occupation troops from the Japanese mainland, requiring help in defending any possible assaults on this island nation. That help came in the form of a 75,000-man national police force.

However, the Japanese were not ready to get back into the military business after their World War II experience, and the constitution under which they now operate was drawn up with a specific prohibition against the establishment of an aggressive military. The constitution restricts military spending to less than 1 percent of Japan's annual gross national product.

With the exception of the early years of establishing the Ground, Air and Maritime Self-Defense Forces, when military expenditures ranged from 1.78 percent in 1955 to under 1 percent of GNP in 1967, the Japanese have met this constitutional provision - on paper at least.

By comparison, Russia spends about 12 percent of her GNP annually on defense. The U.S. spends 6 percent, China and West Germany about 3.5 percent of GNP each.

At a 0.9 of 1 percent GNP ratio in 1980 - the Japanese

military ranks as the seventh-largest in the world. However, it takes a little creative accounting to keep these figures below the 1 percent of GNP ceiling. For instance, one student of the Japanese military told me that if only the retirement benefits paid recent military retirees were added to the published national military budget, the Japanese military would be the fifth-largest in the world.

To push this same military machine up to fourth place - behind the Soviet Union, the United States and China - you do not need to add a single ship or person. The same military expert told me all you would have to do would be to add the money spent on pensions paid to Japanese veterans of World War II.

It is really juggling figures that makes the Japanese Self-Defense Forces look small. As they are now - 43,000 active navy, 46,000 air force and 160,000 army personnel - the Japanese military appears to be in good position to assume much of the defense of its own islands, relying on the U.S. military for support, and for protection against global interference.

The Japanese Maritime Self-Defense Force based at Yokosuka has 48 destroyers and 14 submarines, compared with the 18 to 20 U.S. destroyers and two frigates, and the 11 submarines of the Seventh Fleet. The United States also has three aircraft carriers and three to four cruisers assigned to the fleet, plus numerous support vessels.

A roster of Japanese bases in Japan reads like a muster of U.S. bases a quarter of a century ago - Fuchu, Sendai, Misawa, Sapporo, Hamamatsu, Kure, Fukuoka, Sasebo, Kadena and Naha.

There is a much larger Japanese military establishment than one expects and it is equipped with some of the world's most modern equipment. The Japanese Self-Defense Forces, while barred by agreement with the United States from operating any guided missiles or long-range bombers, are being rebuilt into one of the most efficient military machines in the world.

Now, their operational ability depends upon the presence and assistance of the U.S. military, but if forced into it by U.S. demands elsewhere, the Japanese could - with access to U.S. ammunition supplies and U.S. aircraft build in Japan under license from U.S. companies - mount its own substantial military defense.

Florida Times-Union Sept. 23, 1981

JAPANESE DEPEND ON U.S. MARKETS

TOKYO, Japan - The American ambassador to Japan, Michael J. Mansfield of Montana is an incurable romantic.

During an interview with the former U.S. Senate majority leader at the U.S. Embassy in Tokyo this week, he said, "In my opinion, this is where it all is, this is where it lies, this is where the future is. The Japan-U.S. relationship comprises the most important bilateral relationship in the world. The future of the Pacific depends upon this relationship."

The Japanese, in general, love Mansfield. His talent as a legislator is only surpassed by his talent as a diplomat. Since being assigned to Japan by President Carter in 1977, Mansfield has fallen as much in love with Japan as the Japanese with him.

Mansfield is difficult to interview. He has succumbed somewhat to the mystic impression many have of the Orient - an impression that makes for good conversation, but that masks the fact that Japan and other nations in Asia are made up of people who share the same human problems and emotions as those in the Western world.

Rather than get to the heart of a discussion on the economic problems of Japan, I found Mansfield more likely to drift off into a conversation extolling the virtue of Japanese devotion to decision by consensus, or a dissertation on the historical value of the Japan-U.S. relationship.

Mansfield is a master at saying the things the Japanese want to hear. He has bought into their custom of extreme courtesy, and belittles the American press for not reporting more about the Japanese, which he says is a major fault.

"We need to try and understand the Japanese culture," Mansfield said. It is a constant statement you hear publicly from both American diplomatic and business executives in Japan, and the Japanese officials.

But, despite efforts to promote a heady picture of Japanese progress since the devastation of World War II, there is much to cast a shadow of doubt on Mansfield's elation.

The Japanese number 117 million, about half the population of the United States. They live in an area the size of California. They have virtually no natural resources. They must import nearly everything they use, including a sizable portion of the food they eat.

As one Japanese diplomat told me, "Our only natural resources are people and water."

To survive, the nation of Japan must import raw materials and manufacture products it can sell in the world markets. Right now, the United States is its major marketplace, absorbing about a quarter of Japan's total output of manufactured goods.

The Japanese economy is so dependent upon its U.S. markets that any slowdown in the American economy has a spill-over effect on the Japanese, yet Mansfield attempts to gloss over the issue.

Mansfield, reappointed ambassador to Japan by President Reagan, praises Reagan's economy austerity programs.

"I think Reagan has played it just right," he said.

However, high interest rates in the United State - almost three times Japanese rates - are being felt in Japan and will undoubtedly attract money from Japanese markets to the United States at a time when Japan is accumulating larger than anticipated national budget deficits by government borrowing.

During the oil crisis of 1973, Japan's dependence on foreign oil forced prices here up nearly 25 percent. Inflation caused both cutbacks in production and sales losses in foreign markets.

In order to avoid domestic economic disaster, the Japanese government launched a massive public works program, financed by deficit spending. The programs have become a burden on the Japanese economy.

Japan's budget deficit is four times larger than the deficit in the United States, which has become a major national economic concern for Americans. Last year, the Japanese deficit equaled 33 percent of the total national budget. This year it is expected to reach just over 26 percent of the total Japanese budget. It has been financed by the sale of government bonds to Japanese banks, but one Japanese government official told me the last sale of government bonds had to be privately placed.

The banks have all the government securities they can handle at present, unless the central bank of Japan increases their reserve requirements, making it mandatory for the banks to hold more of their reserves in government bonds. This would further deplete the money available for capital expansion.

An English economics writer based in Japan said that no one, including Mansfield, wants to openly tackle this pending problem of financial deficits, a problem that could be embarrassing for the Japan-U.S. relations.

He viewed it in the light of the old American shell game: "You can hide the problem here and there for a while, but sooner or later it is going to burst loose."

Florida Times-Union, Sept. 27, 1981

IN JAPAN, EVERYBODY GETS
IN ON ACT OF DECISION

TOKYO, Japan - The score was 2-0 in the bottom of the eighth with one runner on second when former New York Yankee star Roy White stepped to the plat and hit a double to right field driving home the two runs that iced the game 4-0 for the Yomiuri Giants and handed Suguru Egawa his 20th win of the season.

The 40,000-plus fans in Tokyo's Korakuen Stadium were ecstatic over their team's defeat of the Taiyo Whales. The Giants were on their way to an almost certain 31st Central League Championship and the All-Japan title in the playoffs with the Pacific League champions later this month.

It was baseball Japanese style, and a better view for an American of the modern Japanese culture than all the recent fuss over movies of the ancient Samurai.

In fact, to believe that Japan today is anything like the movie Shogun is to believe that the United States is a model of Gone With the Wind.

The modern Japanese who packed Korakuen Stadium for baseball games enjoy all the amenities of any American ballpark, including an improved form of video playback on a gigantic outfield television screen, not yet available in American ball parks. They cheer in a mixture of Japanese and English, and many of their words for baseball are taken directly from the American language.

Like American baseball fans, the Japanese love home runs. They worship home-run hitters. Their biggest player of all time is Yomiuri Giant Sadaharu Oh who smashed a career total of 868 homers - besting both Babe Ruth's and Hank Aaron's home-run records in U.S. baseball. Oh stepped away from the plate last year and is now assistant manager of the Giants.

In a half-hour visit with the group of nine traveling fellows of the International Press Institute, Oh told us the closely called, American-style baseball would never be possible in Japan.

"We have our fans to consider," he said through an

interpreter, a comment that goes a long way in explaining another dimension of the modern Japanese culture - best described as collectivism as opposed to the rugged individualism espoused in modern American society.

If anything is more confusing to the American trying to negotiate a trade agreement or a five-course dinner with the Japanese, it is this apparent lack of indecisiveness encountered when trying to deal with an individual in Japan. Quick decisions are made only by baseball umpires here.

An Englishman who hangs out in the gathering spot for ex-patriots from English-speaking nations in the old neighborhood near where Gen. Douglas MacArthur had his headquarters, offers a great description of this confusing aspect of Japanese culture:

"The Japanese invented plastic 2,000 years ago - the plastic smile, and the plastic bow. They never wear out. If you ask a Japanese to do something for you, to study a plan and build something for you, they will get a group together and bow and smile and scratch their heads for a couple of days before they get around to doing anything about whatever it is you have asked them to do for you. It can drive an outsider berserk."

The gentleman is correct. If you have not been exposed to Japanese culture - ancient or modern - you are in for a surprise. Decision by consensus is the way of life. Everyone who can be brought in gets in on the act. It is the single-most important element of Japanese culture that the American businessman who hopes to do business here must learn. It requires patience and understanding if you want to close a deal on relatively comfortable terms with the Japanese.

Not understanding this aspect of the Japanese culture can mean the loss of trade, or at best unnecessary costs. The Japanese are "courteous but not polite," a Japanese diplomat told me at dinner one night. They have learned to use this peculiar aspect of collectivism to their negotiating advantage, and more than one American has fallen victim to it.

So, if you're headed for Japan to do a little business, just remember the baseball diamond is the only place you are going to see any quick decisions. Have a hot dog and enjoy it. You'll feel right at home.

Florida Times-Union, Sept. 20, 1981

JIMMY CARTER'S VISIT TO JAPAN UPLIFTS THE FACELESS CLASS

TOKYO, Japan - It's ironic I had to travel halfway around the world to see a former president who practically lives in my back yard, but that's what I thought when Jimmy Carter came to town.

By coincidence, it was Labor Day. The Japanese do not celebrate our traditional Labor Day; they go to work. Jimmy Carter was working, too.

It was difficult to tell the difference between the Jimmy Carter of the Orient and the Jimmy "Who" who stumped across Iowa in 1976 on his way to victory in the Iowa caucuses and eventually in the presidential election.

At a press conference for both Eastern and Western journalists at the Nippon Press Center in Tokyo, Carter turned in a performance - orchestrated by the ever-present Jody Powell, his presidential press secretary - equal to the occasion. I am sure it was a treat for those journalists from the Far East who are not bombarded daily with reams of babble from the White House.

In the typical Japanese tradition, both questions from journalists and non-answers from Carter dripped with courtesy. If anyone said a harsh word during this conference, it was removed by the interpreter.

It was almost as if Carter were running for office again - as well he might be. But being in Japan when he could have been making hay at a Labor Day parade in the United States doesn't do much to confirm that suspicion.

I learned later in a conversation with Dr. Masuru Ogawa, retired editor-in-chief of the English language *The Japan Times* daily newspaper, that courtesy is the style in Oriental journalism.

American businessmen and politicians - who are always complaining about the American reporting techniques of investigating and questioning - would love Japanese journalists.

Dr. Ogawa said the style in Japan is to ask a question and accept the answer. In other words, the Eastern journalist doesn't drive the questions home until he gets to the heart of the issue.

Instead, he often settles for a cursory explanation. It is highly unlikely the Japanese press will ever produce anything like Watergate.

Carter apparently loved the style of the Japanese press conference.

He alternated between his trademark smile and a stern look in keeping with the Oriental seriousness of the occasion. And, he was not required to answer any tough questions.

At one point, he even commented that he did not detect a question in the Japanese journalist's statement, but that he would comment on the issue anyway. The particular issue in question was global environmentalism, and in true Carter-candidate style, the ex-president said he favored doing something about it.

Carter was on a five-day, unofficial tour of Japan, following a 10-day tour of Communist China. He was invited to visit Japan by a major Japanese television station as part of a continuing series of visits to this island nation by former American presidents.

Carter is popular here for two things: His success in the Camp David accords which have helped maintain peace in the Middle East, and for appointing former U.S. Senate Majority Leader Mike Mansfield as ambassador to Japan.

The Japanese love Mansfield. He apparently gives them what they want. By contrast, older Japanese like Dr. Ogawa, who was educated at UCLA and Columbia University in the United States, refer to the late Gen. Douglas MacArthur as "the dictator" - the American ambassador who gave Japanese what he wanted them to have.

MacArthur's reign over the occupation of Japan after World War II was harsh, but is was period during which he stripped much of the power from the old ruling class and passed it down to the people. The common Japanese still rule today through a parliamentary system of government.

Although there have been other U.S. ambassadors to Japan between MacArthur and Mansfield, it has been under Mansfield's tour that the Japanese industrial might has risen to global significance. With its rise has come a new generation of international traders, travelers, entertainers, bargainers, and elitists in their own right.

They are the new power in Japan. They are a faceless class -

no star attractions but rather a new club with a stiff upper lip. The Japanese press has a tendency to glorify, and not question, the industrial might this generation has developed. Jimmy Carter - through his Ambassador Mansfield - has helped the Japanese sell their new face to the world.

Florida Times-Union, Sept. 16, 1981

CULTURAL RIFT MAY BLOCK
U.S.-JAPANESE MERGER

TOKYO, Japan - If you can get used to listening to a Los Angles Rams-Dallas Cowboys football game over rice cakes for breakfast, you can understand the cultural differences that may eventually block the merger of the U.S. and Japanese economies.

There are those in the United States who advocate the adaptation of Japanese management philosophies to American businesses, but they evidently have not spent much time in this country. If they had, they would recognize some irreconcilable differences between the two economic powers.

Since this is being written on America's Labor Day - while Japanese workers are on the job - there is probably no better place to start than with the differences in the two countries' labor pictures.

To make Japanese management systems work in U.S. industry, you would have to witness a scene such as this:

A couple thousand United Auto Workers gathered in the parking lot of a General Motors plant to sing the GM company song and do calisthenics before their shift starts.

Add to that a cheering throng of the same auto workers who have just heard a group of their own members recommend to GM management that new machines be installed on the assembly line to perform body-welding tasks more efficiently than the auto workers have ever been able to do it.

No matter how you view those two scenes, it is difficult to make them jell - it is just not the American way.

There are other major differences that have as much impact in keeping the two economies separated, even though they are alike in many ways.

For one thing, there are no management stars, so to speak, in Japan. It is no great honor to get your picture on the cover of the national business magazines in Japan. The honor comes in getting your company's name on the cover and that honor is shared by all the workers in the company.

Japanese industries are extensions of the old family-business arrangements, familiar in the United States in the late 19th century and the first part of this century.

Most Japanese devote their entire careers to a single company in exchange for a promise they will never be laid off.

Under these conditions, it makes decision by consensus less complicated since everyone from the janitor to the chairman of the board feels like his is part of the same team.

In fact, chairmen of boards in Japan publicly take pride in saying they do not make decisions; rather, they allow the decisions to come up through the ranks and spend their time rewarding workers for improving the efficiency of the company's production system.

The Japanese are outwardly very humble, but the wise foreigner need not be overwhelmed with this modesty that carries over into corporate policy. Privately, workers and business leaders here will admit that the wise Japanese manager knows when and where to plant his ideas so that those ideas can rise through the consensus decision-making process.

Still, Japanese companies do operate with an ear attuned to quality in their systems. They still have not been able to match U.S. standards of per-capita production, but they are expected to by the end of this decade. There is a definite concern for quality in the Japanese production system today.

It has not always been that way. When I lived here 25 years ago, the Japanese were just beginning to rebuild their industrial base, which was destroyed during World War II. Much of what they produced back then could be classified as junk by Japanese standards, but it found a ready market, particularly in the United States.

It was the sale of the lower-quality products, coupled with U.S. assistance in rebuilding Japan's nationalized steel industry that helped this bombed-out country get back on its feet and eventually challenge the United States in economic stability.

The country still draws regular benefits from the U.S. Treasury - mainly in the form of military expenditures. Since World War II the Japanese have maintained only a minimum defense force while the United States has picked up the tab for defending the Pacific from the threat of communism. That's why you can listen to a National Football League game at breakfast here in Tokyo. The NFL is carried live by the U.S. Armed Forces Radio Network in the Far East.

Ironically, it is the largely individualistic American society that has been responsible for defending the Japanese society, which is primarily collectivist. The Japanese may not have laughed all the way, but their industry has certainly been able to smile all the way to the bank at our expense.

The tides of time are changing rapidly here. This rebuilt nation - even with the massive barrier of its written language - has become more like the United States than any other country in history. It has, in fact, become the modern "Paper Tiger" of the industrial age.

JAPAN EMPLOYMENT *(1981)*

HIROSHIMA, Japan - One of the great hidden myths of the Japanese economy today is the general believe the Japanese enjoy lifetime employment with a single firm.

When life spans were not much more than 50 years here - prior to World War II - lifetime employment was not as difficult to perpetuate as it is today when Japanese people are expected to live well into their seventies.

Actually, the Japanese labor issue goes much deeper than just the lifetime employment situation. There are three factors, which until recent years - particularly since President Nixon cut the yen away from a fixed rate of exchange with the dollar and the world oil crisis in the early 1970s - were cited as the pillars of Japanese production. They were:

1. Long-term employment.
2. A seniority wage system.
3. Vertical unions, or one union for all workers in each company rather than unions organized nationwide for all workers in a single trade or occupation group.

The advent of longer life spans in Japan has brought about a crisis in the seniority wage system. The old system was based upon pay by length of service with the company. Promotions into management were also based on length of service with the firm, and promotions were important if one were to achieve a healthy retirement bonus and to save face in his community.

It also meant that more introductions to the industrial, political and bureaucratic leaders would be available, and the introduction is an all-important item in Japan.

Without proper introduction, a Japanese does not get into the proper schools, and without getting into the proper schools, he does not get recruited by the proper companies, and without being recruited he stands little chance of achieving the high status of an elite industrialist in this island nation of the Far East.

It is a ritual that begins each year as all industries announce simultaneously their recruiting selections.

When life spans were 50 years it made it possible to finance retirement programs that started at 55 with a large bonus, especially if the employee had risen to the executive ranks. Even if he had failed to make it to the rank of executive in a Japanese firm, the employee was more often than not given the honorary rank of executive to make him eligible for a one-time retirement bonus of $100,000 or more.

As life spans lengthened more and more retiring employees have qualified for executive positions, honorary ranks, and tremendous bonuses and the vertical labor unions in each company are fighting to maintain this status machinery.

Retirement ages have risen slightly toward the 60-year-old mark and there is talk of pushing them upward to 65 or 70 to help reduce a huge national debt caused by an over-burden of social programs, the least of which is not social security. Again the vertical labor unions within the companies are resisting this, also.

The seniority wage system has its own built-in, self-destruct mechanisms that many large Japanese firms are beginning to discover. Regardless of the official rate of inflation - now about 5 percent annually - posted by the government it appears to be much higher. Inflation reached 25 percent during the oil crisis in 1973 and marked the turning point of the wage crisis facing Japanese industrial community.

Younger workers faced with higher costs of living, and backed by their strong vertical unions, have fought for and obtained large pay increases to insure their financial survival. This has pushed other workers' wages - based on the seniority system - up accordingly.

Today, somewhere between the ages of 40 and 45, Japanese workers are being paid their first wages that exceed their productive capacity. As they continue to climb the seniority ladder, wages and salaries climb, also, and they are paid sums well in excess of what they can ever produce.

Some companies have tried to introduce merit pay systems to stem this tide, as well as severance pay programs to weed out the unproductive employees, but again such programs have met strong resistance from the vertical labor unions.

The combination of the old lifetime employment system, pay based solely on seniority, longer life spans, and inflation is causing a crunch on Japanese industry. So far, since the early 1970s, the industries have been able to deal with it by trimming out the fat in their operations, by not hiring as many employees as they retire, and by the introduction of more robots and other automation.

But, most companies still carry a lot of expensive deadwood that cuts back tremendously on their overall production capacity. There is strong opposition from the workers and their unions towards any more dramatic cut backs, which leaves Japanese industry faced with a situation that could price them out of their vital world markets in the years ahead.

JAPAN HOUSING (1981)

TOKYO, Japan - For all the problems prosperity has solved over the past two decades here, it has left this island national one gigantic one the solution to which may well divide the country.

Tokyo is a city that has literally risen from the ashes of World War II, at least twice. The first rebuilding of this great metropolitan area of 11 million people took place from 1945 through the mid-1960s. The millions of wood and paper houses destroyed by Gen. Curtis LeMay's Army Air Corps bombers were rebuilt in their original form pushing the majority of this city upward to a full two-story height.

The original landowners, many who were not allowed to return to Tokyo for several years after the war due to food and sanitation shortages in the city, came back to their ancestral lands and began the initial reconstruction period that lasted into the age now referred to by many contemporary Japanese as the "Period of Golden Growth."

But, this so-called golden period brought with it - in addition to unprecedented prosperity - that modern economic bug-a-boo inflation, driving limited housing and land costs sky high.

The dramatic increase in land prices, a high inheritance tax, and a growing metropolitan population, caused major shifts in urban housing patterns and living standards. While the majority of Japanese families had been content with small homes consisting basically of two combination sleeping and living rooms - each containing about 100 square feet - plus a small kitchen and a bath, an increasing standard of living brought with it the desire for more living space.

Japanese today, especially in urban areas, no longer sleep on the floor or take their meals at the traditional low table. They generally retain one or two traditional rooms in their home, but the remainder of the house is much like a Western-style home. They share all the modern conveniences available to any American family.

I spent last weekend at the home of Izumi Tadokoro, chief of the International Affairs Department of the Japan Newspaper Publishers and Editors Association, and other than being allowed to sleep in the family's one traditional-style bedroom, eat with chopsticks at the dining table, and soak in the traditional Japanese hot tub before retiring, it would have been difficult to tell the house from the average home in Arlington or Cedar Hills. But, for what it costs to build such a home in Tokyo today, you could probably buy three or four homes in most Jacksonville suburbs.

With 115 million people squeezed onto a land mass the size of California it is not difficult to see why the cost of land has gone out of sight. We think of California housing as being expensive - the cost of the average house in California is now around $110,000 and shows no sign of coming down, but in Japan just the land for building a home can easily cost that much. In the suburbs of Tokyo, 100 square feet of land costs about $15,000.

With the average family income here of approximately $18,000 per year, it is easy to see why more and more Japanese are becoming frustrated with the housing situation.

As the preceding generations died and attempt to pass their homes on to their children, the children are finding they often are forced to sell the ancestral lands to pay the enormous inheritance taxes. Large development companies have bought up this land, and the city of Tokyo has literally risen again since the mid-'60s as concrete high-rise apartments.

There has been some condominium-style development, but my Japanese is so poor, and most Japanese do not understand cooperative housing enough to discuss it in detail in English, that I am assuming that it represents no significant share of the market yet.

Almost all Japanese you visit with concerning personal economics say housing is the biggest problem facing the nation. Everyone wants more living space in a country with little more to offer. Urban sprawl and limited land area for agricultural production have collided head-on, squeezing the cities ever upward in grey concrete apartment hutches. Prices of housing, including rent have gone out of sight in proportion to the cost of other items in the Japanese budget. From what I have been able to determine from available statistics, and the government apparently does not make too many available in certain problem areas, housing can absorb as much as 75 percent of the average household budget in Japan.

For Americans coming here to work, the costs are a shock. Rents of $6,000 per month are common in areas where the 5,000

American residents of Tokyo live. Most American companies pay substantial housing benefits to their U.S. employees here.

The housing problem has become severe enough to warrant much serious debate in government and academic circles. Much of the debate has narrowed down to two camps - one favoring the traditional right of private land ownership, and the other, much smaller camp, favoring state ownership of land.

Higher living standards enjoyed by the modern Japanese worker, driven by inflationary pressures locked into a national economy financed almost one-third by deficit spending, have done much to break the ancient and sacred tradition of Japanese private land ownership. Even the need for more space in downtown Tokyo has brought about the abolition of an ancient rule that no building could rise higher than the Emperor's palace.

But, prosperity here has also brought with it a national consensus of social concern. If the burden of housing costs continue to rise in proportion to other costs, there could well be some moves in the not too distant future towards state land ownership.

The Japanese do not adhere to any rationale that is particularly consistent with Western logic. It would be easy in this island nation for the people to view the land - as a whole - as a national treasure. As such it would become a ward of the government and would then be parcelled out through bureaucratic processes for living use.

Such a move would bring strong opposition from the wealthy, but rapidly shrinking, numbers of private landowners.

JAPAN'S 30-YEAR-OLD DECISION CONTINUES TO PAY TODAY

TOKYO, Japan - The Japanese nation is closely aligned with the United States today because of a dispute that arose over four northern offshore islands between 1946 and 1951 - islands that today are occupied by some 12,000 Russian troops.

More than 16,000 Japanese residents were expelled from the islands of Etorofu, Kunashiri, Shikotan and Habomai after the Soviet take-over of the islands on Sept. 4, 1945, in the wake of the signing of the truce between Japan and the Allied powers aboard the U.S. Battleship Missouri in Tokyo Bay.

The Soviets moved into the islands while U.S. troops were busy occupying the major islands of the Japanese archipelago. American troops occupied and ran the government of the nation for 5-1/2 years until an accord was reached with the signing of the San Francisco Treaty on Sept. 8, 1951. The treaty established what Japan now calls the San Francisco *taisei* (system).

Japan is a whole nation today because the Russians couldn't get along with Gen. Douglas MacArthur, who served as commander of the Allied forces in the Southwest Pacific and later as the occupation leader during the postwar restoration of Japan. Russia did not enter the war against Japan until after the war in Europe ended.

Because Russian generals refused to serve on an Allied command staff headed by MacArthur, the Soviet Union did not share in the spoils of victory when Japan fell as it did in Europe after the Axis surrendered.

Recently declassified documents from the Potsdam Conference show that Russia was to have received a portion of Japan equal to about one-third of the nation - all north of Tokyo including the four islands it occupies today - when Japan was finally defeated. It would have been a partitioning of the Japanese islands similar to the split of Germany.

But, by a twist of fate on the day before the first atomic bomb was dropped on Hiroshima, the Soviets withdrew to achieve a better bargaining posture in resolving their objections to MacArthur. The war ended nine days later, and the Soviets had no representatives in the final settlement arrangements.

Because of the dispute over the four small offshore islands, which the United States was not interested in but that the Soviets had always believed was part of a bigger archipelago they have resided on for centuries, the Japanese have never signed a settlement agreement with the Soviets. The truce still stands, but peace has never been resolved on paper, although arrangements were made several years ago to permit the re-establishment of diplomatic relationships between the two countries. In a strictly legal sense, Japan is still at war with Russia.

Sentiment over the Soviet occupation of the four islands still runs strong. Japanese Prime Minister Zenko Suzuki became the first Japanese leader since World War II to inspect the islands. He flew near them by helicopter recently and viewed them through binoculars. The flight was symbolic of the current Japanese efforts to regain control of the islands.

However, the Japanese, despite some strong talks going on now, are not equipped to do too much saber rattling over the issue. They maintain a 258,000-man air, ground and sea self-defense force under arrangements with the United States for joint protection of their homeland. A constitutional provision prevents the use of the defense force for aggressive purposes or to force a resolution to diplomatic issues. And this particular issue is not significant enough to bring U.S. forces to bear upon the Soviets who occupy the islands.

But the issue was so strong in 1951 that it was the single biggest factor that led to conservative political leadership of Japan for the last 30 years and the close economic ties of the island with the United States for the last three decades.

By dividing Japan into two camps, the issue helped develop the two-party political system in the country after World War II. The conservatives became the Liberal Democratic Party, which is still in control of the majority rule in the Japanese Diet (parliament) today.

The United States, principally through then-Secretary of State John Foster Dulles, gave the Japanese a choice concerning their political and economic future in 1951.

"We are prepared to combine our power with that of others in mutual committals in accord with the United Nations Charter, so that the deterrent power that protects us will also protect others. Japan, if it is disposed to protect itself against indirect aggressions, can, if it wishes, share collective protection against direct aggression," Dulles offered the Japanese.

Through then-Prime Minister Shigeru Yoshida, the Japanese signed the separate peace treaty with the United States in San Francisco, which gave the Americans perpetual right to station troops in Japan as part of the security settlement.

In so doing, the Japanese handed over the common defense of their archipelago to the United States and its allies, and devoted its national wealth to redevelopment of its industrial machinery.

Dulles recognized the implications of the San Francisco security arrangement 30 years ago:

"You will note that the security program we outline does not require that the Japanese nation should become militaristic and create such land, sea and naval forces as tempted Japan down the road to destruction. Against that, the new Japan has rightly set its face."

He added, "Our own study convinces us that the industry, the aptitude and the ingenuity of the Japanese people can assure the possibility of a rising economic standard through trade and commerce with the rest of the world."

The Japanese chose 30 years ago to trade four small islands and close relationships with Russia for a strong security arrangement with the United States, which would assure the economic freedom to rebuild their industrial machine.

The fuss being made over the Soviet occupation of the offshore islands today is not much more than political rhetoric. The choice the Japanese made 30 years ago has paid handsome dividends. Today, thanks largely to the U.S.-provided military protection, the Japanese enjoy a standard of living equal to more than 80 percent of that enjoyed in the United States - a far cry from the near total devastation of their country and their economy at the end of World War II.

JAPANESE FINANCE (1981)

TOKYO, Japan - In America kids dream of growing up to be president. In Japan they dream of growing up to be finance minister.

The top bureaucratic posts in this country far over shadow in prestige the post of prime minister in the eyes of most Japanese citizens. To be a bureaucrat is the ultimate goal. To be the bureaucrat that controls the country's finances is the most powerful and prestigious position in the nation.

As a result parents push children through the proper education systems, at great expense, to qualify them for taking the entrance examinations to the universities from which prospective bureaucrats are recruited. Everything is flung into the breech when it comes to securing a lifetime post in any of the thousands of government agencies at both the national and local level.

As one young bureaucrat told me, "It is not that the bureaucrats are paid so well, but rather that they have more prestige than anyone else in the country - for all of their life."

When he talked of prestige he meant the deep reverence that bureaucrats are held in by ordinary citizens. They wield almost unlimited power over their constituents, and they are paid homage equal to their perceived stations in life.

Many firms have their headquarters throughout Japan, but all of them maintain large offices in Tokyo just to enable them to be in the proper place to administer to the needs of the bureaucracy.

Top bureaucrats and their lieutenants derive a lot of their power from the fact that Japanese laws are written in such a way as to leave a lot to interpretation. The company that wants to have a government regulation relaxed finds it necessary to appeal to the particular bureaucrat in charge of their case with proper respect.

Proper respect in Japan means lavish entertainment and a steady stream of gifts throughout the year. Such gift giving is not looked upon as bribery, but is intermingled with the normal social customs of this country and is expected albeit played down tremendously.

However, the people I have visited with on this trip say the best way to get a government rule or regulation interpreted in your favor is to make sure that your company representative knows the bureaucrat in charge of your affairs well, and is on hand at all the proper gift-giving times of the year with a present equal to the occasion. The presents are rarely, if every, money, but one bureaucrat remarked that the homes of his superiors were the best furnished in all of Japan.

This attitude towards the bureaucracy has led to its proliferation, and the burden of cost it has brought with it will certainly be one of the hot topics of debate during a special 55-day session of the Japanese Diet called this week.

With a national budget 33 percent in deficit last year and expected to be over 27 percent in deficit this year - the Japanese fiscal year beings on April 1 - the cost of government has become a major issue here. The taxpayers have already been promised no tax increases during this fiscal year.

The major bill to be considered by the special session was originally entitled "Bill for temporary measures concerning reductions, etc., in state subsidies, etc.," but has already been amended to read "Bill for temporary measures concerning reductions, etc., in state subsidies, etc., as part of the measures to be taken for the time being to promote administrative reform."

The rewording was done to put the bureaucrats on notice that the government would be looking for ways to trim back some of the fat in government agencies, but it is doubtful whether or not it will have any impact on the bureaucracy.

Japan watchers say the bureaucrats are so strongly entrenched in the country's government structure that they rarely miss a beat, not even in wartime, or during periods of feast or famine.

Florida Times-Union, Oct. 6, 1981

POLITICS HELPS PUT JAPAN'S RAIL SYSTEM IN RED

TOKYO, Japan - Politicians are the same in any language. They need to develop some way of systematically repaying the people who elected them to office.

In America, congressmen since the beginning of the nation have used public works such as dams and highways to bestow their gratitude on their constituents, not to mention using such projects as a means to buy more votes and assure their re-election.

In Japan, the politicians have learned to use the national railway system as a means of satisfying the voters. Many Japanese members of the Diet, the Japanese parliament, have gotten there - and remained there - on the promise of linking their villages in the country to the major cities of the nation via a spur to the national railroad network.

The train is to the Japanese what the automobile is to the American. Most trains in this island nation haul people, not freight.

And, they run on time. There is a national law that requires the Japanese National Railways (JNR) to refund in full the ticket price to every passenger on any train that arrives over three hours late.

Japanese trains are clean and efficient. By any standards they are the most modern in the world. The Japanese Shinkansen, or Bullet Trains, are the pride of the nation. Japanese compare their success with developing trains, which travel at speeds up to 140 mph across the land, to the American success in developing space vehicles.

The government-owned JNR operates all the major trains in Japan and licenses and controls all of the small, privately owned railroad companies that provide links to JNR points in remote areas of the country. The private trains are called "accommodation trains" because they bring passengers to the national rail network. As such, they receive subsidies from the government to maintain their operations.

Japanese politicians have learned how to use this combination of rail benefits to their advantage, but it has been a tremendous drain on the national budget.

Hardly any of the railroad lines in outlying areas of the country pay their own way. For years, the JNR depended on fares from the major metropolitan areas to pick up the losses from operations in the country. But inflation has taken its toll; so have the Japanese lifetime employment seniority-pay system and five Japanese rail unions.

The revenues from metropolitan lines have not been sufficient in recent years to offset the losses piled up by the constant addition of more and more railroad spurs to the far reaches of the land where politicians want to reward their constituents for their loyal support.

The result has been that JNR ran more than $3 billion in the red last year and was forced to come up with proposals to help eliminate this deficit, termed "colossal" by the government.

To accomplish spending cutbacks - no one wants to raise the fares, which seem extremely low to foreigners - JNR has presented its unions with proposals to trim nearly 70,000 workers from its ranks, dropping total employment in the national rail system to about 350,000 by 1984.

The cuts are to be made mostly by attrition, but ducking the real issue has been accomplished here as it is in the United States during periods of fiscal belt-tightening - by transferring much of the workload from the federal payroll to private payrolls via contract work. The enables the government agencies to put the real cost of running the railroad, or any government business for that matter, off the books or out of sight since the price of contract labor gets transferred to some other part of the national budget and does not, in the Japanese case, show up directly under the JNR label.

So far, JNR has offered to transfer such things as freight-car loading, train-car inspection and maintenance, track maintenance, ticket printing, some station operations, traffic control, and railroad-crossing security to outside contractors, who most likely would be expected to pick up the surplus employees leaving the national railway system's payroll.

Japanese politicians have become as adept at playing the fiscal shell game as their American counterparts.

Florida Times-Union, Oct. 3, 1981

CHRYSLER MIGHT LEARN FROM JAPAN'S MAZDA

HIROSHIMA, Japan - There are no government bail outs of ailing automobile manufacturers in Japan, but if Chrysler Corp. has a first fiscal cousin here it is Mazda, better known in local quarters as Toyo Kogyo.

Bunzo Suzuki, manager of international public relations for Mazda, is as familiar with Phillips Highway and its auto dealers in Jacksonville as he is with the sprawling Mazda facilities here and its 28,000 employees. Suzuki is a regular visitor to Jacksonville. He gave up a day from his busy schedule this week to conduct me and eight other traveling fellows of the International Press Institute through the complex.

The tour, arranged by our hosts - the Japanese Editors and Publishers Association - was a rare treat. In trying to get a tour of an auto plant lined up for us the Japanese hosts were turned down by the two leading automobile manufacturers in Japan - Toyota and Nissan (Datsun). Auto manufacturers here are shy of the American media for several reasons. Top management does not feel the U. S. press has given it fair treatment in explaining Japan's unusual relationship between management and labor, and the auto industry here harbors an unspoken resentment over the U.S. coercion of voluntary restrictions on the import of foreign automobiles.

Toyo Kogyo Co. Ltd. is Japan's third largest auto manufacturer and one of the elder statesmen of Japanese industry. Prior to World War II, the company was a leading manufacturer here of three-wheeled light trucks, a hybrid motorcycle-style pickup truck.

During the war, the Hiroshima plant was converted to the manufacture of torpedo parts for the Japanese Navy. Ironically on Aug. 6, 1945, when the world's first atomic bomb was dropped here killing an estimated 200,000 people, the Mazda plant located about four miles from ground zero in the heart of this coastal city, which was virtually destroyed by the blast, sustained only minimal damage.

At the war's end, nine days after the A-bomb fell on Hiroshima, the Toyo Kogyo Co. Ltd. returned to the manufacture of civilian vehicles and enjoyed a successful career culminating in the OPEC oil crisis of 1973. The Arab oil embargo threw Japanese industries - with virtually no natural resources of their own - into a tailspin. The post-war Japanese economy, which had enjoyed unprecedented prosperity throughout the 1960s, began to crumble. Inflation soared to over 25 percent.

Like Chrysler in the U.S., to which Toyo Kogyo has no direct links, Mazda had geared up to build larger cars, which were not fuel efficient like the products of its domestic competitors, Toyota and Nissan. The company began losing money - it was in trouble for the first time in recent history, and there was no way to turn to government for a bail out.

It was at this point that Japan's unique, and possibly misnamed, lifetime employment system - backed by its company wide, or vertical, labor unions - was used to save the company while new fuel-efficient models could be designed and factories could be retooled.

It is this unique feature of Japanese industry that is most misunderstood by the Western world. When an employee goes to work for a major Japanese company, he trades job security for company loyalty. In other words, it is understood that he will be employed by the company until he retires - currently at age 57 with Mazda - in exchange for pay raises based solely on seniority and fringe benefits including such things as inexpensive company housing, free medical care, discounts on nearly all necessary goods and services through a genuine discount company store, low-interest home and educational loans, and a whopping - an average of over $50,000 - one-time cash retirement payment plus a monthly retirement pension.

All these benefits are jealously guarded by the one union that represents all Mazda workers, 25,000 of the company's current total of 28,000 employees. The Toyo Kogyo Workers' Union, while loosely affiliated with other unions in some of Japan's other auto companies, represents and bargains only for Mazda workers in all trades and occupations within the company.

It maintains a seven-story headquarters building and facilities on the Toyo Kogyo plant grounds built on reclaimed land from the

Inland Sea.

The union headquarters was built and paid for by union members. The union has an income of $3 million in annual dues to maintain its operations, and it is highly organized and worker-oriented.

The problem most Westerners have in understanding the so-called vertical, or single-company, union found in Japan is they have the tendency to think because the Japanese unions limit their activities to a single company, they somehow or other belong to that company or are controlled by that company's management.

Nothing could be further from the truth, especially in Mazda's case during the economic crisis of the Mid-1970s when the company was losing money and facing disaster.

Despite the loyalty that workers show for their companies in exchange for so-called lifetime employment in Japan, they and their unions refuse to give up certain benefits even in times of economic crisis.

One such benefit is the semi-annual bonus, which amounts to 35 percent of a Mazda worker's annual pay and up to a 50-percent-or-more added payment in other Japanese manufacturing firms. The Toyo Kogyo Worker's Union would not budge on the bonus issue even when the company had to struggle against what appeared to be insurmountable odds to pay it during the mid-1970s.

What the union did bargain with was an issue they use today to prevent the introduction of a merit-pay system into the company's seniority-based pay scale: the right of company management to reduce costs by re-allocating employees to other jobs, cutting back on surplus employees by attrition only and the introduction of robots to the assembly lines.

The changes saved Mazda's corporate life and greatly improved its productivity. In 1974, Toyo Kogyo had 37,000 employees and produced 700,000 cars and trucks. Today the company has 28,000 employees and this year it will turn out 1.2 million Mazdas.

One of the tricks used by management at the bottom of the sales downturn in the mid-1970s was to transfer 5,000 blue- and white-collar workers to its sales force, which in Japan sells cars door-to-door. Such a move is akin to Chrysler's Lee Iacocca putting 5,000 United Auto Works on the street to peddle K-cars.

The Japanese auto-workers-turned-salesmen produced an impressive sales record of more than 200,000 units. Some of the salesmen remain voluntarily on the street today as part of an extension of the original plan that will be phased out later this year.

Toyo Kogyo now has 160 robots performing welding tasks on its assembly lines. The robots work two shifts a day and require no company benefits.

Union officials told me that they do not resent the introduction of robots. They can control the growth of the robots' use because union members man the robots' switches.

The union leaders did, however, hint that they might resist any massive introduction of robots in other areas of the assembly line if it meant significant cutbacks in employees and, thus, loss of union members. Even through the Mazda plant is an open shop, 100 percent of the eligible employees currently belong to the union.

The robots have been a blessing to the overall production at Toyo Kogyo. By using the robots, the company has been able to diversify the number of models it can produce on a single assembly line.

It is not unusual to see RX-7s, 323s, 626s, and the popular new model, the Cosmos, all coming off the same assembly line. While older welding machines can handle a single model on single line, the robots can be programmed to distinguish between different models as they roll onto their station and perform the different welding tasks required on each model.

The ability of the Japanese auto industry and its unions to make adjustments not permitted by the disenfranchisement of the U.S. auto industry and its multitude of horizontal unions also enabled Mazda to shift it focus to improving quality when economic conditions might have dictated otherwise.

By allowing cutbacks in employees by attrition and the shifting of employees from one job to another, the union gave the company de facto approval to a reduction in the massive inspection force employed by most other auto manufacturers.

Mazda grasped the opportunity to introduce the quality control, or QC, circle concept to its auto-production processes. The next worker on any assembly line is treated as the client of the previous worker under the QC concept.

There are no inspectors on the line as there were in the pre-

QC days. Instead, every worker on the line is an inspector. Instead of tagging a defect found in a previous worker's work, any person on the assembly line can push an emergency button and stop the line.

A special team rushes to the area and corrects the defect on the spot. The line is re-started and when the vehicle rolls off the assembly line, it is test-driven on a treadmill-style test track at the last station on the assembly line and it is ready for the market.

About half the Mazda production is for domestic consumption. The other half is for foreign markets, and the cars are driven right from the assembly line onto ships anchored in the Inland Sea adjacent to the Mazda plant. Last year a quarter of a million Mazdas were shipped to the United States with Jacksonville the destination for many of them. About the same number will make the long ocean voyage this year.

Toyo Kogyo has 1,600 QC circles in operation at its Hiroshima works, where its car and truck assembly is currently done. In addition to the worker-client inspection processes developed by the QC concept, a massive production-improvement suggestion programs has been introduced. Last year more than 900,000 suggestions were made by QC circles and more than 75 percent of them were incorporated into the production process.

Workers make the suggestions more out of their loyalty to the company than for the small monetary reward offered. The maximum cash bonus offered by the company is $400 for an outstanding suggestion that proves useful, but Suzuki said no person, or QC circle, has ever qualified for the maximum bonus. Most receive the minimum bonus equivalent to about $4.

To visit with the Japanese, on their own turf is an experience that leaves one with the impression that the Japanese believe they have found the answers to renewed prosperity in their auto industry.

Viewing the Mazda experience from a modern Western-style motel room a few miles away where English is spoken and Western economics is more clearly understood, I could see several stumbling blocks ahead.

The advent of longer life spans and the desire to work beyond the retirement age of 57 today, tied to rising inflation, shrinking markets and the lifetime-employment, seniority pay-scale concepts, only appears to be postponing an insurmountable cost in higher-priced but lower-productive years ahead for Japanese workers.

Florida Times-Union, Oct. 11, 1981

OGAWA-SAN TELLS REDNECK HOW JAPAN BEAT WEST

One last tale from my recent Japan trip.

To set the stage for it, I have to describe the main character - Masura Ogawa.

Ogawa-san (-san added to a Japanese person's name is equivalent to Mr., Mrs., Ms. or Miss preceding an American's name - an expression to show respect) is the Mount Fuji of Japanese journalism. He is the retired editor-in-chief of The Japan Times, the top English-language newspaper in Japan.

As such, he writes a front-page column for the paper each Sunday. The range of Ogawa-san's prose runs from in-depth dissertations on the intricacies of floating international currencies to downright sword rattling concerning rearmament of the Japanese military, a subject on which he personally claims much support.

He is an old warrior, a veteran of the Philippines campaign when his country was the victor. He doesn't have much use for former Gen. Douglas MacArthur, whom he refers to as the American "dictator" of the Japanese occupation.

Ogawa-san can recite poetry, sing a bawdy jingle, and throw down sake with the best of them at the top geisha houses in Tokyo. He can also take a nap in a sitting position during a conference and never miss a word, whether it's in English or Japanese.

He's gray on top, round in the middle, and one of the most interesting hosts you could ever have. His English is better than mine, to the point that we had to employ Don James, managing editor of the Wichita Falls (Texas) News-Record and Times, to interpret some of my Redneck expressions.

If Ogawa-san has a short suit, it's that he hasn't mastered Redneck. I can't fault him for that. In every other category he is *Itchi-ban* (No. 1).

One day we while we were swapping tall tales, with James translating my transgressions of the English language, Ogawa-san jumped from straightening me out on why Japanese kill whales to why Japanese can take any product and improve upon it. There really is no relation between the two to my way of thinking, but to

Ogawa-san it was a perfectly logical transition.

The story goes something like this:

When the shogun returned the rule of Japan to the emperor in 1868 - called the Restoration by the Japanese - the doors were opened to the outside world.

(That's the Japanese version. In truth, the shogun returned the rule of Japan to the emperor because the doors to the outside world had already been opened by foreigners who were getting ready to come down hard on the shogun. Such circumstances on the home front made retirement a happy alternative for the shogun, and since the emperor had been out of work for a few centuries, he was the logical choice for a successor.)

Left with a country suffering under a deteriorating feudal system, the emperor cast about for advice. It seems an English engineer named Dyer-san (according to Ogawa-san) found his way into the emperor's court.

After taking a close look at Japan in the late 1800s, Dyer-san told the emperor that Japan was so far behind the rest of the civilized world that it would be useless to try to develop new systems and products.

Dyer-san's advice was that the emperor send emissaries to other countries to study how they worked, and bring these emissaries home to teach his people how to "imitate."

"When Japan has imitated itself up to equal footing with the rest of the civilized world, then there will be time to develop new things," Ogawa-san quotes Dyer-san as having told the emperor.

The emperor so attuned the country to this philosophy that it became part of the unwritten Japanese national creed, and today still governs a lot of the country's policies, according to Ogawa-san, who immediately - and I presume logically to his way of thinking - launched into a ribald ditty about why newspapermen drink, smoke and chase the ladies.

I made a mental note to look up the background on this Dyer-san character who apparently laid the ground work that enabled the Japanese to beat Detroit at its own game. But, after searching for two weeks, I have been unable to uncover the first bit of evidence that Dyer-san ever existed. I've tried English, Japanese and American reference books. Nothing.

I'll bet Ogawa-san is now telling the girls down at the geisha house how he finally bagged a Redneck - the translation of which is probably not printable in a family newspaper.

One way or another the lovable old cuss is going to win the war single-handedly, and I tip my hat to him. He got me one-up, fair and square.

It's people like Ogawa-san whom you meet along the way that make travel exciting. Still it's good to be home again.

I knew I was home last week when I had to pay a nickel for a glass of water at Bressler's ice cream parlor in the lobby of Independent Square - a truly American gesture.

(Just to keep the record straight, Ogawa-san, after reading a copy of this column, consistently avowed until the time of his death nearly a decade later that he had never told me the Dyer-san tale.)

The following is the complete text of the book The Ephemeral Bliss of the Free Fall, written following a tour of Japan as the leader of a Rotary International Group Study Exchange team in 1991. It is written in the first person, much of it as I traveled, unlike the other third-person essays in this compilation of my writings on Japan.

The Ephemeral Bliss of the Free Fall
By Dave Whitney

Somewhere between San Francisco and Tokyo, the twenty-second hour of daylight begins to get to you. Sleeping is not the same with just the window shades drawn on a jumbo jet.

There are six of us on this trip from the Florida Keys and the Bahamas. We're a Group Study Exchange team sponsored by the Rotary Foundation of Rotary International. We're repaying a visit six Japanese made to Florida in October 1992. I am the team leader.

It's my third trip to Japan, the first for the other five team members – Whitney Bain III from the Bahamas, and Ron Pullman, Rick Ramsay, Paul White and Tim Wilson from the Florida Keys.

My mind drifts back to the first trip I made. It took more than two weeks aboard a troop transport from Seattle to Yokohama in 1956. Even as agonizing as the long flight is from Miami to San Francisco to Tokyo, it is not nearly as tedious as crossing the Pacific at six knots on an old tub. My last trip to Japan was in 1981 as a member of a team sponsored by the International Press Institute and the Japan-America Society. We spent a month interviewing top leaders in politics and industry and writing about it. My speciality was economics. I look forward to returning this trip to see first hand what has taken place in Japan's economy over the past 12 years.

I wonder if we will see Mt. Fuji on our approach to Tokyo's Narita Airport in the late afternoon. My first view of Mt. Fuji came when my ship sailed up Tokyo Bay in the early morning hours of a fall day in 1956. The tip of the mountain could be seen off to the west-northwest as we met the pilot boat that would send aboard the Japanese pilot to bring us to the dock at Yokohama's North Pier. It was a beautiful, serene sight. One of those picture-postcard views from the mind file that stays with you forever.

Our approach to Narita in 1981 - on my 45th birthday - allowed us a quick glimpse at Fuji-san in the distance. Somehow seeing Mt. Fuji on the way in seems to be a signal to me that all is well in Japan. Japanese tell me that if you see Fuji-san you will someday return to their home islands.

Today we have been flying above a heavy cloud cover. The flight attendant announces our final approach to Tokyo/Narita. We shove all our loose odds and ends under the seat and into the overhead and buckle in. The 747 enters the cloud bank and I sit back waiting for it to break out hoping to catch a fresh glimpse of Fuji-san.

The approach seems to take forever. I hear the pilot make a couple of course adjustments, lower the flaps, then the landing gear, and finally cut the power as he flares to settle on the runway that jumps up at us out of the fog.

We have just made a zero-zero landing in a socked-in Japan.

There is no Mt. Fuji.

- Hai, so desu -

President Bill Clinton is being assailed in the Nippon press for some caustic remark he supposedly penned in his notes from a meeting with Russian President Boris Yeltsin in Vancouver.

Clinton apparently accused the Japanese of not always meaning "yes" when they say "yes."

From the Japanese response one would think Clinton had initiated a major international incident. My experience with the Japanese has been that they don't have a whole lot to cry about.

The Japanese don't have a word for "yes" from our perspective. The closest thing they have in their language is *hai*, pronounced HIGH in our language. It is one of their most used words, especially when followed by *so desu*, pronounced SEW DESS in American. Even when *hai* is used alone, in the more reflection-sensitive Japanese language, *so desu* is generally implied.

When many newcomers to Japan hear what they think is "yes" – *hai* – what they are really hearing is "Yes, I'm listening" or "Yes, I hear you" or "Yes, I understand."

The Japanese use what we think is "yes" in the same manner some Americans use "you know" when they are talking. Some Americans will inject a "you know" into the middle of a conversation to ask, "Are you listening?" A Japanese will inject a "*Hai, so desu*" into the same conversation to say, "Yes, it is so" or Yes, I hear you." Some Americans will punctuate their conversations with "you know" asking, "Do you understand?" A Japanese will punctuate another's conversation with "*hai*" to say, "Yes, I understand."

The use of the word *hai* by a Japanese does not necessarily mean agreement. It can, but don't count on it.

Clinton is close.

- Hai, so desu -

Japan is the only country I have ever visited where if you took a poll of members of various religious sects or denominations you would find that the total number of people who admit to being a member of some religious group would add up to more people than there are in all of Japan. It is the only country I have ever visited in which religions are compatible with each other.

Citizens see no problem with practicing more than one religion, or parts of several different religions.

Shinto is Japan's native and national religion. Buddhism is as much a national philosophy as it is a religion. The late comers among religious sects in Japan are the Christians who arrived in the 16th Century and were banned by the 17th. Christians returned in this century, and although Christianity has been the premier religion of exclusion introduced to the Japanese, many Japanese find the teachings of Christ compatible with both Shinto and Buddhism and, with the exception of a few fundamental Christian groups, do not generally get caught up in the exclusionary aspect of Christianity.

While in Japan I enjoy indulging in the opportunity to practice religious beliefs across a wide spectrum of offerings. As a Unitarian-Universalist in the United States, I am a puzzle to most of my fellow Americans. In Japan, I am never asked what my religion is. I am, instead, simply allowed to indulge in the many religious offerings made available in Japanese society.

I try, but am not very good at remembering the rituals, to visit at least one Shinto shrine and participate in one ceremony of gratitude or thanksgiving on each of my visits. I have never received a *koan*, or theme, on which to contemplate from a Buddhist priest. I indulge, instead, in *zazen* meditation in which I try to empty my mind during meditation.

One of my major fascinations with religions in Japan has always been with the influence of Confucius on the society. Ask any Japanese if he practices Confucism, and he'll respond in the negative. But Confucius, who lived five centuries before Christ, was the patron saint of bureaucracies.

Confucius said there were only five relationships in life that required mutual obligations: ruler-subject, parent-child, husband-wife, older brother-younger brother, and friend-friend.

Obedience to superiors was an accepted absolute. Of the five relationships that Confucius outlined, only friend-friend was not a hierarchical relationship.

Over the years Confucian thought evolved into a philosophy of right and wrong taught as ethics courses in Japanese schools up to the end of World War II. After the war, the Confucian-based ethics that spawned *bushido* – The Way of the Warrior, and emperor worship – were dropped as part of the Japanese curriculum. Still, though, today the basic obedience demanded under Confucian doctrine of the five relationships, permeates the Japanese social order.

Before this trip is over, our inability to observe - as a matter of daily acceptance – these hierarchical relationships will undoubtedly cause problems.

- Hai, so desu -

Japan has one of the finest train systems in the world. I have lived in Japan for months at a time and never had to depend on a car. In the old days, in the Army, there was a motor pool of jeeps and other vehicles to draw from. Driving on the left hand of the road is easy enough to learn. We had motorcycles and other forms of transportation, but if you wanted to get somewhere, there was always the train – dependable and for the most part comfortable, especially the Green Cars – equivalent to our first-class seating.

The Japanese that meet us at the airport include several we already knew from their trip to Florida in the fall of 1992. My new *senséi* – teacher, instructor – Tohru Shimizu was among them. Shimizu means "spring water" in Japanese. It's a fitting name for Tohru. He's the only Japanese I have ever met that will greet you with a hug, an unusual public display of affection for a Japanese, although it is not unusual to see two men walking down the street holding hands.

Shimizu is an unusual Japanese. He is a refreshing drink of fresh spring water in a country packed with men who seem to be stamped endlessly out of the same suit-and-tie mold. Shimizu is an entrepreneur, the head of a chain of nine supermarkets. He owns Molly Maid – a franchised network of home cleaning services. He's betting that down the road, as the Japan economy continues to tighten internally and more two-wage-earner families develop as a means of financial survival, his Molly Maid franchises will flourish. Contrarian thinking for a Japanese.

It is important if you want to survive within the Japanese culture that you have a *senséi*. My former one was Masaru Ogawa, editor emeritus of the *Japan Times*. Only the Emperor got lower bows. Ogawa-san was one of those people who could open doors – any doors – for you. Ogawa-san died two years ago.

I met Shimizu-san when he led the 1992 Japanese group Rotary International Group Study Exchange team that visited Florida. We have corresponded frequently, mostly by fax, and he has gone out of his way to help tailor our trip to fulfill the wishes of the young businessmen who are traveling with me.

A very similar word to *senséi* in the Japanese language is *sensai*. It means one's former wife. For those in the group who have wives, they are all former wives for the next month, or so it would seem. Women still have little status in Japan. When we were putting together this team we received a letter from the Japanese Rotarians requesting specifically that we bring an all-male team. Although we're accustomed to women in Rotary in the United States, it's a custom that does not translate to the Japanese.

Shimizu is not in charge today. Dr. Shiro Watanabe, the local Rotary Group Study Exchange chairman, is the *honcho* on the scene. He's the Rotary governor's representative. The others in the group who meet us are subservient to him in the Japanese tradition. Dr. Watanabe greets us with the formal bow, handshake, and the Japanese smile that is as difficult for them to maintain as it is for us to keep a straight face. Japanese usually grin when they are nervous. They take one look at the pile of luggage we have brought and break out in big smiles.

We have to get from customs to the train station down a level or two beneath Narita airport. We grab individual baggage carts and pile on our stuff and hustle them down escalators, across airport concourses and up to the entrance to the lower level train stations. Here we are greeted with waist-high poles that prevent us from taking the carts down to the trains. The Japanese each grab a bag, we shoulder the others, and down the steps to the trains we go.

We've got reserved seats on the Narita Express, a modern state-of-the-art train. It's a train I have not seen before. It's been in service about three years. In streamlining, the Narita Express falls somewhere between the newer versions of the boxier regular express trains on Japan Railway and the *Shinkansen*, or bullet train. It has a distinctive red-and-white paint job. It's sitting on the track when we arrive, but we can't enter yet.

Workers are cleaning the cars as they do at the end of every run. Japanese trains are spotless. The Narita Express is no exception.

When boarding time arrives, we pile our luggage in the luggage compartments at the end of the car and take our assigned seats. On the bulkhead of the passenger car is an electronic map that shows the path of the train southbound to Chiba, Tokyo, Yokohoma, and our destination Ofuna. The trip will take two hours.

At one end of our car are rest rooms – both Western and Japanese style. I've never figured out how anyone could squat and use the Japanese *benjo*, nothing more than a hole in the floor, especially on a train flying across the countryside. Likewise, I've never figured out why the Japanese put glass windows in the doors of the Western-style rest rooms on their trains. It seems a simple "Occupied" sign would suffice, but they seem to prefer to see that there is really a human being taking up the space. Privacy, as in all Japanese life, is not a consideration. For the rest of the team members it is a subtle introduction to things to come.

Also at the end of the car are vending machines. Here I solve one of the major problems I have always faced in Japan – finding a cup of coffee. Something new has occurred since my last visit in 1981 – coffee in a can. At 110 yen – about a $1 at today's exchange rate – I can get a can of hot or cold "Georgia" coffee at the punch of a button. "Georgia" is the brand name because it is a product of Coca-Cola whose American headquarters are in Atlanta. There are Japanese brands as well. One, "Boss," will eventually earn me the title "Boss Coffee" from my traveling companions.

The first duty to attend to on the train ride south is the customary gift giving. I have in my bag gifts from our stateside sponsors for the district Rotary governor in Kanagawa Prefecture. Following the Japanese rigid chain-of-command, I present these to the governor's on-site representative, Dr. Watanabe. Also to honor his presence as the senior member of our greeting group I present him a golf watch from my stash of gift items.

Similar presents – including baseball caps from various major league teams whose members are clients of Ron Pullman – are made to the other Japanese who accompany us on the ride. Pullman is a financial strategist who handles investments for several major league ball players. Those Japanese who have children get frisbees from a collection a local bank gave me before I left the Florida Keys.

I'm wearing a Cleveland Indian baseball cap that Pullman got from one of his Indian clients. I may be one of the few remaining Indian fans in the world – dating back to the days of Satchel Paige. The conversation turns to baseball, the other national religion of Japan. I am asked what my favorite Japanese team is and assume it is a leading question, since "the" national team in Japan is the Yomiuri Giants, and Shimizu-san knows that I once spent an evening in the locker room and at a game with the great Sadaharu Oh who hit more home runs than Babe Ruth or Hank Aaron. Oh-san swung a compressed wood bat, something that is no longer used and is seldom mentioned in Japanese baseball circles.

Instead of "The Giants" I reply, "The Hiroshima Carp." The truth is I don't have a favorite Japanese baseball team. I just like some of the team names – Nippon Ham Fighters, Swallows, Buffalo, etc. The semantics of Japanese team names are – when translated to English – at times humorous. Take the Nippon Ham Fighters. At first glance one would assume it is a national team – Nippon being interchangeable for Japanese – like the Yomiuri Giants. What is a Ham Fighter? The thought makes for some great mental pictures, but actually the team is the Fighters, and it is owned by a meat processing conglomerate named Nippon Ham.

The Yomiuri Giants, home-based in Tokyo and revered by most baseball fans in Japan, are owned by the publishing and broadcasting conglomerate Yomiuri. Yomiuri makes certain Giants games are nationally broadcast, nurturing the team's image – a lesson apparently not lost on CNN's Ted Turner when he bought the Atlanta Braves a few years back.

Teams in Japan's two leagues – the Central and Pacific – are generally owned by private industry, and many take their names from their owners, much like the Buick Open in American Golf and the Federal Express Orange Bowl in college football.

The train races through the unlit nighttime countryside to Chiba, the northeastern port city on Tokyo Bay, then after a short run west makes the turn south to Tokyo and begins to pick up the suburbs. Once they start, they never stop. The first thing I notice is that there is no longer any open space between cities or suburban sectors. The houses are packed side-by-side as if it were the heart of Tokyo, yet we are nearly an hour away and traveling at speeds in the neighborhood of 70-75 miles and hour.

Each town or suburb has its own train station, but the Narita Express flies on through. Around each train station is a suburban shopping center. The streets are filled with automobiles. Most appear to be new or nearly new. What impresses me most is the proliferation of signs in English. As we whiz through many suburban centers, with the exception of their compactness and the traditional signs in Japanese characters, it would be difficult to tell them from similar suburban centers in the U.S. The scale, like the reserved seats on the Narita Express, is about three-quarters American.

Eventually the conversation turns to my previous visits to Japan. One of the Japanese seated in my group wants to know if I enjoyed Japanese women. "Did you find out it runs (he makes a sideways sign with his hands referring to a vagina)?" He asks laughing. *Ah so desuka?* - Is that so? The dirty old man syndrome, so much a Japanese thing, raises its ugly head. I answer with a palms up gesture. They all laugh.

When the train stops in Tokyo, a young couple board with their small son. The boy is wearing a Hiroshima Carp baseball cap.

"Do you think he will trade?" I ask one of my Japanese companions. He answers with a shrug. Trading items, especially clothing does not come naturally to the Japanese. They will give you gifts constantly, but trading seems to be a missing art. I make it my goal to swap the kid hats before we get to Ofuna.

As the train surfaces on the south side of Tokyo Station, it is apparent how much the city has grown upward since my last visit. All the way from Tokyo to Yokohama I am glued to the window absorbing the mass of development that has taken place.

Sometimes it is difficult to remember what was in a certain place the last time I visited it, but about one thing I am sure: there never was this much here when I visited in the past. Some of the areas we are rolling through were still rubble left from the war when I first visited in the 1950s. By the time I returned in the early '80s it had been rebuilt, but now it is stacked higher and tighter than I can recall. There are definitely more people – millions more – living and working here.

As the train nears Yokohama I notice the young boy's parents get out of their seats. They are going to leave the train before we get to Ofuna. If I am going to trade my Cleveland Indians baseball cap for the Carp hat I need to get moving. I step over the legs of the man sitting next to me and walk up the aisle towards the Japanese boy. The eyes of our hosts follow me. I don't believe they are quite sure if I am really going to do this. I kneel next to the boy, who is standing in the aisle hanging onto the arm rest on a seat. I point to the cap on his head and then the one on mine and ask, "*Booeki?*" It's the best I can do. It's a word for trade between countries. He's got his eyes fixed on the big smiling Indian – Chief Wahoo - on my hat. He smiles and his hand comes forward to touch the Indian. I look up at his father and ask, "*Dooi?*" May I have your permission? The father nods in the affirmative. The young boy and I swap hats. Mine comes down over his ears, but he's smiling from one to the other. His father, also smiling, picks him up and they head for the door of the train as we pull into Yokohama.

I have a Carp hat, my big trade of the trip.

- Hai, so desu -

It's raining when the train gets to Ofuna. We transfer our luggage by carrying it off the train, up the steps to the station and then outside to a string of waiting taxi cabs.

It's also dark so the first real view we get of Japan is that of a large statute on a hill outside Ofuna station, a steady stream of people hidden beneath umbrellas pouring out of the station, and several more Japanese Rotarians who are on hand to greet us and load us into the cabs. Japanese cabs are meticulously clean. They used to have hand-embroidered lace covering the backs and tops of the seats. The cab drivers used to wear white gloves. Now the seats just have white covers. Most of the drivers have forsaken the white glove routine.

We motor from Ofuna to Fujisawa, a town I remember as being a way stop between Camp Zama and Enoshima – a resort island off the southern coast of Kanagawa Prefecture. Tonight I don't recognize any of it. There is no countryside as in the old days, just cars, buildings and people, packed tightly together.

We arrive at the Fujisawa Grand Hotel and the first thing I notice is there is a 7-11 next door, also one up the street about a block. Grand may be a word that is a bit overdone in reference to this hotel. It is nice, but hardly grand in the five-star tradition. The hotel is a relatively new one. It has banquet facilities, accommodations for weddings including a wedding shop where you can buy gifts for the bride and groom, and a decent Western-style restaurant.

We check in and are shown to our rooms. They are traditional Japanese in size. This is not a luxury hotel. It is more in the "businessman's" range of hotels. The rooms contain a single bed that would be comparable in size to something between our twin and double. There is color television, a small writing table, a hot plate complete with tea pot and bags of tea and coffee. All of it is packed into an 8-by-10 space. You enter the room through a narrow hallway from the corridor. The hallway passes a small hanging closet and the bathroom, which has the traditional deep Japanese style tub, and Western-style plumbing.

Japanese hotel bathrooms seem to be stamped out in a factory somewhere. They are all essentially the same in the Western-style hotels - small, but efficient. Altogether, taking in the bathroom, hallway and bed area, the room is about 8 feet by 16 feet in size. It has one window that can be opened manually. I learn before the night is over that the window serves as the air-conditioning unit for the room.

After a cup of coffee in the hotel restaurant our hosts depart, reminding us that we have visited Japan at the best time of year – cherry blossom time. They tell us they will meet us at 6 p.m. the following evening for a welcome party and we are on our own.

My first stop is the 7-11 next door. I buy a jar of instant coffee to keep my pot going in my room. An 8-ounce jar of Blendy – other than Columbian beans – costs $8.50, a bargain in a country where coffee costs $5 a cup and you don't get free refills.

On the way by the desk I check on the room rates. The going rate for the room I am in is $79.65 a day. A review of the hotel menu – offering both American and Japanese style meals – posted outside the restaurant in the lobby shows meals average $13.27 for breakfast, $15.93 for lunch, and $30.97 for dinner.

It's about midnight Japanese time, but my inner clock is ticking away somewhere around 11 a.m. I'm not really tired, but should be from the long trip from Miami. My stomach reminds me it's lunch time. Memory tells me there is always something open in Japan. It's safe to walk the streets here at night.

The rain has stopped. I head up the hill towards the brightly lit *pachinko* parlor that generally indicates there is a railroad station nearby. I pass the second 7-11. I could always stop there for a Japanese hot dog, but Japanese hot dogs aren't my cup of tea. They seem tasteless - maybe too much soybean filler. Who knows for sure when you tackle the Japanese diet?

I climb the steps up to the *pachinko* parlor. They lead to a concourse over the bus stops below. Japan is a country that was built in layers. I walk a block down the concourse to the entrance to the Fujisawa train station. There are two couples necking in the park. Several *sarariimen* – suits, ties, umbrellas and briefcases – are staggering out of the train station on their way home. They have been out drinking business with their bosses, a Japanese business tradition or handicap depending on how you view the issue.

At the train station I turn east down another flight of steps to street level once again. This is a typical narrow old-style Japanese street. It goes past the high-rise department stores and empties out on the main east-west street again. I pass a McDonald's that is closed. Across the street is a Kentucky Fried Chicken, also closed. The statute – wooden Indian style – of Col. Sanders standing in front of the restaurant has a Rotary button on its lapel.

Continuing east I pass several narrow, old-style Japanese streets. Down each is a club or two still open. I can tell from the signs, most in Japanese but with beer and whiskey signs in English. These are not tourist stops. They don't need me. I continue to walk passing several Japanese restaurants that are closed. I stop at several and take a look at the food offerings that are displayed in plastic in the front windows. The food hasn't changed much since my last visit here in 1981. The prices have. I make some mental notes.

Just about the time I am ready to head back and opt for a 7-11 hot dog, I round a curve in the street and a couple of blocks ahead of me is a Denny's sign. The lights are on. It looks like it is open. Visions of a juicy British Burger dance through my head. When I get to it the restaurant looks like an American Denny's but in Japanese scale. Inside I take a seat at the counter.

The waitress hands me the traditional Japanese hot towel and a menu. No British Burgers here, but there is a picture of a bowl of beef stew that looks tempting. I order it with hot tea. It arrives about 20 minutes later still resembling a dish of good, old-fashioned beef stew. I dig in. No taste - none at all. Even the brown gravy is bland. It fills my stomach. That's about all I can say for it. I walk to the counter and plunk down the
equivalent of $12.39 cents in yen for the meal. There's no tipping.

- Hai, so desu -

Back in my room I still can't sleep. It's nearly 2 a.m. Japanese time, but my inner clock won't recognize the flip-flop of time zones. The room is hot. I look for the air-conditioning switch. There is one on the headboard, but it only goes down to 22° C. In fact, I'm not sure it's even an air-conditioner. Opening the window works better. It's cool outside - about 45° in our language.

I plug in the portable computer and decide to play with it for a while. Testing the fax-modem to send a message to my office back in the Keys I discover that the Japanese have a digital telephone system in this hotel. It won't accept the analog dialing instructions from the computer. I dig for the books to see if I can reset the computer so it will work with the digital system. In a matter of minutes I have the correct dialing string coded into the communications software and give it another try. Still won't work, maybe I'm doing something wrong. I'll see if Paul White can give me a hand tomorrow. He's light years ahead of me in computer knowledge.

Roaming around the keyboard I call up the calculator. The prices I saw in restaurant windows on my walk around town tell me things have gotten more expensive in Japan. Just how much more I need to figure out.

We bought yen coming into the country at 113 yen to the dollar. In 1956 when I first visited Japan the exchange rate was 360 yen to the dollar. In 1981 240 yen to the dollar. Today the exchange rate is at its lowest level in history - the Japanese yen is at its strongest point against the dollar.

To figure out what this was doing to the purchasing power of the dollar, I used the cost of a bowl of soba – the Japanese equivalent to our hamburger or hot dog, a noodle soup with vegetables and sometimes pork.

In 1956 I could buy a bowl of soba in a neighborhood restaurant for 40 yen, or 11 cents American. In 1981 that same bowl of soup cost me 600 yen, or $2.50. Now a bowl of soba costs about 750 yen, or $6.64. That's an increase of 5,936 percent over 37 years, or 160 percent annually compared to an average annual inflation rate of just over 10 percent in the U.S. over the same period.

The purchasing power of the dollar in Japan is declining at warp speed.

Consumer prices in the U.S. rose 399 percent between 1958 and 1993. Not necessarily a record to be proud of, but a little easier on the individual wage earner than the quantum leap Japan's economy has taken. On the other hand, wages in both the U.S. and Japan have escalated in concert with consumer prices.

Generally when they get out of synch we have a recession or some variation of "hard times." Right now the Japanese are about two years behind us in the current global recession.

Currency is where the immediate difference is felt. Although the Japanese currency has inflated much more rapidly than ours, so has their earnings so they have moved more easily into today's markets internally than those of us who only visit here occasionally. We have to trade our dollars for Japanese yen when we get here, and if we are used to the older, more liberal exchange rates, then we get a double whammy from deflated exchange and inflated prices.

When I first came here in the '50s, 100 yen was the smallest bill in circulation. There were still some *sen* – one hundredth of a *yen* – coins in circulation. One in particular always fascinated me. I believe it was a 5-sen piece because I recall it was made of plastic and had a square hole in the center like today's 5-yen and 50-yen coins that are made of metal. Today I ask Japanese about *sen* pieces and no one under 75 years old seems to remember them. I know they existed for two reasons: I used them, and I still read about them in histories about Japan in the '30s and '40s.

Today the smallest bill in circulation is a 1,000-yen note. The old 500- and 100-yen notes are now coins. They are the size of U.S. quarters and vending machines handle them just as U.S. vending machines handle quarters. They buy between two and three times what a quarter will buy from a U.S. vending machine. The major problem I face is that I find myself dropping my change in my pocket as if it were quarters. By the end of the day, when I empty my pockets I find I am carrying $30 or $40 worth of Japanese money around in loose change.

The only two other paper notes in circulation in Japan are the ¥5,000 and ¥10,000 bills. The ¥10,000 note has always been the largest bill used in Japan. In the '50s it cost me about $28 to buy one. Since my monthly pay, including overseas allowances, was only $108 I didn't buy many ¥10,000 bills. When I came back to Japan in the early '80s I could buy a ¥10,000 yen note for about $40. At that time in my life it took me less than two hours to earn $40, so there were plenty of ¥10,000 yen notes bought and spent.

Today there is so little difference between a ¥10,000 Japanese bank note and a $100 bill that it's hardly worth worrying about.

If the yen strengthens just a tad more against the dollar, the two bills will be equal in exchange. It takes me more than two hours today to earn $100, so I'm sliding backwards in this game – rapidly. My purchasing power in Japan has been better than halved by the exchange rates, and cut at least in half again by the increase in prices here.   Japan is no bargain for the return visitor.

All of this tinkering with prices and exchange rates should have put me to sleep, but it hasn't. I try television next. There are 10 channels on the set in the room plus three pay channels. The set has a bi-lingual switch. There is not much on at 3 a.m. The bi-lingual switch does not produce anything in English. I flip through the pay channels. Cable television is just coming to Japan. There are less than a half dozen channels available and this hotel is apparently not a cable subscriber. Instead it has three pay channels. The first has a movie in Japanese. The second is just starting. The title says it is a "Ricky, Ricky Film." English maybe.

It opens with a Japanese girl seated in a lawn chair on the balcony of a high-rise apartment porch somewhere in what appears to be a Japanese city. She is being interviewed – in Japanese – by what I assume is a Japanese newscaster. Their conversation is so fast I can't follow it in my limited Japanese.

Within a couple of minutes they are inside the condo unit, stripped to their birthday suits and going at it hot and heavy. That's when I remember that the "r" in Japanese is pronounced like an "l" in American. I've tuned into the Licky-Licky flicks not Ricky-Ricky films. I can't wait to tell this one to Rick VanGrouw my managing editor who is stuck back in the Keys running the *Islamorada Free Press* for me while I watch skin flicks in Japan.

This is hard-core porn with a minor exception. Whenever the camera meanders into a scene where pubic hair can be seen the area is blurred out. It's like watching a baseball game on television with

the batter diffused every time he hits a home run. Japanese hard-core porn is as bland as Japanese hot dogs despite the fact that millions of Japanese ride the railroad trains pouring through two-inch-thick pornographic comic books and no one seems to pay any attention. The Japanese aren't normally prudish
people, but pubic hair is a big no-no.

I opt for the third pay channel – an old Western movie in English. It finally puts me to sleep.

- Hai, so desu -

Before we can be officially welcomed to Japan by a largegroup of Rotarians our team is escorted into a side room off a large banquet hall at the Fujisawa Grand, seated around a large table facing a group of Japanese Rotarians charged with explaining what they had planned for us.

They give each of us a schedule of our activities for the next month. It's in booklet form with the pages on the right written in *kanji* – Chinese characters used in writing Japanese – and the page on the right is written in English. The first thing I notice in the day-to-day activity log is that there seems to be more activities in Japanese than there are in English.

The second thing I notice is that the schedule of our activities does not match up with the outline given by Rotary International for Group Study Exchange teams. Instead of a one-day-a-week vocational day that seemed to be the heart of the experience to the team members I find instead a lot of visits to companies and plants that deal with things loosely related to our various careers and occupations.

For instance, I am a newspaper editor and there are two visits to newspaper printing plants, which I know from past visits to Japan have nothing to do with the editorial side of newspapering.

There are courtesy calls to mayors, a visit to an aerospace center, sightseeing, a sumo tournament, visits to U.S. military installations, a baseball game and a trip to Hiroshima I had requested to give team members a chance to visit the atomic bomb museum and walk ground zero.

There are a dozen or so Rotary clubs to visit, something we expect and are prepared for.

I question the lack of vocational exchange opportunities. My questions are passed over lightly. This is my first sit-down formal meeting with the Japanese and I am having a little difficulty dealing with jet lag and remembering just how Japanese meetings go. There is really no room for discussion. Meetings with Japanese are well scripted events and the Japanese that perform do not deviate from the basic script.

Question-and-answer periods are not part of the everyday Japanese routine. Japanese do not wing it well, so they avoid getting put on the spot.

I don't push the issue. After all this is our first night in town. I don't want to make waves by disturbing the *wa* – the harmony – of the situation. *Wa* is important in Japan.

Initially I thought there might be some saving grace in the fact that the schedule we were given had "AM" and "PM" slots marked "Free" every few days. None of the evenings appeared to be taken up so I assumed team members would be free after the afternoon plant tours to strike out on their own and sample Japanese culture.

I would learn later the "Free" times were when the Japanese had scheduled our transportation, usually by bus with a half dozen Japanese Rotarians, to our next stop and many one-night stands.

And, I would soon learn to forget about having evenings off since the local Rotarians were responsible for feeding us. Hidden somewhere in their *kanji* schedules they have us booked into sit-on-the-floor, 12-course Japanese dinner parties nearly every evening. Those follow 10-course sit-down lunches they have scheduled for us almost every day.

One can only eat so much raw fish.

I get off on a bad foot from the start. We are marched from the first meeting with the Rotary leaders into the large banquet hall across the corridor. The center table, about 40 feet long by 10-12 feet wide situated under a large crystal chandelier is loaded with food much the same as we would expect at a large formal cocktail party in the States.   Around the room are smaller round tables containing large bottles of beer and glasses. There are no chairs. The meeting is opened with a toast by the Japanese Rotary governor. I don't drink and neither do four of my five team members. We hold up the opening ceremony while the Japanese find some orange soda that we can use for the opening *kanpai*, or toast.

The Japanese can't seem to understand that we don't drink simply because we chose not to. To them the drinking is part of their job. Their evening routine as businessmen, or *sarariimen* – is to go out with their boss after work and drink for several hours.

In Japan it is a disgrace for a workingman to show up in his neighborhood in the early evening. It means he is lazy, he is not working hard, he is not doing everything he can to earn a living for his family. So, they go from work to the local restaurant and drink business for a few hours before going home. They have difficulty understanding why we don't do the same.

We get the *kanpai* out of the way and get down to introductions. Members of our team have scripted Japanese speeches on cue cards and we do our introductory talks in Japanese much to the amazement of our hosts. Despite our foreign accents it appears they understand most of what we say. They laugh in the appropriate spots – when I apologize for my poor Japanese, when Paul White tells about being an aeronautical engineer and managing a Chinese restaurant because our space program is not hiring, and when Tim Wilson explains that he and his wife own their own production company with her as president and him as vice president.

Tim has prepared a video of the Florida Keys, with the sound track in Japanese, that we show. It holds the attention of about a third of the crowd. The others are more interested in getting back to drinking and eating. The program, which started at 6 p.m., is promptly over at 7 p.m. As quickly as they assembled, the 100 or so Japanese hosts disappear.

We decide to drop our coats and ties in our rooms and go out on the town. The team meets in the lobby of the hotel and no sooner than we get out the front door we are met by some of the Japanese Rotarians who were at the welcome party. They, too, are on their way to get something to eat and invite us to join them.

We go to a restaurant in Fujisawa where we sit on the floor and round-after-round of drinks and Japanese food is set before us. We sample raw fish, *yakitori* – skewers of barbecued chicken pieces, livers and gizzards, rice, *tempura* – deep fried shrimp and vegetables. The party lasts until about 9:30 p.m. when the Japanese take their leave and we head back to the hotel.

It is a pleasant evening, punctuated often by "What do you think of Japan?" It's a question the Japanese constantly ask us. As often as it is asked one of our team members comes up with a different answer. At times the Japanese want to argue about our interpretation of their country. Other times they just nod their heads and are non-committal.

The biggest point they seem to want to get across is that Japan is now the second strongest economy in the world, that they are indeed a world power. I don't belabor the point.

- Hai, so desu -

A group of Japanese Rotarians picked us up at our Fujisawa hotel at 9 a.m. We are riding one and two to a car accompanied by one or two Japanese. I am riding in the front seat of a Japanese luxury car with the top ranking Japanese. I have an interpreter – a young Japanese woman who spent a college semester in Texas. We are going sightseeing at Enoshima, an island shrine and tourist attraction directly south of Fujisawa on the Japanese coast.

This is our first day of sightseeing with the Japanese. As always, they are polite, but they have a schedule that they insist must be kept. It's not the brand of sightseeing that we're used to in America. This is the packaged tour routine, planned right down to the rest stops, which are few and far between.

I'm riding in the front seat with the Japanese leader who tells me he will be 75 in a week or two. I watched him throw down enough booze last night to fell the average person. This morning he looks fresh and crisp. There is not the slightest trace of a hangover. He is dressed in the customary grey, pin-stripe suit of a business executive even though it is Saturday and we were told to dress informally. His fellow Japanese also showed up this morning in their suits and ties. Our team is wearing slacks and windbreakers. We don't do ties on Saturday, especially when we were led to believe this was a casual day of sightseeing.

Riding in the front seat of a car I'm not driving in Japan takes a little adjustment. The Japanese drive on the left side of the road. Japanese cars have right-hand drive. Although I get into the car on the side I am accustomed to in the States, I find myself faced with nothing but a padded dash. When the car starts to move I instinctively want to grab a steering wheel and ride the corner of the brake pedal with my toe. I feel totally out of control as the car rolls out into traffic that is bumper to bumper and moving down the wrong side of the street.

Thankfully traffic doesn't move that fast in Japan, so the adjustment usually comes easily, but there are times - like when a truck is coming at us on a street hardly wide enough for two cars to pass. I want to shove the brake pedal through the floor when there is no brake pedal on my side.

It is only about five miles from Fujisawa to Enoshima, but I struggle with my out-of-control feelings until we make the turn onto the causeway that runs from the mainland to the island. It's a familiar sight, more crowded and built up than I remember it, but nonetheless a familiar sight that takes my mind off getting adjusted to riding in the suicide seat on the wrong side of the road in a car driven by a man who reminds me of a geriatric cabby in Sarasota, Florida.

It was cool last night, but by the time we reach the island the sun has come up and it is getting warmer. The car we are riding in has every bell and whistle the Japanese make, but despite the fact the temperature inside the car must be pushing 90 to 95 degrees Fahrenheit, the driver has neither turned on the air-conditioning nor rolled down a window beyond a small crack at the top of the window on the driver's door. Normally I would crank my window down, but I'm all turned around in this car and have decided to wait and see what the driver does.

He does nothing, and gives no indication that he realizes the temperature
is reaching sauna levels inside his car.

I have other things to worry about. I know there is a shrine on top of the mountain that is Enoshima Island. I know there are a lot of steps – something like 350 – up the side of the steep hill that leads to the shrine, and still more beyond that leading to a garden and amusement park atop the island. I know that once you have seen everything there is to see on top of the island – including climbing the observation tower, there are a zillion
steps coming back down although there is a choice of climbing back down the same system of stone slabs that goes up to the top, or taking a leisure walk down the roadways that wind around the back side of the island, some with grades so steep I have always wondered how some of the little, light four-cylinder Japanese utility vehicles ever got to the top.

I also know I had my right angle removed nine years ago and my right leg is fused to my foot. I have never given it the type of workout that I sense is coming up today. I can see the small mountain I most likely am going to have to climb straight ahead.

The biggest difference I noticed on the drive down from Fujisawa is that there is no open countryside anymore. Thirty-five years ago, the last time I visited this area, it was a nice drive through the countryside on winding, narrow two-lane roads. The roads are still narrow by U.S. standards, but wider than they used to be and jam-packed with homes and businesses on each side.

The growth in this area of Japan has been phenomenal. Just how much I wondered until I picked up this morning's *Japan Times* over a cup of coffee in the hotel restaurant. There are about 40-50 million more Japanese on the main islands than there was when I first came here in 1956. Thirty million of those live in the Kanto Plain area, an area surrounded by mountains around Tokyo Bay.

Japan's population growth has been steady since World War II, leveling off only last year, according to the Japanese Management and Coordination Agency that just released its preliminary figures for the last fiscal year, which ended Oct. 1, 1992.

The nation's population marked its slowest growth rate in the post-war era. Japan's population increased by 410,000 during the year to 124.45 million. Although the Japanese used to bill themselves as "the 100 million" during World War II, they stretched the figures quite a bit. There were about 75 million people living in Japan when the Japanese attacked Pearl Harbor.

During the war between 5 and 7 million of these went overseas. How many returned is still speculation. So, by conservative estimates, there are about 50 million more people living in Japan today than there was at the end of the war in 1945.

Today, the number of elderly citizens aged 65 or older make up 13.1 percent of the population – the highest ratio in post war Japan – while the number of people under 14 has hit a postwar low of 17.2 percent.

There are 61.1 million men and 63.36 million women in Japan. From the looks of things, as we pull into the narrow street that winds its way up the hill through a gauntlet of little shops to the foot of the steps that continue on up the mountain to the Shinto shrine, and eventually to the top, a good many of the 122 million Jpanese are on vacation today.

It is a Saturday, more and more a day off for Japanese workers. When I first came to Japan it seemed like the Japanese worked seven days a week. When I visited in 1981 they were still working six days a week. Now there is a movement to pare the Japanese workweek, which averages 44 hours for industrial workers,

back to 40 hours. For the first time in my nearly four decades of dealing with the Japanese I am hearing locals talk
more and more about leisure time. They want more of it, and they want to enjoy it.

One of the local Rotarians, a professor at Tokyo University, I visited with last night told me that for the first time this year he heard students say they were going to shop corporate opportunities. The students were looking for the corporations that would offer them the most time off, something totally out of keeping with the old Japanese traditional of work, work, work.

A pretty good mix has the day off today. We are guided by a man walking in front of the car through a crowd of people packing the shops along the narrow walkway up the hill. He waves our car into a tiny four-car parking lot in front of an ancient Japanese hotel. The crowd around us is a mix of young and old. There are a lot of couples, young to middle-aged, some with small children who appear to be enjoying a day off. There also are a lot of older couples, people who appear to be retirement age who are visiting Enoshima as tourists.

Most obvious to me is the change in Japanese dress code. This crowd could be a crowd in almost any tourist center in the world. Many of the older men stick to the tradition of coats and ties, but those under 50 are dressed in more leisurely attire, tennis sweaters, windbreakers, sweat shirts, and slacks. The women in the crowd are dressed mostly in leisure clothes, many of them wearing slacks. There is not a kimono in sight. The children are dressed in American fashions ranging from jeans to National Basketball Association sweat shirts.

We stop at the hotel, which is owned and operated by a fourth or fifth generation descendant of the founders. He is a Rotarian. We are greeted by a group of local Rotarians in the coffee shop over coffee and pastries and then get a tour of the hotel. It has both Western-style rooms and Japanese-style suites. They overlook the inlet that is formed by the causeway to the island. It is a plush, albeit several centuries old, hotel. In one room, off the lobby on the main floor, I find a tunnel that leads back into the center of the mountain that is Enoshima Island.

Just as I am tempted to sneak off on a tour of the tunnel, one of the Rotarians informs me we are running behind schedule. It is time to start the march up the hill.

The shops along the street could be souvenir shops along Duval Street in Key West or Bourbon Street in New Orleans. There are more Oriental than Occidental souvenirs, but I swear I have seem many of them in shops in the States. The prices are high, but the tourists seem to be indulging themselves with abandon.

When we get to the other end of the street, itself a series of staircases, I spot the racks of sake jugs that mark the shrine high up the side of the cliff in front of us. There are hundreds of steps leading up to them. Our 75-year-old Japanese host takes them in stride. I am winded half way up, but struggle to make the top where we are herded into a hall off the shrine and seated at tables in a side room. Here they serve us tea and explain that we are going to go into the shrine and be blessed by a Shinto priest.

I quickly try to remember the ritual and must appear stumped. My interpreter, who is sitting across the table from me, senses my confusion: "Do you remember the ceremony?"

"Vaguely," I answer. "I forget which way to turn the branches and when to bow and clap my hands."

She smiles and points to a wall behind me: "Look over there. It's written on the wall."

And, it is. Not only written, but explained in drawings. I am relieved. The last trip I made to Japan I was not the group leader, so I could simply watch what he did and repeat it. This time, as team leader, I know I am going to have to go first in everything, even when it is not fully explained.

Following the ceremony at the shrine, we continue our climb to the top of the island where we find a botanical garden and amusement park. The rest of the team members opt for continuing the climb to the top of an observation platform. I'm bushed. My legs feel like rubber. I decide to take a rest.

The other five team members line up at the ticket window where one of our Japanese hosts buys them tickets to the botanical garden and the observation tower. I slip off to the side to watch the Japanese tourists and compare them to those I am familiar with in the Florida Keys. Just as I reach a vendor's booth under a long tent to the side of the entrance to the botanical gardens, our senior host comes running over to me waving his arms and shouting: "You are to tour the gardens."

"*Arigato*, thanks," I say, "I need a break."

"You must tour the gardens," he says, giving me a stern look. The remainder of the Japanese are beginning to gather behind him waiting to see what I will do. I take a can of Boss Coffee from the vendor and hand her a ¥1,000 note. She counts out my change.

"The garden is next on your schedule," I am reminded by my 75-year-old host who shows no sign of having been stressed at all by the climb to the top of Enoshima Island.

"*Hai, so desu*, I know, I know," I reply. "My legs are tired. I am going to take a rest. I will tour the garden after I have taken a rest."

"You only have 20 minutes to take the tour," I am reminded.

"You must be back here by 11. We are scheduled to eat lunch at noon."

"*Hai, so desu*, I understand. I will be here at 11. I am going to take a rest and then I will get back on schedule."

It seems to work. The senior Japanese motions to his entourage and they head under the tent to a table in the far back corner. I finally have a few minutes to myself. I finish my can of coffee and dispose of the can in the container outside the vendor's booth. Then I sneak back to the entranceway to the botanical gardens where people are constantly coming up the hill and splitting off to the right to go into the gardens and climb the tower or off to the left to find a place to rest under the large tent bounded on three sides by vendors selling refreshments or souvenirs.

I have several shots of black-and-white film left in the camera I am carrying. It's a Japanese camera. I start framing faces with the zoom lens and notice that the faces are not much different than those I see in Florida. The first woman I focus on is wearing fashionable wire-rim glasses, a brimmed, white canvas cap to shade her from the sun, an off-white linen jacket over what appears to be a white rayon blouse, madras slacks, and Nike walking shoes. She appears to be in her late 50s or early 60s. Her facial features indicate she is Japanese, but her appearance suggests she could be a middle-aged housewife from Nebraska or Iowa who is simply on vacation.

What is most likely her husband is standing off about 15 feet taking a picture of her with the observation tower in the background.

He is using a Nikon camera with what appears to be a standard 50-millimeter lens. He is dressed not unlike a middle-aged Midwestern businessman off on a weekend jaunt – casual slacks, comfortable walking shoes, a yellow polo shirt under a good imitation of a Member's Only grey jacket. On his head is a Giants baseball cap. His physical features, too, are Japanese but his demeanor is much more relaxed than that of any of the Japanese I have been involved with since I arrived a few days ago.

This couple could be an American couple who have taken early retirement and are out enjoying the world, but they're not.

The Giants baseball cap is not a souvenir. It has been worn enough to collect the tell-tell dents and marks of a fan's hat. No tourists from overseas this couple. They are members of the growing upper middle class in Japan, a class that has gained significantly in numbers since my last visit here. My bet is that this couple has a year-old Japanese luxury car parked somewhere at the bottom of the mountain. They do not use its air-conditioner during the Fall, Winter, and Spring months, of course.

A proud set of young Japanese parents are chasing their young daughter up the short flight of stairs that leads to a small pool in the center of the walkway going into the gardens. I am sitting off to the side atop a short stone fence. The little girl, who appears to be two or three years old, is dressed in a brightly colored jumper. She wears small, fashionable tennis shoes. Sleeves of a ruffled blouse flare out from beneath the shoulder straps of her jumper. The girl's hair is neatly cropped in the traditional Japanese page-boy style.

Her mother is dressed in jeans and a sweatshirt on which an English slogan is emblazoned. One of the words, "sport" has been misspelled "spirit" on the shirt. The girl's father is dressed in slacks, a loose-fitting, long-sleeved dress shirt, and has the arms of a sweater, draped down his back, tied around his neck. He wears no tie.

Both the mother and father wear stylish walking shoes. The three could be a middle-class, upwardly mobile, family from any major metropolitan area in the U.S. Their facial features are the only indication they are Oriental. Their height is average, not the shorter-than-*gaijin* (foreigner) I am used to from my old days in Japan.

I snap some pictures of the people about me and climb down off the stone wall. It is time to tour the botanical garden. On my way across the patio that leads to the garden entrance, I cast a sideways glance towards the refreshment tent and the group of Japanese Rotarians seated at the table in the back corner. They are having a few beers. Ah, a little hair of the dog that bit them last night.

I pay ¥200 to get into the garden and skip the ticket for the observation tower. A system of paths leads through the garden to the tower and an amusement park at its base. I stroll along the paths, watching the other people touring the gardens. It is evident from physical characteristics that most of these tourists are Oriental – Japanese, most likely – but from their dress and holiday mannerisms, they are pretty much like the tourists that I see every day at home. Gone is the old traditional grey that for so long dominated Japanese dress. Today's modern Japanese dresses with style. The more expensive the label – Gucci, Yves St.-Laurent, Ralph Lauren – they wear, they more they make it visible.

I look up and see the other members of the team, and our interpreter, waving from the top deck of the observation tower. The 20 years difference in our ages shows. They look like they could do another mountain. I am thankful that the remainder of the long walk ahead of us is all downhill.

As I round a curve in the stone walkway I see the amusement park ahead. To my left, behind a hedge, I see a young Japanese boy, probably around 10 years old, race by in a go-cart on a track that has two hairpin turns laid out in a space not much larger than a McDonald's drive-in window. Ahead of me is a small, fenced area in which younger children are playing on wooden models of train engines, fire trucks, and cars. The youngster who is playing engineer in the train freezes when I raise my camera and focus on him. His laughter turns to a bland stare. He looks over towards a woman who appears to be his mother for approval before he looks back at me. She nods. He looks at me and smiles for the camera.

My watch says it is nearly 11 o'clock. It's time to catch up with my Japanese hosts. I head back for the gate. They are waiting on me when I get there. The leader is pointing at his watch and saying we are getting behind schedule. "We must go," he admonishes everyone, and heads for some steps that lead down another path through more shops and a walk around the backside of the island.

The walk back down the small mountain top that is Enoshima Island takes us through a small shopping village, across a wooden bridge from which I get a glimpse of sports fishermen several hundred feet below us casting large surf rods into the waters around the island. There is no surf. They are fishing from atop a flat stone peninsular that juts off from the base of the mountain we are walking down.

The walk continues down narrow, one-lane roads that are steep and full of sharp curves. A short fence on the ocean side prevents us from slipping over the sharp cliff that descends to the ocean from the waterside of the road. Every time someone hesitates to look at something we are reminded that we are running behind schedule and prodded on by our hosts.

By the time we get to the bottom, my legs are killing me. Walking down constant inclines with a leg that has no ankle is a painful experience. I have just set a personal record for distance in this category. The pain is intense, but there is no time to rest. We are loaded into the cars and drive off the island, down the beach road on the mainland to a large hotel. The noonday sun is hot, but the Japanese continue to drive with their windows up and their air-conditioners off.

I head for a rest room after we walk from the ground-level parking lot, through a large atrium area, and down three flights of parallel marble stairs separated by a wide slow flowing stair-by-stair waterfall that ends in an outdoor reflecting pool at the underground restaurant level of the hotel. I am just about to unzip my fly when one of our Japanese hosts steps into the rest room, looks at me, and says: "Come. We must go. They are waiting for you so they can have the toast and start lunch."

Geez, I thought the schedule at least suggested this was going to be a leisurely day of sightseeing.

Lunch is one of those Japanese meals that goes on, and on, and on. It starts with a plate of *sashami* – raw fish – followed by a plate of *sushi* – rice rolls filled with raw fish and other seafood, and vegetables. Then the traditional bowl of *mizu supu* – soy bean soup – is served. A small dish of relishes accompanies the meal, then a bowl of rice. Next comes a platter of *tempura* – fried shrimp and vegetables. Then a plate of *yakitori* – barbecued chicken, chicken livers and chicken gizzards on skews – is served. That's followed by a plate of *unagi* – smoked eel. I am stuffed before we are half way through.

It seems to fascinate my Japanese hosts that I use *hashi* – chopsticks – with no problem. I am constantly explaining that I have been here before, that I have used chopsticks in the past, but my hosts never seem to remember.

At one point I am eating a piece of raw fish that looks an awful lot like the bait we use to catch yellowtail snapper in the Florida Keys. It looks exactly like bonito, a fish that we do not normally consider a food fish. I have caught a lot of bonito. They are fun fish to catch. I've used them for shark bait, and particularly when cut in small pieces to stuff sand balls when we are sand balling for yellowtail. I never considered bonito edible.

I turn to the man next to me. "I think I am eating bait," I say, holding up a piece of the fish with my *hashi*.

"That's a fine fish. That's *katsuo*. Very good," I am told.

"I think it is bonito. We use this for bait where I come from. We don't eat it."

"No, it is *katsuo*, a good fish to eat."

"Maybe so, but I still think it is bonito where I come from."

I ask the interpreter, sitting at the end of the table, if she has a Japanese-English dictionary. She digs through her purse and comes up with one. "Look up *katsuo* and see what it means in English, please," I ask.

"Bonito," she replies.

I am eating bait – raw. I smile and continue.

I learn later that serving a guest the first bonito of the spring season is a very honorable gesture in Japanese.

The waiters and waitresses keep a steady supply of beer and *sake* flowing. A small drinking bout breaks out between one of the Japanese and Ron Pullman. They are pouring *sake* for each other in the traditional friendship style of the Japanese. As soon as one bottle is emptied another is put in its place. After a couple of bottles the Japanese begin watching Pullman out of the corner of their eyes. The old story is that *gaijin* cannot handle their *sake*.

The Japanese, and many Americans, believe we can drink *sake* sitting down, but when we stand up we pass out from it. It does have a kick.

After Pullman has downed the contents of a couple of bottles the Japanese begin to warn him how lethal *sake* can be. He smiles and asks his Japanese drinking partner to keep pouring. I wonder if either one of them will be able to keep up with the afternoon schedule. We have some more walking ahead – down the beachfront highway to an aquarium and then across to the oceanfront marine auditorium for a dolphin and whale show – all in the hot sun.

Lunch lasts a couple of hours. It ends as abruptly as it started. We are reminded that we have a schedule to keep. The hotel manager gives us a brief tour of a Japanese wedding chapel on the underground restaurant floor of the hotel and then it is up three flights of steps to street level and off to the aquarium down the beach.

I look for the elevators, but my Japanese hosts insist on taking the steps up to ground level. I tried the same thing yesterday in city hall in Fujisawa when we went to visit the mayor, but the Japanese insisted on using the stairs to cover the four flights up to the mayor's ceremonial reception room overlooking the downtown business section of the city.

When we hit the street, Pullman and his Japanese drinking buddy set the pace on the way to the aquarium. They start out down the sidewalk as if they were in a marathon walk. They never miss a step or waver an inch off the B-line course they have set for themselves. The rest of us follow.

When we reach the aquarium, our Japanese hosts buy us tickets and inform us we have 15 minutes to tour the place and then we have to cross the street for the marine show in the waterfront auditorium.

We split up as we stroll through the large marine tanks in which the various saltwater species of the area are displayed. By the standards that I am used to at Marineland in St. Augustine and Sea World in Orlando and San Diego the Japanese aquarium is dirty. The rocks and other structure in the tanks are overgrown with algae. The fish on display are alive, but many look unhealthy with scars and often open sores. Many of the species the Japanese have on exhibit are the same we have off the Florida Keys.

My favorite is the tarpon. The Japanese call it a "bastard mullet." Like bonito, I am sure they eat it. In the Florida Keys the tarpon is strictly a sports fish – one of the ultimate challenges for anglers especially when it grows to over 100 pounds. The tarpon the Japanese have in their tanks probably weigh no more than 20 pounds.

We leave the aquarium, climb up a flight of steps, cross the highway on an overhead walkway, climb down two flights of steps to the entrance to the marine stadium that is set below the highway level, climb up three flights of steps to the top of the stadium, walk around to its north side where the bleachers face the ocean, and then climb to the top of the bleachers where we are going to watch the show standing up leaning against the top rail of the stadium.

From this vantage point, we can see everything in the stadium, everything in the seaside town behind us, and all the ocean activities in front of us. Enoshima Island sits a couple of miles off to our left.

The sun is hot. It is a warm spring day. Most of us brought jackets because it was cool when we left the hotel in Fujisawa this morning. None of us are wearing them now. The Japanese are still in their coats and ties. Even though the sun is out, it is a hazy day. The haze has not burned off as it normally does where we come from. This haze has to be a variation of smog, although I am accustomed to not seeing it in areas along the ocean where steady breezes help disperse it. Not here. It's staying in. I cannot see any horizon on the ocean in front of me. The water simply disappears in an apron of haze or smog.

A Japanese marine mammal show is not unlike those at marine attractions in the U.S. The porpoises and whales perform the same tricks that we are familiar with in the States. However, the Japanese seem to crowd about twice as many big fish in half the space we do. Even the dolphin here must become accustomed to the confining space limitations of the Japanese.

The major difference in the marine shows we have at home and this one I am watching is the actors who try to spin a story out of the various tricks their charges have mastered. Here the two main characters are young Japanese girls dressed in day-glow dresses. They bounce around the marine stage and chatter back and forth in the whiny, high-pitched female voice that represents Japanese "cute." Their antics make the children in the audience laugh and most likely fulfill some of the mentally erotic desires of the Japanese men in the audience.

The show lasts about half an hour. We climb back down the bleachers, and the three flights of stairs to the ground level of the marine stadium. We cross the area in front of the stadium and start up a flight of concrete stairs to the street level. On the third step, the knee on my good leg lets go with a crack that sounds like a rifle going off. It's a knee that has bothered me off and on since I played football in the service in Japan in the '50s. It just quit. I take a fall, but recover by grabbing a handrail. My legs are gone, but I pull myself to my feet and continue to follow the Japanese. They cross the street and head back for the hotel a few hundred yards down the beach.

When we get to the hotel, we enter at the front ground floor lobby. There is a Japanese wedding taking place down three levels and the guests are walking up and down the three flights of steps that descend from the lobby around a circular atrium to the restaurant and wedding chapel level underground. The Japanese head down the steps and we follow. At the bottom, they stop. We gather with them. The hotel manager comes and thanks us for our visit. We thank him for his hospitality and then turn around and climb back up the three flights of steps to the lobby and head for the parking lot.

Crossing the parking lot I notice a van parked with curtains drawn over all the windows. I have seen very few camper vans in Japan. This is one of the exceptions and I walk over to it. As I am looking at it, I come around to the left side and on the ground, in front of the sliding door that is closed, sit a pair of shoes. The Japanese apparently observe their custom of taking off their shoes before they enter their homes even when their homes are temporarily campers.

We load up in the cars we each came in and head back for Fujisawa. The day is still hot, but the windows remain up and the air-conditioning remains off. We have a warm ride back to the hotel.

- Hai, so desu -

I've been here three days and my eyes haven't stopped burning since Day 1. I remember the pollution in Tokyo in the '50s. It was so bad people, who customarily wore face masks when they had a cold would wear them just to filter some of the dirt out of the air. Out here, in what was then the country, the air always seemed to be clear. When I returned in the early '80s I was impressed with how clean the air, even in Tokyo, was compared to the old days.

The first couple of days here this time I thought my red eyes were due to a lack of sleep. Then it dawned on me that when the morning haze never seemed to burn off my case of red eye must be due to the pollution. After all, when we met with the mayor of Fujisawa this morning he said the biggest problem he had to deal with in city government was the environment. He assured us, though, that industry was taking care of its pollution.

My first reaction was to close the window in my room to see if that would help my eyes clear, but the room got so hot I had to open it to cool the place down. It looks like I'm going to have red eyes for the rest of the month. There is plenty of pollution here. I found it when I walked down the street to check out a river at the foot of the hill. The banks of the river are solid concrete. The water running through it is bile green. It is more a sewage canal than a river.

On a visit to a relatively new city hospital today I noticed how streaked the buildings were - a chronic case of acid rain. All the buildings in Japan have that grayish look that comes with old age, even the new ones.

After our crushing day of sightseeing at Enoshima today, I soaked my soar legs in a hot tub, and with nothing else to do this evening decided to try and walk the soarness out of them by catching a train north to Sagami-ono, a small town in which I used to spend a lot of time. In the 1950s it was the home of Zama Hospital Camp, one of the finest medical facilities west of San Francisco. Most of the activities centered on the base. Americans lived in the base housing projects that resembled suburban neighborhoods in the States.

In those days there were a hundred homes around the local railroad station. The rest of the area, as far as you could see, consisted of rice paddies one of which I got a close-up view of one night when I slid a motorcycle through the cinder intersection, clipped a guy wire on a telephone pole and went end over end into a rice field that had recently been drained.

Sagami-ono was a favorite hang-out because there was a small restaurant called the Italian Garden located at the intersection where I took the road west to Camp Fuchinobe, my resident base, or the road south to Camp Zama which was then U.S. Army Headquarters Far East. I had an office on both bases and Sagami-ono was the halfway stop.

The Italian Garden was owned and operated by an ex-patriot named Mac-san who, instead of returning to the States to live after World War II, got a work visa and stayed in Japan to build the restaurant. He served the best pizza – cut in squares instead of slices – in Japan. It came in one flavor: pepperoni. Those of us who had ration books helped keep Mac-san's bar stocked by bootlegging a little American whiskey to him. It helped pay for the pizza in the days when my monthly pay, with overseas allowance, was a whopping $108 a month. Of course there were offsetting advantages. Cigarettes cost $2 a cartoon. White Horse scotch was $1.85 a fifth and beer was $1 a pitcher.

We drank beer, rode motorcycles and hung out at the Italian Garden bending Mac's ear for the lack of anything else to do when we were off duty.

When I left in 1958 Mac said he had two years left on his current visa and would have to go back to the States and then return on a new one if he wanted to stay in Japan. I always wondered what happened to him. When I was in Japan in 1981 I took an express train from Tokyo to Zama and then caught a local up to Sagami-ono. The few rice paddies that remained were being turned into housing subdivisions. The old Camp Zama
Hospital had been deserted and stood grown over with weeds and vines. The Italian Garden was still there at the intersection. I knocked on the door, but no one was home.
So tonight is the night I hope to find out what happened to Mac-san if the old Italian Garden is still there.

The train has made a dozen stops since we pulled out of Fujisawa. The conductor has just announced the next stop will be Sagami-ono. I eagerly look for something familiar but there has been nothing but a steady parade of homes, factories, and train stations since we left Fujisawa.

The train begins to slow and the ambient light becomes brighter. The neon lights glitter with an intensity that I cannot connect to Sagami-ono. When the train pulls into the station I see a huge - six or eight story - shopping center complete with a long covered mall extending out from one side of the station. It is fairly new. Construction areas are still marked. The exit to one side of the station is lined with corrugated tin sheets to protect people coming to and from the train station.

My intuition tells me the Italian Garden should be on that side of the station, but nothing looks familiar. I decide to exit on the other side although I can't ever remember using that side in the past. I recall that it was nothing more than farms in the '50s and pretty much the same in the early '80s. Today it looks like the entrance to any of hundreds of railroad stations in Japan. I notice, too, there are a lot more train tracks coming into and going out of Sagami-ono than there used to be.

Outside the station I recognize nothing. I walk across the small park in front of the station and buy a pack a cigarettes, the one thing that is actually cheaper in Japan than the U.S., and a can of Boss Coffee from a pair of vending machines in front of a Japanese book store. I go back to the small park, sit down on a brick bench, and light a cigarette. A young couple is necking on a bench across the walkway from me, People are coming and going from the railroad station. They seem not to notice.

Nothing that I can see registers in my mind. I finish the cigarette and decide to go back in the station, climb up the steps to the walkway that crosses the tracks, down the steps on the other side, and try the opposite exit. Once there I walk out into a huge covered mall that runs two or three blocks straight ahead past two-story shops and businesses directly into a massive stairway. The stairway goes up one story onto a grand walkway that apparently crosses a major thoroughfare and then disappears
into a department store that would be the envy of Macy fans.

The whole street is brightly lit in multi-colored neon. Hundreds of shoppers are strolling through the shops and fondling the dry goods on clothes racks many store owners have wheeled out onto the sidewalks under the covered mall. It is a dazzling sight. I recognize nothing.

I reason that if I have just walked out of the old Sagami-ono train station that all I have to do is turn down a little road to the right that takes a slight bend to the left, walk a couple of blocks, and I would be standing at the Italian Garden. I did that when I returned in 1981 and it led me right to the old watering hole. The problem now is that the old street to the right that takes the bend to the left isn't visible anymore. A wall of corrugated construction tin blocks my access to it if I could see it.

The only other choice I have is to walk up the mall and see what the street is that passes under the overhead walkway to the gigantic department store. When I reach it I find a four-lane highway with bumper-to-bumper traffic. It might be the old two-lane highway that ran from Sagami-ono to Zama, but it doesn't resemble anything I remember. If it is the old highway, then all I need to do is turn right, walk a few blocks, and I should come to the intersection through which I once slid the motorcycle. I know from my last visit that has changed. Instead of a surface intersection it is now a junction of the north-south highway – the one I should be walking along now – and an east-west express highway that runs from Yokohama to the east westward through Sagami-ono and on past Fuchinobe to Sagamihara.

In the distant street lights I see an overpass. That could be the east-west highway and the Italian Garden should be on the southeast corner of the intersection. I see nothing but new shops, restaurants, and stores lining the highway I am walking along.

On the opposite side of the highway I see three Italian flags hanging from a new building. Maybe Mac-san has gone big time and built a new Italian Garden across the street from the old one?

I walk past a Century 21 real estate office, a Denny's and am within a block of the intersection, but still no Italian Garden. I am directly across the street from the building with the Italian flags, but can find no sign that identifies it. I turn towards the intersection again and, in the light that has diminished the farther I have walked from the huge shopping mall, I see a dirt parking lot leading off the highway just ahead of me. I walk past a row of bushes, look to my right and there is the old Italian Garden. The building looks just like it did when I left in 1958 and again when I saw it in 1981.

The only thing different is that the parking lot is filled with Mercedes, a Jaguar and a half dozen Japanese luxury cars. If Mac is still around it looks like he has hit the big time. No jeeps, motorcycles, or bootleg whiskey in this neighborhood anymore.

I walk in the front door, and stare at the room. The customers are all Japanese, well-dressed, affluent. The restaurant has the same black walls it had when I was last here in 1958. The tables have the same red-and-white checkered table clothes. There are no GIs in uniform, no *gaigin* here. What used to be an extension off the bar is now the master's station. I walk over to it and am greeted by a tall Japanese woman dressed in a low-cut stylish black evening dress. She appears to be in her mid to late 20s.

"Do you have reservations?" She asks in English.

"No," I respond. "I just wanted to see the restaurant. I used to come here in the 1950s."

"Oh," she replies. "I don't believe this was built until the 1960s."

"No, I used to come here in 1956, '57 and '58 when I was stationed here in the Army," I tell her. "An American named Mac owned it. He's not still around is he?"

"I've never heard of him. My mother-in-law owns the restaurant. She has owned it for 33 years."

"*Hai, so desu.* That explains it," I reply. "*Arigato.*"

"Would you like to make reservations?" She asks.

"No, thank you. I just wanted to take a look at the place."

I left finally knowing what had happened to Mac. Thirty-three years would put the date at 1960. That was two years after I left, the same two years that Mac-san had left on his visa in 1958. He didn't go back to the States and renew it. He must have sold the restaurant to a Japanese national, taken his money and gone home. He probably sold it to the mother-in-law of the girl whom I talked to in the restaurant. The girl wasn't even alive in the '50s. She probably thinks her mother-in-law built the restaurant, or maybe it's a case of her mother-in-law not wanting people to remember that the Italian Garden was originally built by an American. That would be the Japanese way.

I decide to take a shortcut back to the station, to try the old back street from the Italian Garden to Sagami-ono Station. It is still there although now it's packed with houses and shops.

Instead of coming out in front of the station like it used to it comes out as an alley adjacent to another department store that is part of the huge shopping complex that has been built on the site of the old Zama Hospital.

My eyes still burn so I decide to take a fling at trying to find the pharmacy department in the store. I board an escalator and begin riding up floor by floor looking for the pharmacy. I find it on the seventh level up. I walk up to the Japanese man behind the counter. He is dressed in a white coat like you would expect a druggist to be in the U.S.

"*Visine o kaitai no desu ga*, I'd like to buy some Visine." I tell him.

"*Hai, so desu*," he replies moving down the counter cabinet between us. He reaches down and produces a bottle of Visine with everything expect the brand name on the label printed in Japanese.

"*Ikura desu*, how much?" I ask.

"Eight hundred fifty yen," he replies in English.

That's almost $8 for a bottle of Visine that we pay a little more than $2 for in the States. My eyes are sore enough I buy two bottles. I put the first Visine drops in them right there in the department store.

Back at the train station I buy a ticket for Fujisawa and am careful that I pick out the right track. I am ready to head back to my little room at the Fujisawa Grand and hit the sack.

The next train scheduled for Fujisawa is an express. That means I won't have to suffer through all the stops we made on the way up to Sagami-ono. When the train pulls into the station I jump on looking forward to a short 20-minute ride back to the hotel.

The train pulls out of Sagami-ono heading south but shortly after it leaves the station I feel it slow to pass through some switches, something I don't remember it doing on the way up.

Then the conductor announces the next stop is Atsugi. Atsugi is not on the run to Fujisawa. It's on the line going west out of Sagami-ono, not the line running south to Fujisawa. It's a good 10-to-15 minute ride down to Atsugi where I will have to get off the train, climb up the stairs, cross over the tracks, go down the next flight of stairs and wait for the next train back to Sagami-ono to catch the right train to Fujisawa.

Forty-five minutes later I am back in Sagami-ono. Since I haven't left the train station at either stop, my ticket to Fujisawa is still good. I go through the routine of looking up the stations on the railroad map on the wall and asking the railroad man at the ticket counter which track the train for Fujisawa leaves on.

"One," he tells me in English.

That's the same track I thought I took the last time, but maybe I messed up. I take the steps down to Track 1, make sure the sign says the train on that track goes to Fujisawa and wait patiently for the train to pull into the station. When it arrives I board.

Again the train heads south out of the station and again, a little way out, it slows, passes through some switches, and heads in a more westerly direction. The conductor announces the next stop is "Hon-Atsugi," one stop beyond Atsugi. I'm on the wrong train again.

An hour later I am back in Sagami-ono. Maybe I'm cracking up. I've taken this train in the past. It goes to Fujisawa. The sign on the track says it goes to Fujisawa. I retrace my steps, put more Visine in my eyes. I end up back on the same station platform that I was on the last two times I caught the wrong train.

There is a trainman walking along the platform. I catch up with him. *"Fujisawa yuki no ressha wa nanban homo kara demasu ka* - What platform does the train to Fujisawa leave from?" I stretch my Japanese to its limits to make sure I get this right. He motions on down the platform we are walking along and then disappears into a small office.

I continue walking, passing several overhead signs saying the trains heading south on this platform go to Fujisawa. I get to the Let's Kiosk - the platform newsstand - and ask the woman behind the counter, *"Fujisawa yuki no ressha wa nanban homo kara demasu ka?"*

"You on right platform. Take last four cars," she answers in broken English. I buy another pack of cigarettes from her and tell her "thanks."

So, I have been catching the correct train but not the right cars. The train that pulls into Sagami-ono on the track marked Fujisawa heading out of the station gets split before it pulls out.

I've been getting on the wrong end of the train. I don't ever remember split trains running out of Sagami-ono in the past, but then it's hard to recognize this as the Sagami-ono I used to know.

A lot of things have changed since I last visited Japan. It's often difficult to understand and accept the changes but at least this time I catch the right train to Fujisawa. It's a local. It makes every stop between Sagami-ono and Fujisawa.

- Hai, so desu -

The Japanese give us Sunday off. Ron Pullman has an appointment to meet with an executive of a Japanese insurance company. He has lined up one of our interpreters to go with him. One of our Japanese hosts will take them. Pullman is a financial strategist. Among his clients are several major league baseball players. He wants to explore investment opportunities available between Japan and the U.S.

We meet for breakfast in the restaurant at Fujisawa Grand. The team wants to go to Tokyo for the day. They have been reading tour books and have spotted a couple of things they would like to do in Tokyo. The main thing they are interested in is seeing the rogue bands that gather in Harajuku Park to play all kinds of music on Sunday afternoons. I want to pay a visit to St. Albans, an Anglican mission in Tokyo, to see if I can locate some people I met there in 1981. St. Albans is in the Roppongi area, near the Tokyo Tower in the central part of the city.

Harajuku Park is south of Shinjuku on the west side of town.

Everyone in our group knows enough Japanese to get through a train station and ask directions to his next stop. We decide at breakfast that we will go our separate ways and meet in front of Harajuku Station at 1:30 in the afternoon. Tim Wilson, Whitney Bain, Paul White and Rick Ramsay will take a train to Shinjuku. I will take a train to Shibuya. Pullman will go with his Japanese host and the interpreter to meet with the insurance executive. We will each find our way to Harajuku on our own by 1:30. It is a good test of our ability to get around in Japan.

My only instructions to the team members is that each carry enough money to cover a $50 cab ride, which should be more than sufficient to get them to a familiar central train station - Shinjuku or Tokyo - from which they can catch a train back to Fujisawa if they happen to get lost.

Pullman's Japanese escort and interpreter come and pick him up. I get my walking stick from my room - my legs are killing me from yesterday's sightseeing at Enoshima and my venture up to Sagami-ono last night. On the way to the train station I tell the guys about my little episode with the split train in Sagami-ono. They have a good laugh over it.

We catch a local north to make connections with the trains to Shibuya and Shinjuku. The others have a good map of the Japanese railroad system in the Tokyo area and Kanagawa Prefecture. I check it for the station I want to get off at to catch a train to Shibuya. My stop is before theirs.

We are all standing in the rear of a second-class car talking when I think I hear the conductor call my stop next. The train stops, I say "So long" and "Good luck" to the other four and dash down a flight of stairs to catch an express on the track below. It is pointed in the right direction and ready to leave so I jump on. As we speed down the track the conductor calls out a stop I don't recognize. I watch as the train pulls into a station. The sign pointing towards the stop I have just come from has Minami in front of the name of the town. *Minami* means south in Japanese. I am on a train headed for Yokohama not Shibuya. I got off the northbound train a stop too early. I didn't hear the conductor say *minami* when he called out the town I was looking for and missed the correct connection by a stop. I end up doing the same thing I did last night when I caught the wrong trains out of Sagami-ono. I get off the train, climb the stairs to the crossover, cross the tracks, go down the stairs to the tracks that carry the trains going the other direction, and wait for a train back to the stop where I made the mistake.

There I catch a later edition of the same train we left Fujisawa on, ride one stop north, get off, and catch the correct train to Shibuya. My mistakes eat up time on Japanese trains, but they don't cost any more money as long as I don't leave the station.

When I leave for a destination in Japan, I put two 100-yen coins in the ticket vending machine at the entrance to the station and buy the minimum ticket. When I get to my final destination, I go to the fare adjustment machine, put in my ticket, pay off the balance owed, and use that ticket to get through the automated exit machines or past the railroad employee who sits at the gate clicking his ticket puncher in a rhythm not unlike that of an Appalachian mountain native playing the spoons.

If I want to ride first-class, I use the same system, find an empty seat in one of the Green Cars, and wait for the conductor to come by. He can write me a ticket for my destination and take my money, so I don't worry about standing in line at the reserved seat ticket window. I have always found that my rather loose way of travelling the Japanese train system allows me to remain flexible and makes travel more enjoyable for me.

I like remaining a little loose when I am on my own in Japan. It is a pleasant break from the more structured existence with the Japanese. I make a mistake now and then, but it just gives me a chance to see a little more of the country, to observe a few hundred more Japanese as they go about their daily lives. It doesn't cost me anything since I am here to observe the culture of Japan. Railroads are the mainstream of that culture.

Since I was here in 1981, the trains have been privatized. Japan Rail – *JR* – the heart of the network of national trains will go public in a month or two. There are many independent train companies operating lines that tie into the *JR* network. Japan's railroads used to be the pork of politicians.

We expect our politicos to bring the bacon home in the form of a military base, a dam, or large government grants when we send them to Washington. Japanese used to expect their politicians to have a railroad line built to their remote area of the country when they elected a local representative to the Diet. Most received what they expected. Japan now has an excellent network of railroads that reach into the most remote corners of the islands. The trains run on time and the rides are relatively inexpensive. Until now running the trains at a profit has not been a major concern of the government.

Privatization will change that, but it is too early to tell what the long-range effect will be on the pocketbooks of the average Japanese.

When I get to Shibuya I am amazed at how much the station has grown. I had been told that this had become the busiest station in Tokyo, but had no way to imagine what to expect when I arrived. I haven't been in this station in over 30 years. Then it was a large station in relation to others in the country, but nothing compared to what I run into.

It is largely an underground station with several layers of tracks. An underground mall stretches for what seems like several blocks. I look for the exit to the main part of the station and surface at the point where five main streets intersect in the Shibuya shopping district. I surface in the midst of at least a couple million people milling about through the skyscraper department stores and small shops that line the old streets off the main arteries. It reminds me more of Times Square than the Shibuya that I remember.   The only things that indicates this is Japan are the facial characteristics of the people and the fact they wait for traffic lights to change before crossing the street. Even with a few hundred thousand people packing the intersections waiting to cross to another department store, there is no jaywalking. When the light finally changes at the five-point intersection, the people move like a flood in all directions. No one breaks the traffic light protocol.

Rather than make two subway changes to get to Roppongi and St. Albans, I opt to take a cab. It is not a long ride. I walk around to the taxi area at the station and slide into the back seat of a waiting cab. The driver asks me where I would like to go.

"Tokyo Tower, *dozo* - please."

When I first came to Japan in the '50s Tokyo had ¥70 cabs. The exchange rate was pegged at 360 yen to the dollar, so you could ride a cab all day long for a pittance in U.S. coin. We called the cabs "*kamikaze*" because the traffic laws of the day were that if the driver blew the horn and then hit someone it was not his fault. The taxies were Datsun and Renault four-door, four-cylinder subcompacts in which we literally flew around town. In those days there were few wide streets in Tokyo. Most were wide one-lane alleys which opened onto two-lane thoroughfares. In the heart of the city there were some four-lane boulevards, but they were a rarity.

When I returned in 1981 most taxies were Nissan – the company that used to build the Datsun - Cedrics and Glorias, full-sized four-door automobiles. The basic fare was ¥500 yen and the exchange rate was ¥240 to the dollar. There had been some improvement in the streets in Tokyo, but few expressways had been built to take the pressure off the surface streets. No one zipped around town in those days. Most of our money on taxies was spent while the meter ticked away and we waited in traffic.

Of course, this is Sunday so there is not much commercial traffic on the streets. The cab I am in is meticulously clean as Japanese cabs have always been. The driver wears his traditional white gloves, the white covers on the seats are spotless. But, instead of the white embroidered lace which used to adorn the tops of the seats, a plastic imitation lace is being used. The minimum fare is ¥600 yen. The exchange rate today is ¥111 to the dollar.

The driver moves out into traffic without using his horn, or trying to force his way into the lane that heads in the direction of Roppongi. He is more courteous than any of the cab drivers I rode with in the old days. We move with the flow of traffic onto an eight-lane street heading east. Eventually he pulls up a ramp onto an expressway and the traffic moves along at about 50 miles an hour. In no time, he is pulling off the expressway near Roppongi crossing. We make a right turn down the wide street that goes through the heart of Roppongi. I quickly recognize it from my last visit in '81. The buildings are taller, but overall its appearance remains that of an international settlement.   We pass the Hard Rock Cafe and Tony Roma's – A Place for Ribs on our way towards the Tokyo Tower. I catch a glimpse of the Hamburger Inn, an old landmark I couldn't find when I was here in '81, but for some reason it seems out of place. I make a mental note to check it out later since I had been told in '81 that the old Hamburger Inn had been demolished. In the '50s the Hamburge Inn was the only place in town we could find a real American hamburger. We watched the Japanese build the Tokyo Tower while we munched on burgers. The Tokyo Tower was billed as Japan's equivalent to the Eiffel Tower in those days, but it has never lived up to its billing. Even the Japanese will tell you today it is one of the bigger tourist rip-offs in town.

As we crest a hill, I see St. Albans through the intersection ahead. The meter reads ¥1,300 yen, about $11.75 cents at today's exchange rate. There is no tipping in Japan. Any taxes are included in the price you are charged.

I arrive at St. Albans, which sits next door to St. Andrews, a Japanese Episcopalian Church, just after Sunday services have ended. Christians represent less than five percent of the Japanese population, although Sunday is an accepted day off for most Japanese. Instead of entering through the sanctuary, I walk around St. Albans and enter the community hall at the rear. A woman walks up to me and introduces herself as the rector's wife. I tell her what I am looking for and she calls her husband, Rev. William H. Hargett, over. He turns out to be from the area of central Ohio where I grew up. He knows of the group I am interested in making contact with, but tells me they no longer meet at St. Albans. Instead, they meet now at the Franciscian Chapel, an international meeting place on the other side of Roppongi. I'll have to wait until I can get loose some Saturday night to find them.

We visit a bit about the growth of the international settlement that is centered in the Roppongi area. The rector tells me he now has 28 counties represented in his congregation. When I leave the church, I notice the building across the street that was once the headquarters of the Japanese Imperial Navy is now a Masonic lodge. One of our team members, Rick Ramsay, is a Mason. He had asked if he could attend a Masonic
meeting while he was in Japan. Now that I know where the lodge is, I can steer him right to it.

I've got a little time before I have to meet the rest of the team at Harajuku Park, so I decide to walk down the hill and around the corner to the old subway station I used to use when I visited St. Albans and was staying in Shimbashi. I need to freshen up on the Tokyo subway system. It essentially runs in circles around the city with the subways intersecting with regular trains at main stations throughout the Tokyo area. Each subway station has a map on the wall of its route and interline connections. Sometimes the stops on the line are labeled in both Japanese and English, making getting around the city easy for a *gaijin*. My experience has been that the closer you get to the center of Tokyo, the more English you find on the subway and railroad signs.

Since I have the time, I catch the subway in to Tokyo Station, my favorite of all Japanese railroad stations. There is a whole subterranean city beneath Tokyo Station. I arrive on a level two or three stories below ground level and climb the steps up to the main terminal. There seem to be many more tracks at ground level than I remember, but the old terminal building is still there. It is a magnificent Victorian structure, stretching more than two blocks. Its red brick exterior has been maintained in excellent condition. I walk across the concourse where Japanese soldiers at the end of World War II stacked their arms and boarded trains to their homes throughout the country, cross through the terminal building where the large, round clocks still hang, and see if I can locate the rest room in which I had my first unisex experience back in the '50s. I had arrived in Tokyo

Station on my first trip and had to relieve myself. I found a rest room, entered and was confronted with only a trough filled with stones along a wall. As I was doing my business, a Japanese woman walked by and said, "*Konnichiwa* - good afternoon," and walked on by. I froze in the middle of relieving myself thinking at the time that maybe I had gotten into the wrong rest room.

Not so.

In the '50s, both men and women used the same rest rooms and seemed to think nothing of it. In fact, until 1957, Japanese men simply unzipped their flies and relieved themselves in the street, often tipping their hats to people passing by. It was a custom that took some getting used to. Today the unisex approach has been abandoned, at least in Tokyo Station. There are separate rest rooms for men and women, but they have no doors. Since space is at a premium, the standard urinals in the men's room are close to the door. If you use one of the first two near the door, anyone walking by can get a good look at what you are doing.

Modesty is not a long suit with the Japanese.

I leave Tokyo Station through the main front entrance that opens onto the old Marunouchi district of Tokyo. To my left is the main Post Office building. Down the boulevard in front of me I can see the entrance to the Imperial Palace grounds two blocks away. The rest of the district in front of me is packed with neat, square office buildings. This has become the financial center of Tokyo, that part of town foreign investors travel to in hopes of making a connection in Japanese yen.

Back in the station I catch a *JR* train over to Shinjuku and switch to a local for the short run south to Harajuku Station. I arrive at Harajuku a half hour early so decide to grab a bite to eat. I leave the station at the north entrance that spills out into one of the narrow shopping streets of the district. It is packed with people. They are dressed in everything from Yuppie-fine to punk. It is the first time I have ever seen a young Japanese woman with day-glow pink hair, a mini-skirt, and a ragged denim jacket.

I work my way down the packed street of shops and find a Kentucky Fried Chicken. I check the wooden statute of Colonel Sanders out front. He is wearing his Rotary lapel pin. In addition, he sports a Shriner's button. I order three pieces of chicken and what I think is a biscuit for ¥500. The biscuit comes in a rice paper sack about the size of the standard french-fry pack we are accustomed to in the States. I take my order and find a seat upstairs among a throng of Japanese – adults with children, punk rockers, and older Japanese couples who look as if they are on a Sunday shopping trip.

The biscuit turns out to be some type of fried rice cake. It is bland. The chicken is not as spicy as the KFC regular that we have in the States. The pieces are smaller than we see at home. They fit the Japanese scale of two-thirds to three-quarters American. When I finish my meal, I deposit my trash in the bin nearby, stack my empty tray on top, and look for a rest room to wash my hands.

The rest room is Western style, but I find after washing my hands there is nothing to dry them on. I shake them as dry as possible and on the way back through the restaurant to the street grab a couple of napkins and finish the drying job.

I had noticed the lack of paper towels earlier in a rest room in a Japanese train station and marveled at a young Japanese man who simply raised his coat tails and wiped his hands on the seat of his trousers. Maybe that's a new custom here. There seems to be a shortage of hand towels in all rest rooms although there is the occasional blow dryer built into a rim over the wash bowl that also contains the faucet. To activate the blow dryers, when you can find them, you simply wave your hands beneath them.

I work my way back up the street packed with shoppers to the road that runs parallel with the railroad tracks. Harajuku Park is on the other side of the tracks. The main entrance to Harajuku Station, where we are supposed to meet, is up a small hill to my left. I cross the street when the light changes and begin to climb the hill. I am about 10 minutes early, but as I approach the station I see Paul White, and then behind him in the crowd, Tim Wilson, Rick Ramsay and Whitney Bain. Just as I approach them, Ron Pullman comes walking across the street. We've all made it. We've each successfully navigated our way through a megopolis of 30 million people on our own. We've passed the test.

"How did it go?" I ask Wilson.

"Oh, we only ran into what we thought was a problem once. We took a train to Akasaka to look at cameras and electronics. We saw some fantastic hotels and stores, but on the way back had a little trouble finding the subway station. I went up to a Japanese man, and in my best Japanese, asked him which way the railroad station was -

'*Tetsudo no eki wa doko desu ka?*' The Japanese man looked at me pointed, and in perfect English, said, 'Straight ahead.'"

"How did your meeting go?" I asked Pullman.

"Oh, man, it was a bummer. I tried to explain some of the investment strategies I have been working with and the guy only wanted to give me a lecture. All he wanted to tell me was how pushy Americans are, how we have no patience, how rude we are, how we don't really understand investments. I finally broke off the interview. He didn't want to share ideas. He just wanted to give me a lecture on how superior the Japanese are in investing."

"Too bad," I comment. "We don't seem to be making much headway in exchanging ideas."

"We're not going to if this guy is any example of what we've got to look forward to," Pullman says. "These people definitely feel they are superior to us and they're not going to let us forget it."

We head for Harajuku Park over the bridge that crosses the railroad tracks running into and out of the station. The bridge is an old stone one, left over from some former era in Japanese history. On the bridge some vendors have laid out their wares on blankets. One in particular is interesting. He has a supply of watches from the Soviet Union amidst other souvenirs from Eastern Bloc nations. I spot a watch that interests me. It has a red-and-white face with a red Soviet flag and "USSR" emblazoned across it. I make a note to check the price of it on the way out of the park.

The entrance to the park where the bands play is to the left as we cross the bridge. The entrance to the shrine in Harajuku Park is to the right. We all head to the left towards the cornucopia of music. We find a long street curving around the south side of the park packed with bands of every description. Tim Wilson has his video camera rolling.

One of the first groups we come to is a group of Japanese males dressed in leather jackets, jeans and motorcycle boots. They have set up a large set of speakers and are playing heavy metal music to which they are break-dancing on the pavement. They seem more concerned about their hairstyles than anything else. Most have ducktails reminiscent of the '50s in the States, but one has a hair-do that is stacked nearly a foot on top of his head and combed forward in a style I have never seen before. He spends most of his time combing it as he saunters along in front of the crowd that has gathered.

On down the street we find a band playing decent rock-and-roll music, but their dress is a bit outlandish. One, dancing in front of the band, is dressed in a blouse made from an American flag. As we approach, I notice that most of the band are wearing platform shoes of various garish designs. At first they appear to be an all-female band, but after watching them up close for a few minutes I realize that this is a group of Japanese transvestites. They are a strange collection, but they play decent rock-and-roll.

As Wilson films the bands, I keep looking at some of the clothes they wear. Most are take-offs of popular American clothes - Levi's, NFL sweat shirts, Harley-Davidson vests and jackets. Some are probably the real thing. I spot one singer in a rock band wearing a Baylor University sweatshirt. That's Wilson's alma mater. I point it out to him and he gets it on film.

Behind the bands is the main park. I'm walking along a sidewalk lined with food vendors that separates the street where the bands play from the fence that surrounds the park. As I come to a point where the wrought iron fence ends in a stone wall before which a group of small shrubs and concrete benches form a small rest area, I spot a man leaning against the stone wall who looks like many of the "weed sleepers" who visit the Florida Keys when it starts to snow in the North. He has long dirty hair caked to his head, his face and hands are unwashed, his clothes are ripped, torn, and splotched with layers of stains. He is definitely homeless, the first I have seen in Japan. I point him out to White and Ramsay when they catch up with me.

"We saw a whole bunch of them back over on the other side of the park," Ramsay says. "They are living in boxes just like they do in Miami."

"Yeah, but they do it in Japanese style," White says. "They take off their shoes and leave them outside the door to their box."

We cut through the rest area to the wider paved area that leads into the main part of Harajuku Park. There are large signs as you approach the gate to the park that say "No goods are to be sold in the park." There are police milling about among the crowd of at least a couple of thousand people outside the entrance to the park.

Whitney Bain and I head for the rest rooms off to the left of the park entrance in a stone building. Here again, there are no doors on the rest rooms. You use urinals that are clearly visible to the public milling about outside. No one seems to care. There are wash bowls in which you can wash your hands, but no towels here, either. I watch again as a young Japanese man washes his hands and wipes them on the seat of his trousers.

Outside we start up the wide walkway away from the entrance gate to the park. It is packed with people, many of them appear to be Middle Eastern rather than Japanese. To the left, down a walkway off the main road, there are people packed like sardines gathered around outdoor cook stoves and charcoal pits. The aroma of Middle Eastern cooking saturates the air. From the midst of the throng drifts the rhythms of Persian music.

We have come across the Persian Market. I had read about these in English-language Japanese newspapers and magazines, but was under the impression they were located in Ueno Park over on the east side of Tokyo near what used to be the major black market area where we could sell an occasional $20 greenback for about $100 worth of yen back in the '50s. Back then U.S. military were paid in script, which could be exchanged for yen, but greenbacks were contraband. Once in a while some one would receive one in a letter from a friend in the States and we would sell it on the black market. Greenbacks were in great demand in Tokyo in the 1950s.

This Persian Market is an unexpected find. Wilson and I work our way over into the throng of Middle Eastern men who are gathered around stacks of merchandise that is still in its original containers. I find brand-new Japanese cameras, stereos, and other electronics being haggled over in the old-world market style. Wilson climbs up on a rock to get a better vantage point from which to film the scene. A Persian man walks up to him, pulls, his sleeve, points to his video camera, and tells him to put it down. The man tells Wilson to get out of the area.

We work our way back to the main road dividing the Persian Market from the park entrance and look around for the other members of our group. Whitney Bain is standing in the middle of the road with a perplexed look on his face. I go over to him.

"What's up?" I ask.

"I was standing right here just looking around," he says, "and a man walked up to me and wanted to know if I wanted to buy some hashish. What's going on?"

"They're selling drugs. That's what's going on. The Iranians who live and work here in the oil business have their own black market. It's operating right out in the open here. That's what's going on," I say.

"But drugs are illegal," Bain says. "There's Japanese police right over there and they're aren't doing anything about it. Why not?"

"For two reasons is my guess," I tell Bain. "First, the Japanese are extremely dependent on the Middle East for their oil. They have none of their own. They don't want to start an international incident that might damage their oil relationships simply by starting to bust the Iranians that are here. Second, it probably makes sense to the Japanese to let the Middle Easterners operate their black markets here in an area the Japanese can keep an eye on rather than harass them and drive them underground. Can you imagine how hard this scene would be to control if you drove it underground in a city this size. I don't imagine those Japanese police are missing too much, but at least this way they know what is going on and they can keep an eye on it. They admit it's a problem, but their hands are more or less oil-tied when it comes to doing anything about it."

"It's hard to believe. I've never had anyone just walk up to me and offer to sell me drugs," Bain says.

"Keep your eyes open. You'll see more of it." I'm watching a *gaijin* – an American military type – across the park who appears to be doing a little drug dealing on his own. He's standing in a group of Persians and stands out mainly because of his close-cropped brown hair, a pair of flyer's sunglasses, and a flight jacket he is wearing. Only the *Yukuza* – the Japanese equivalent of the Mafia – and tourists wear sunglasses in Japan. This guy's no *yukuza* and no tourist. He knows his way around.

I watch him talk with the Middle Easterners. His hand comes out of the pocket of his flight jacket and he palms some bills to one of the Persians. The man leaves, the American continues to stand around with the rest of the group. They chat back and forth, but the American appears nervous. He stands first on one foot, then the other. His head twists from side to side as he scans the crowd. He turns his face towards me, but I can't tell whether he is looking at me or not because his eyes are hidden behind his sunglasses. So are mine, so he can't tell if I am looking at him or not. I turn my head slightly and continue to watch him out of the corner of my eye.

Eventually the man who took the money returns. He has a paper bag in his hand. He gives it to the American. The American shakes his hand, studies the crowd around him for a minute, and then marches off towards the stone bridge that leads out of the park. My best guess is that a drug deal just went down.

There was a Japanese policeman standing not 50 feet from where it all took place and he didn't pay any attention to it. I know he saw it. Japanese police just don't miss things like this. My bet is that the drugs are headed for one of the few remaining military bases the U.S. has in Japan, or at least to the Japanese neighborhoods in which the Americans party near the bases. As long as they pass from the Middle Easterners to the Americans, the Japanese are apparently willing to turn their heads.

The team has seen enough of Harajuku. They are hungry and I suggest we catch a train over to Roppongi so I can show them the international settlement where they can find some English-speaking people if they get homesick while in Japan. Besides, I want to check out the Hamburger Inn. On the way out of the park I buy the Soviet watch I had my eyes on earlier. I give the man ¥3,500 for it, about $32 American. He tells me he is from East Germany.

In Roppongi we walk east from Roppongi Crossing toward the Tokyo Tower and stop to check the prices of souvenirs at the Tokyo Hard Rock Cafe that sits back off the main highway next to Tony Roma's. Souvenirs, Hard Rock Cafe – Tokyo T-shirts, sweat shirts, jackets and caps are sold outside the restaurant in a alley-side booth. Business is brisk. So are the prices.

I spot the Hamburger Inn and head on east towards Tokyo Tower. We pause at the intersection across the street from the Hamburger Inn. Tim Wilson has spotted a *sushi* shop on the corner opposite the Hamburger Inn. He is a *sushi* fan and wants to eat there. We split and agree to meet at the Hamburger Inn when we are finished eating.

The Hamburger Inn is definitely not the old one I used to patronize in the '50s. This one has Japanese owners. They tell me they have preserved the old name, but the old Inn was a couple of blocks up the street towards the Tower. That's as I remember it. The old one was closed for a few years, the new owners tell me, but they are uncertain just how long it was out of business. That explains why I couldn't find it in 1981.

I order a couple of hamburgers, hoping to get a good beef burger like in the old days. The counter at which I am sitting curves around 180 degrees after being laid out at a 45-degree angle to the intersection corner on which the restaurant occupies the first floor of a multi-story office building. On the walls are pictures of Harley and Indian motorcycles, and American automobiles from the 1950s.

Across the counter from me sits an Oriental man eating hot dogs and french fries. He strikes up a conversation with me.

"Where are you from?" He asks.

"Florida."

"Ah, I want to go to America someday," he says.

"Are you from here in Tokyo?" I ask.

"Now, yes, but I am Korean. I come here to learn about American ways, to work on my English. My wife is Japanese," he says, pointing to the woman sitting next to him.

"Do a lot of Japanese come here to study their English and American ways?" I ask.

"Yes, we meet a lot of people from different countries here," he explains.

The woman with him asks where the rest room is and is told it is down the hallway directly behind where I am sitting. She gets up and leaves.

We talk about American food – "It's hamburger, not hambulgel" – I tell him. "Got to watch those r's if you want to sound American."

"I work on it," he says.

I feel a call of nature and get off my stool, turn and start to head for the rest room.

"My wife is in there," the Korean says.

"Okay," I reply, realizing it must be a one-holer unisex rest room. "I'll wait."

My order comes. The hamburgers are not really hamburgers. They are more textured vegetable protein than meat. They are virtually tasteless. This certainly isn't the old Hamburger Inn. I finish the hamburgers, study the pictures on the wall, watch the Korean eat another hot dog, and wait patiently with my legs crossed. His wife seems to be making camp in the rest room.

A motorcycle cop pulls up in front. Rick Ramsay, a deputy sheriff back in the Florida Keys, goes out and looks at the cop's bike. They exchange a few words – more hand gestures than words – and Rick comes back in. Still the Korean's wife remains in the rest room. It doesn't seem to bother him that she has been gone so long.

Wilson comes back from the sushi parlor across the street. We visit for a few minutes. About the time I think I am going to have to pull the old Japanese – pre-1957 when it was outlawed – stunt of whizzing in the street, the Korean man's wife comes down the hall from the rest room. I make a B-line for it.

It's a traditional-style Japanese *benjo* – a hole in the floor – but done in modern tile. I do my thing and turn around to wash my hands in the lavoratory only to find a used sanitary pad lying in it. I don't believe I'll ever get a good handle on Japanese toilet protocol.

Before we head back to Fujisawa the gang wants to stop in a multi-story tape, video and CD store in Roppongi. It is beginning to get dark. I have little interest in the store so duck out a back door that leads to a narrow Roppongi street lined with nightclubs and small businesses. I hear the strains of American Big Band music coming from down the street and head towards it. At the Blue Crab a Japanese band is playing on the balcony. The sounds are America of the '40s and '50s.

I go back to the video store and get Tim Wilson so he can get some of it on video tape. Then I sit down on a flight of steps across the street, light a cigarette and enjoy the music. The band is playing for a wedding reception. They play for another half an hour. A Jaguar pulls up, the band leader gets in and disappears. Members of the band break down their instruments and load them into two vans parked in a small alcove off the street next to the Blue Crab.

When everything is loaded, the guests line the canopied walkway down from the balcony to the street and the bride and groom, dressed in stylish Western clothes walk to the street. There they pause, turn around and say *"arigato"* to each of the band members individually, handing each a small envelope. The band

members load in the vans and drive off. The bride and groom climb into the back of a limousine that appears out of no
where on some silent cue. The nightclub workers go back inside, close the French doors that lead to the balcony, and all is quite except the sounds of the city night.

Roppongi won't wake up again until around midnight. It's still early evening. The guys come down the back street from the sound store and we head for the train station.

- Hai, so desu -

Paul White and I are pouring through the manual to my old Macintosh Portable and its internal fax/modem. Paul is turning out to be our team tech. He delights in taking things apart and seeing what makes them tick. He has a field day trying to figure out Japanese electronics. This time he's determined to solve the puzzle of why I can't transmit faxes from my computer via telephone lines to the United States.

"Let's try this," he says. "We can code in some delays, use this string of instructions to the modem to dial blind, and see if we can't get around the need for the computer to wait for a response before continuing with the dialing."

With the book in one hand, Paul pokes out a new set of instructions to the computer, resets the modem, and says, "Give it a try."

I set up the document I want to send to the office back in the Florida Keys, select the modem, and hit the "send" button. The computer starts dialing, then pauses, dials some more, pauses again, and then dials once more. The noise coming from the speaker is more like an old truck grinding through its gears as it tries to navigate a steep hill than a sophisticated computer attempting to dial through to the States, but it seems to be working.

"Negotiating with the FREE PRESS," the fax/modem monitor informs me.

"Hey, it looks like we've made it," I say.

"Good," Paul answers, "That string (coded operating instructions for the modem) should be good as long as we're in Japan."

"*Arigato*, thanks," I say.

"*Do itashimashite* - you're welcome," Paul replies as he leaves.

Finally we've made the connection.

- Hai, so desu -

The Liberal Democratic Party – the LDP – has controlled Japanese politics for four decades. The Japanese live by the conviction that no foreigner – no *gaijin* – can ever become a Japanese. They preach that to be Japanese is to be "unique." The Japanese sing in a united, and exclusive, voice. Often the song has no meaning to us although the Japanese singing it have a way of bestowing on it a feeling of utmost importance.

Starting with Dr. Shiro Watanabe who greeted us at the airport, District Rotary Gov. Tomiji Oinuma who gave us a hearty welcome our first night in town, and the mayor of Fujisawa who held an audience for us the following morning, we listened to the chorus of the season: "You are fortunate to be in Japan at the most beautiful time of the year – cherry blossom time."

It's the opening for every greeting in early April. It has a bit of truth to it. Japan's cherry blossoms are indeed beautiful. To the Japanese it is a time of celebration, the end of winter, a renewal of the soul.

To the *gaijin* the cherry blossoms are pretty, but hardly the be all to end all. After mid-April it's back to the eye-burning air and acid-rain drenched grayness of everything in sight.

An early April edition of the *Japan Times* – one of the major English-language daily newspapers in the country – carried a cartoon on its editorial page called "The Cherry Blossoms' View of the Universe."

One cherry blossom high up the tree says: "Oh, I'm so happy! Somebody wrote a *haiku* about me last night?" A *haiku* is a 17-syllable Japanese poem that contains at least one word referring to the particular season it addresses.

Another cherry blossom nearby says: "What? That was about me." Then adds, "After all, I'm a much more delicate blossom than you!"

Off to the right a third cherry blossom opines: "Here's my advice: make the most of your looks while you've still got them."

Another philosophies: "How pleasant it is to be a brief moment of beauty in a course human existence!"

And yet another cherry blossoms observes: "It's so much more elegant to die early than late. ADIEU!"

The Oliphant of the cartoon by Leigh & Leigh is a small pedal from a single cherry blossom drifting off towards the ground below with the comment: "Ah! The ephemeral bliss of the free fall!"

That seems to be the song of the season this trip to Japan. We're riding across Yokohama on a toll expressway that is stacked higher than any toll expressway I remember from my previous visits to Japan. The outside lane has a concrete barrier higher than the bus protecting the neighborhoods stuffed beneath the expressway that is built on stilts instead of fill. We skim along at rooftop height of surrounding six-story office buildings.

I turn to the Japanese host riding in the seat next to me and say: "To me it looks like you have paved all of Japan since I was last here. Everything is concrete – the roads, the river beds, the highway barriers, the hillsides."

"*So desu*," he answers. "The government and the contractors are very close. They have a lot of money."

I'm aware that the English language newspapers have been carrying blow-by-blow accounts of the higher ups in the LDP who have been found to have millions in gold stashed away, bank accounts that would make the Kennedys look like poverty cases, and who have been caught with their hands stuck in the rice jar. I mention this to my Japanese host.

"*Ah so desu*," he mumbles buying a little time to arrange his thoughts as is customary with the Japanese we deal with on this trip. "The contractors have the politicians tied up. They get first pick at the money every year."

"Then what is being said about the close relationship between the LDP leaders and the construction businesses is true?" I ask.

He shrugs his shoulders.

"Is there any opposition strong enough to unseat the LDP?" I ask.

He shrugs his shoulders.

"Has the LDP been in power so long it can get away with something like this and the people don't get upset?" I ask.

He shrugs his shoulders.

"Do you feel there is a need for a change?" I ask.

He shrugs his shoulders. The bus comes out of a toll booth cut into a hillside and as we break out the other side of the hill we have a good view of hundreds of cherry trees in bloom in the suburban area to our right. My Japanese host points out the window: "You are fortunate to be in Japan at the most beautiful time of the year ..."

Ah! The ephemeral bliss of the free fall!

(Japanese Prime Minister Kiichi Miyazawa's government was toppled in a vote of no confidence in parliament six weeks later.)

- *Hai, so desu* -

Japanese buses are great, especially the buses the local Rotarians rent to haul us around all day. By American standards they are half buses, maybe - short and stacked high to meet the Japanese need to pack as much in as little space as possible. The buses are often overstatements. Today's has a video disk player in the front, a public address system, plenty of air-conditioning, and a chandelier in the back. It seats 16 people up front, two on each side of the aisle, and nine in the back, three each along both sides and three across the back in three long seats – individual but they can be made into a long seat by raising the middle two arm rests - all arranged around a long table directly under the imitation crystal chandelier. This particular bus is done in three shades of mauve.

It is about as long as the familiar rental car buses we see at American airports. It is almost as high as a double-decker. It is no wider than half a narrow Japanese street on which two cars can barely pass without taking off one or the other's rearview mirrors.

Visibility from our high perch is excellent as we crawl through Japanese traffic. All traffic in the Kanto Plain – the area around Tokyo Bay in which 30 million people live and work – is like Los Angeles at rush hour.

We've been weaving our way through one Japanese town after another headed back to our hotel in Yamato for cocktails with some more Rotarians who will take us under their wing beginning tomorrow and move us to another hotel in another town.

The bus pulls up a hill, through what appears to be a residential neighborhood, and around a tight turn. All of a sudden I am looking at the approach lights to a runway – the gradually descending pillars that support the red lights that create "The Rabbit" that guides airplanes caught in foul weather, or the dark, to the end of the runway. About a hundred yards off to my right, on a taxiway, are three P-3 Orion sub-hunters lined up for take-off. On their sides are painted the Japanese "meatball." I've seen these planes before. I wrote about them a dozen years ago when they were in Jacksonville, Florida – when the U.S. Navy turned them over to the Japanese at Jacksonville Naval Air Station and then trained the Japanese Navy pilots how to fly them.

I was working for the Florida Times-Union in Jacksonville, the same newspaper I was working for when I received the International Press Institute fellowship to come to Japan in 1981.

As the bus drives across the end of the runway, just outside the perimeter fence, I realize that I have seen this runway before. It is Atsugi Naval Air Station. This is the runway from which it was rumored that Japanese Vice Admiral Onishi, the inventor and commander of the kamikaze corps, took off and flew to his death instead of facing surrender at the end of the war. Actually Onishi apologized to his men for taking the easy way out and disemboweled himself after Emperor Hirohito broadcast his surrender rescript in 1945.

It is the same runway used by the first Americans, an advance party for Gen. Douglas MacArthur, to land Aug. 26, 1945, and set in motion the process of occupying Japan. But, it had never set as close to civilization as it sits today.

The U.S. Air Force Base at Tachikawa, about 30 miles to the north, was ringed by houses and industry when I served in the Army in Japan in the '50s, but not Atsugi as I remember it. Atsugi was a defendable Navy and Marine air station the last time I was here, probably during the fall football season of 1956 or '57. The Atsugi Marines were the toughest football team in the old Intra-Service Football League. It was a tough base to get on, and an even tougher one to get off of if you weren't supposed to be there.

That's all history now. Neighbors can sit in their apartments and study most of what is going on on the base with their naked eyes. No more open fields here. No strict security measures that prevent prying eyes from getting a good look at whatever it is that is about to be launched. Not many Americans, either, these days.

- Hai, so desu -

Why do I keep coming back to Japan?

Is it because of the beauty? Not necessarily. There are moments of beauty in Japan, but if I want natural beauty I have more of it in my backyard in the Florida Keys and the Everglades than I have found in any of the other corners of the world I have explored.

Is it because I am looking for new answers to old questions? Maybe. I've never fully understood why the young woman – I've forgotten her name – down the street from us in Sunbury, Ohio, had to lose her husband to the war or why another man on our street, Chuck Reese, had to come home with an arm missing after serving as a Navy flyer in the South Pacific.

My first visit to Japan was not a planned event. I originally had an Hawaiian assignment. I was happy with that. But the only places married guys in the military intelligence group I served in could take their wives in the 1950s was to Hawaii and Alaska. There was a guy in my class named Stanford or Stamford that was married. He drew a Japan assignment and couldn't take his wife. I wasn't married. I simply made a swap with him. It was that stroke of fate that first brought me here.

Do I keep coming here because I have some fascination for Japanese people? I have had some good Japanese friends – Ogawa-san and Shimizu-san among them. But I have had good friends from South Africa and other distant lands and never felt compelled to visit them or spend the amount of time I have spent in Japan.

When I examine this issue from time to time I always wind up back at the couch in the living room – now in the Library of the Florida Keys Masonic Lodge No. 336 of which I am a Past Master. I was kneeling on this very same couch in my grandmother's living room on Dec. 7, 1941 – Dec. 8 in Japan, although I didn't know what or where Japan was back then.

I was five years old. It was a Sunday afternoon. I was looking out the front window of my grandmother's house, across the street, watching Mid Perfect – a
blind man who wove and repaired wicker furniture in the dark in his living room – rock in his rocking chair on his front porch. It was a clear day. I only wanted to go outside and play.

My grandmother walked into the room. "The Japanese have attacked Pearl Harbor," she said. I still wanted to go out and play.

But something about the tone of her voice told me not to ask. Not to say anything. I had no frame of reference concerning war. We had no television in those days. The radio, when it was turned on, was usually turned to news programs and things I did not understand. But I think I knew instinctively on that day that what my grandmother had said would account for a large portion of what lie ahead for me. A cerebral concept way too deep for me to comprehend. But I understood its significance at that moment. It is one of the first distinct incidents that I remember from my childhood.

When my grandfather died at the age of 96 in 1977 he left me the couch knowing that he lived in Ohio and I lived in Florida. I don't think I ever mentioned to him that early memory, yet my grandfather left one of the largest physical items in his estate to me, one of more than a dozen heirs and the one that lived farthest from him. I considered letting the family sell it for its antique value – it must be close to 100 years old today. There were offers, but each deal seemed to fall through. I finally worked out a way to get it shipped to Florida. It has survived two wives, one divorce, a daughter, and numerous dogs, cats, birds and other pets. Every time I have mentioned I might get rid of it, a wife or my daughter have talked me out of it. I see that couch almost everyday of my life and each time I look at it I am reminded of that memory of Pearl Harbor Day. Am I spooked by it?

Maybe. *(In 2008, when I moved from the Florida Keys to upstate Lakeland, the couch went to the Masonic Lodge Library. My grandfather, as was my father, was a Past Master of his Masonic Lodge.)*

Why am I even thinking about that damn couch today? I am 12,000 miles from it. I am halfway around the world in Japan. Yet a conversation earlier today triggered my stream of thought.

I was riding through Kawasaki with a Japanese friend. We were talking about how the city has been rebuilt. Every available inch of building space has been used. The only direction left for the city to grow is up.

I made the comment that that is exactly what Kawasaki has been doing since the day I first saw it in 1956 when much of it was cleared, open area that had been bombed out during the war.

My friend looked at me and said, "One of the things that has always puzzled me, and I think a lot of older Japanese, is why – after bombing us into the ground – you Americans moved so quickly to help us rebuild. We did not expect it."

"I don't know," I replied.

"We were surprised. Many didn't understand it at the time. Many Japanese don't understand today," he said.

"I don't understand it, either," was all I could say. And then I started thinking about the couch again.

- Hai, so desu -

Information is hard to come by in Japan, especially for a *gaijin* or foreigner. I know this from my past visits. The Japanese will tell you just what they want you to know, no more, no less.

If you want to find out anything else, you dig it out on your own.

Luckily for English-speaking people there is a link at least to our language. Every morning from 7:00 to 7:30 a.m. we get the latest U.S. and world news from the Far East Network - the U.S. AM radio station that serves the few American forces left in Japan. From 7:30 to 8:00 a.m. I read the *Japan Times*, a national English-language daily newspaper serving Japan's international community. There are other English-language newspapers – the *Asahi Evening News*, the *Marinuchi*, and a weekly business newspaper. Most are not available outside Tokyo, so you grab them whenever you can at the Let's Kiosk news stands in railway stations where they periodically show up. There are also English language magazines of various types from which you can glean some information.

Confirmation of what you find in publications can often be found in government statistics, some of which are released in booklets printed in English. Further confirmation can be found in casual conversations with Japanese residents although I have found that when you probe too deeply your source will either clam up, or seek anonymity if the conversation gets too serious.

Japan is not an open society.

Even the *Japan Times*, with which I had a close relationship for years through my friendship with Editor-in-Chief Emeritus Masaru Ogawa, is suspect when it comes to reliability. Prior to, and throughout, World War II – the Greater East Asian Conflict to the Japanese – the *Japan Times* was the *Japan Times-Advertiser* and operated under the wing of the Foreign Ministry. With that tie, there was never much doubt that it was in many ways a propaganda device for the Japanese government.

Ogawa-san died in 1991, but before his death we discussed this former relationship between the *Times* and the government. He assured me the paper became independent following the war, and that under his guidance operated as an independent newspaper. But we used to banter back and forth about the tone of some of his front-page Sunday columns that occasionally rattled old Japanese war swords.

"There's a constituency for it among my readers," he would tell me in his perfect Stanfordian English.

I spent nearly three years in Japan in the '50s in military intelligence. My job was to analyze information, learn what was going on around us, and report it to my superiors. The techniques I used in those days are still valid today. Granted I don't have access to telephone taps, and teams of surveillance technicians, but the tricks I learned to gather, process, and distill information about Japan and the Japanese work just as well today as they did nearly four decades ago.

I digest everything I can find in English. I read in my room, in the hotel lobbies, in the restaurants, on the trains, on the tour buses, and am constantly looking for a Japanese who has at least a cursory knowledge of English and can confirm some tidbit of information I have gleaned from other sources.

I always carry a pocket-size portable radio so I can tune into the morning news on Armed Forces Radio. Listen to it for about a week and you can get a pretty good idea of how few American military are left in Japan. Unit and individual awards are announced as part of the military's desire to bolster troop morale and from these announcements you can learn unit numbers and their locations. It is not too difficult to set up your own U.S. Order of Battle identifying American forces remaining in the Japan area, and where they are located, from these announcements.

Armed with this knowledge, and my past history in Japan, I have a pretty good idea of what we have returned to the Japanese and from that have the advantage of being able to spot major relocations of segments of the Japanese population and industrial strength. There have been some mega changes in the last 37 years.

Working in reverse, from what Japanese tell me today back to what I learned about Japan in the '50s, and later during my stay here in the early '80s, I can get some idea of whether I am getting straight information or whether I am being honeymooned by the Japanese. It's not always easy to tell the difference because most Japanese you visit with appear most serious about everything they discuss with you. There is not much levity in Japan.

Dispelling myths becomes somewhat of a sport. One myth that I have never believed is the "Japanese Miracle" that has been touted so highly by hordes of English-language writers for the past two or three decades. To me there is no miracle to what the Japanese have accomplished, and these accomplishments are not nearly of the magnitude we have been led to believe.

There is no doubt that Japan's economy is second in size only to that of the United States. But what that economy represents is often quite different than we have been led to believe.

For instance: Japan has largely used its real estate to collateralize its wealth, but there simply is not that much real estate in Japan. Japan is about the size of California, but probably no more than 15 percent of it is habitable. It is a mountainous country. Yet today the total value of all real estate in Japan is nearly three times the total value of all real estate in the United States. That alone has a profound effect on how people live and work, on the productivity of a country, and on the relative value of a yen or a dollar.

The rapid increase in the value of Japanese real estate may have been good for the country following World War II. After the war, during the time of the U.S. occupation that lasted from 1945 to 1950, Japan adopted a new constitution and took major steps to break-up the old *zaibatsu*. *Zaibatsu* are powerful financial groups, with roots going back to the old days of the *shoguns*, that had controlled the country for centuries. They owned the land, the industry, and controlled the politics of the country.

With the reforms brought under the occupation and Gen. Douglas MacArthur the outside world was led to believe that these powerful groups had been broken up. But to this day there remains some resentment to what MacArthur tried to do in breaking down the stranglehold the *zaibatsu* had on the country's economy. Many older Japanese still refer to the new Japanese Constitution as "the MacArthur Constitution."

Only the rapid appreciation of real estate values prevented the old *zaibatsu* from getting their old land back after it was meted out to the people who lived and worked on it under MacArthur's rule.

"They (the *zaibatsu*) just didn't have enough money to buy it all back," one Japanese businessman told me as we rode a bus from Yokohama to Sagamihara one day and I was commenting on how the rice paddies had all disappeared and new cities and industry had sprung up in their place. It's an area in which only 1.8 million lived at the end of World War II. Today 8.4 million people call it home.

A I travel through it I find the name of many of the *zaibatsu* that have existed for most of Japan's modern history – Mitsubishi, Mitsui, Asahi, Sony, Hitachi, Fuji, etc. These conglomerates own industry, land, banks, and interests in most of the medium and small-sized enterprises in the country. One would think they would have been wiped out in the destruction wrought by World War II, but they weren't.

One of the cleverest tricks, that has rarely been reported, was the financial coup they engineered at the end of the war. During the two weeks between the time Japan surrendered and the American occupation forces took over the country, the Diet – Japanese parliament – met and agreed to pay off all contracts, including those for undelivered war material, owed the *zaibatsu* from the long war against first China and eventually the United States. With this nest egg, even though the *yen* was virtually valueless, the *zaibatsu* were ready to resume business when the opportunity became available. That opportunity came when the *yen* was tied to the dollar at a fixed rate during the Occupation but still there just wasn't enough, as the Japanese businessman told me, to buy all their feudal holdings back, mainly because real estate values inflated faster than the buys could be made.

The fact that there was any major shift from a feudal land society to a more egalitarian ownership of Japan is a myth. The same groups that have been in power for centuries still own, and largely control, the country. Once the *zaibatsu* regained control of the land, and their development companies proceeded to build homes, they not only controlled the land, but almost the total indebtedness of the Japanese people.

Of all the loan debt in Kanagawa Prefecture – a political subdivision of 8.4 million people southwest of Tokyo that includes Yokohama – in 1988, the last year I could find figures for, 95.4 percent of it was housing loans. There are 2.7 million homes in the prefecture. Of these 53.3 percent are owned, the remainder are rented.

The average per capita income of residents of Kanagawa at the end of 1988, expressed in dollars at the prevailing exchange rate

at that time, was $19,000. Average family income was just under
$48,000, which would indicate that more than one member
of many families was earning income outside the home.

The superiority of the Japanese educational system is another
myth that needs to be explored. The largely accepted theory is that
Japanese youth spend all their waking hours on their books in an
attempt to get passing marks on their college entrance exams. Once
admitted to college they are assured a job with a major corporation
and can live out the remainder of their lives in absolute security.

The fact that Japanese students study ardently is true. The
fact that they all, or a large percentage, go to college is not.

In Kanagawa Prefecture, which is a good mixture of Japanese
urban and suburban society, only 27.7 percent of the high school
graduates went on to college in 1989. Enrollments in all schools,
from kindergarten to university, indicate that most students
discontinue their education after high school. They are the people
that drive Japanese industry, the workers, not the supervisors.

Parents, particularly those that we come into contact with
who either work for large corporations or own and operate their own
medium-to-small business many of which are owned in part by the
zaibatsu, still push their children to go to university.

As one father proudly told me, "Sometimes things work out
better than you can hope for. My son failed to pass his college
entrance exams last year and we did not know what we were going
to do. But he studied for an extra year and this year he got high
marks and will now go to a better university than we had hoped."

As he told me this walking down the street in Ofuna one day
it seemed like a great weight was being lifted from the father's
shoulders.

Don't doubt for a minute that the Japanese education system
is not a good one. Excellent is up for debate. The whole system,
which operates on much the same grade level plan as do schools in
the United States, is based more on memorizing what one is
taught than in teaching students how to think. Individual creativity is
not nurtured.   Conformity is required from kindergarten on.
Students wear black uniforms to school, reminiscent of the old days
in Prussia. Only in the past year has anyone thought to deviate from
the standard black book bags carried by students from the day they
start to school. This year some department stores offered the book

bags in other colors and some mothers, who do all the buying for their children, took the plunge and bought brightly colored bags for their young charges.

Newspapers have been carrying reports of how these youngsters are being ostracized by their peers because they are failing to conform to the standard color all other students have worn for eons.

Young men who have gone on to university and completed their studies and been hired by major corporations as *sarariimen* tell me their four years at university was one big party. Young women – and there is an increasing number although they are still definitely in a minority - tell me they have taken their education more seriously, many opting for exchange semesters in other countries, and have little hope for landing any job above serving tea as OLs – office ladies – in major Japanese corporations. Most that I come into contact with are working on their English and looking for a way to get out of Japan in hopes of pursuing professional careers in some more equalitarian
society. The United States is high on their list.

Young and middle-aged *sarariimen* tell me they are not hired by major corporations for any particular specialty they have acquired through their studies. Instead they are hired as a class, which will determine their pay for the rest of their corporate life since pay is based on seniority and rarely on merit within the Japanese corporate structure. They are then assigned to whatever the company wishes. They will serve three years in personnel and then be transferred to marketing. Three years later they may
end up in research and development.

They spent inordinate hours at work. They are in their offices from early in the morning until late at night. Several nights a week they go out drinking to supposedly discuss business with their boss and colleagues. They get home at midnight or later, bath, grab some sleep, jump on an early train and return to their offices the next morning. Those that are married see little of their wife and children with the exception of an occasional Sunday if they are not involved in some extracurricular company activity.

That the wives run the households is no myth. They run the household budget, do the shopping, ride herd on the children, and expect their husbands to bring home the paycheck. The Japanese worker at all levels is hobbled to his job. Family comes second.

It is an old tradition that is beginning to wear thin in some quarters. For the first time in history some Japanese wives are beginning to sue major corporations for *kareshi*, or killing their husbands early from overwork. Other wives, however, are not interested in their husbands being around the house. They refer to retired husbands as "dead leaves" – the most difficult thing to sweep off the sidewalk – or worse yet as *oki gomi*, "big garbage."

That even this small amount of information that is contrary to the image that Japan has fostered of itself over past centuries is now beginning to appear in conversation and in some of the English-language publications available in Japan is significant. In a country in which meaningful information is so hard to come by, this indicates there are deeper, underlying cultural problems that are yet to be revealed.

- Hai, so desu -

The war – World War II to us, The Pacific Conflict, Fifteen-Year War, or Greater East Asian Conflict to the Japanese – is never that far away. It ended nearly 50 years ago, but it seems that it has always dominated my life. I was nine years old when the war ended. I can remember tying a small American flag to the handle bars of my bicycle and the waves and smiles I got as I delivered my afternoon editions of the "V-J Day"-bannered *Columbus Citizen* along my afternoon paper route in Sunbury, Ohio, a small town of about a thousand people 22 miles northeast of Columbus in the then-rich farm area of central Ohio.

Eleven years later I walked down the gang plank of the American troop ship *MSTS Mitchell* and rode an Army bus through still bombed-out areas of Yokohama. For nearly three years I travelled the trains, highways and back roads of Japan working with, and visiting with, veterans and survivors – from both sides – of the war. I spent nearly a year of my time in Okinawa, a piece of the former Japanese Empire that was destroyed by both sides towards the end of the war.

Twenty-four years later I returned to Japan. The jingoists still drove up and down the streets of Tokyo in loudspeaker-equipped trucks playing war music and extolling passersby to join their cause, to keep Japan Japanese, to return to old ways, to bring all eight corners of the world under the roof of the old Japanese Empire's Greater East Asian Co-Prosperity Sphere.

My *sensei*, Masaru Ogawa wrote an occasional sword-rattling piece in his customary Sunday front page column of *The Japan Times*. He claimed – in the early 1980s – he still had a constituency that held that the war never really ended.

I visited aboard a Japanese destroyer in Yokosuka that was far superior to anything the U.S. had afloat at that time. I made my first trip to Hiroshima where younger Japanese asked me: "How could you have done this to us?" My answer: An invitation to Hawaii and a visit to the *U.S.S. Arizona* memorial.

It's now a dozen years later. Japan has been rebuilt to the point that a first-time visitor, if he or she did not make a deliberate trip to Hiroshima or Nagasaki, could never tell a war of the magnitude of World War II had ever damaged this island nation. But the war does not go away. In the English-language newspapers there are two topics relating to the war that are currently being discussed throughout Japan, a third that has grown out of the war and threatens Japan's outwardly professed desire for world peace.

"Comfort women," women of other Asian nations – many from Korea – conscripted by the Japanese Army and Navy to provide comfort for their men overseas in combat, are attempting to get redress for the abuse and humiliation they suffered nearly a half a century ago at the hands of the Japanese. After the first woman came forward, a steady stream of others have broken 48 years of silence and joined in a struggle to obtain some form of restitution from the Japanese government.

The second issue is a visit scheduled for the end of April by Japanese Emperor Akahito to Okinawa. Akahito is the son of Emperor Hirohito who led the Japanese nation through World War II. It will be the first visit by a Japanese Emperor to Okinawa, although Akahito visited before as crown prince.

Okinawa has been a Japanese prefecture since it was annexed by the Japanese in 1879. It was occupied by the U.S. following World War II and was returned to Japan in 1972. There is much speculation – demands from some groups – that Akahito will apologize to the Okinawans for the damage done to their island by Japanese forces during the closing days of World War II.

Both the U.S. and Japan blasted the main island of Okinawa into unidentifiable fragments as the Americans positioned themselves for the invasion of the Japanese home islands. The Japanese were responsible for the loss of a conservatively estimated 100,000 Okinawans, many forced to march in a protective wall in front of Japanese troops as Allied forces advanced across the island. Japanese soldiers assassinated Okinawans as spies for speaking a foreign language. At the time, many Okinawans over 60 spoke only their former Ryukyuan dialect learned before Okinawa became a part of Japan.

Okinawan children killed their parents to prevent their capture by Allied forces. Parents killed their own children and grandchildren. Husbands killed wives. Okinawans joined the Japanese in suicide in the closing days of the campaign because the Japanese had convinced them Americans were barbarians and would do unspeakable things to them if they were captured.

It was all done in the name of the Emperor.

Okinawans succumbed to the Japanese pressures during World War II. They were freed from Japanese domination by the U.S. occupation. Many Okinawans thought someday they might regain their status as an independent nation but instead were rejoined to the Japanese body politic when the U.S. occupation of Okinawa ended nearly three decades after the war.

That turn of events has always been a curiosity to me. The Okinawans I got to know back in the '50s had little love for the Japanese. They were, however, proud of their ancient nation of Ryukyu. I used to say that Okinawa would eventually become the 51st State if for no other reason than that would be the only way we would ever recoup any of the zillions of dollars we spent rebuilding the island.

Yet today, the Japanese press bemoans the fact the Okinawans, now considered Japanese citizens, "suffered under U.S. occupation for 27 years." America not only spent 27 years rebuilding Okinawa, it turned around and gave it all back to Japan.

I doubt if any Japanese Emperor can ever adequately apologize for anything the Japanese did to other nations and other people during the war. It is not The Japanese Way. As much as Japanese like to hear us say we're sorry for Hiroshima, I've never had any Japanese freely offer an apology for Pearl Harbor in the name of his Emperor.

There have been several revisionist histories written by both Japanese and Americans. Some have added new twists to the way the war was played out, but the ones I find most ironic are the ones that tell – and I believe these to be true – that many people in the nations of Asia occupied by the Japanese during the war are grateful today to the Japanese for having liberated them from colonial – Caucasian – imperialism. Many Japanese today believe this.

In less than a single lifetime, people seem to have forgotten the real suffering they endured at the hands of the Japanese occupation forces. At least 100,000 – maybe as many as 150,000, about 25 percent of the population of the Ryukyus in the 1940s – Okinawans never lived to struggle with those memories.

The final personal irony to this unfolding chapter in Japanese-Okinawan relations is that Emperor Akahito will travel to Okinawa to plant a tree in a special Spring ceremony held nationwide. He'll plant that tree in a peace memorial park that is located on the former site of a military intelligence unit in which I once served. We lived in American-built buildings on the small isolated base at this site. We gave it back to the Japanese with the rest of the island although we still retain several military bases on Okinawa to the chagrin of the Japanese press.

The hangover problem from World War II that is being thrashed around in the Japanese press today is the prospect of North Korea acquiring the atomic bomb. Intensive research and study over the past 20 years of anything I could find concerning the Japanese atomic bomb program during World War II provides an extra twist to this story.

One of the misconceptions Westerners seem to foster about the Japanese is that they were for so long imbued with only the ability to copy the works of others, primarily the works of Caucasians. We Westerners have a tendency to view the Japanese as late arrivals in the world of technology. Someday that thinking may cost us dearly. It almost did us in in the early days of World War II when we refused to accept the fact the Japanese had – on their own – developed a superior fighter aircraft in the Zero.

Although we have been led to believe that the Japanese never got off first base in the quest to explore the building of an atomic bomb, research leads me to believe otherwise. The Japanese were technology sophisticated enough to develop the bomb on their own. There is one documented interview with a former Japanese officer on his way home from Korea following the surrender who claimed he witnessed the explosion of a
Japanese atomic device near an island off Hungnam, North Korea, four days after the bomb was dropped on Hiroshima.

By that time, the Japanese had lost most means by which they could have delivered an atomic bomb over long distances. However, they continued to view the weapon - *genzai bukudan* - as a defensive possibility when Allied forces began to invade the Japanese home islands. Knowing their *kamikaze* forces were running out of planes and pilots, the Japanese realized, following the battle of Okinawa, that a big bomb like *genzai bukudan* would be required to put a dent in the Allied invasion force once it approached Japan proper. They continued their research and development of the bomb.

Because Allied air raids had dealt Japanese industry such a devastating blow on the home islands, the Japanese atomic program was moved to North Korea, considered at the time part of Japan. Japan had annexed all of Korea in 1910. When the Russians entered the war during the last days, they moved directly into what is now North Korea, dismantled the local Japanese industry, including what they could find of the Japanese atomic project, and trucked it off to Mother Russia.

There is speculation among historians who deal with the dawn of the atomic age, that what the Russians captured and spirited away of the Japanese atomic program enabled the Ruskies to acquire the bomb so soon after America developed it.

So, if it upsets the Japanese that North Korea may become a nuclear power, they need only to look back into their own military history and examine what motivated them to be the first to put such a weapon on North Korea soil.

Even though the visible scars are gone, the war does not disappear here in Japan.

- Hai, so desu -

We've been staying in the Yamoto Grand Hotel, another mid-range Japanese *bisiness hoteru* about 20 miles up the road from Fujisawa. Nice, but not fancy. Decent-sized rooms, but no service help.

It's the end of our first week and I've written a report that the people in my Rotary Club back in Key Largo might enjoy. I set up the computer and fax/modem, plug it into the telephone in my room, and push the "Send" button.

The computer and fax/modem are operating on the customized dialing instruction that Paul White devised in Fujisawa. They enabled us to get around the digital Japanese phone system in the Fujisawa hotel and dial direct to my office in the Florida Keys.

The computer dials away but halfway through the process a voice comes over the loudspeaker in the computer: "*Moshi, moshi.*" It's the Japanese equivalent of our "Hello, hello," when we answer a telephone.

"*Moshi, moshi,*" the voice continues, breaking my computer-generated dialing string. I unplug the computer.

My telephone rings and I pick it up. A Japanese woman's voice – high-pitched as is their style – on the other end says in broken English: "You no fax from room."

"I was using my computer," I said.

"You no fax from room. You bring fax to front desk," the voice on the other end says.

"*Hai, hai,*" I reply and hang up.

I'm not faxing anything from this hotel.

- *Hai, so desu* -

Curiosity drives me across Japan as a veteran of the U.S. military, a curiosity to discover what happened as a result of those nearly 1,000 days and nights that were deducted from my normal Stateside life because someone, or some group of someones whom I had never met, determined that those days were to be spent here instead of in some beer joint off campus at some American university.

We're riding on a bus across a flyway that crosses an old familiar road. At this intersection in 1957 I slid a motorcycle around the corner on some lose cinders, caught the headlight on a telephone pole guy wire which flipped the bike end over end and threw me and the motorcycle into a nearby rice paddy. Why I wasn't beheaded I'll never know. The only evidence I have of the accident is a small scar on my right little finger. I didn't even break the bottle of scotch I had tucked into my Hong Kong-tailored white cashmere bomber jacket. The bike was totaled.

Back then I could sail down this road between the rice paddies at 100 miles per hour. Today the road has been widened to four lanes. The traffic moves at a crawl. There are no more rice paddies. Only homes and factories.

We are headed west towards Sagamihara, through Fuchinobe where I was once stationed. I am anxious to see if anything is left of the old base at Fuchinobe. I asked back in 1981 when I came through this area, but a cab driver at Sagami-ono station told me to save my money, the old base had been turned into a park.

As we clear the flyover, I catch a glimpse of what used to be the back entrance to an American housing area near the old Zama Hospital Base. I know the hospital is gone. It is now a major regional shopping center. I ask one of the Japanese on the bus if the old housing area is still in use.

"By Japanese," he tells me.

Just as we pull beyond it I see the only graffiti I will see during this trip to Japan. It is on an old building – Western in style – that used to set alongside the old two-lane road that ran by the American housing area. Its windows have been knocked out. Its roof has caved in. It is deserted. It is covered with graffiti, spray-painted in Japanese characters. My guess is that the comments are not pro-American.

A few miles up the road I catch a glimpse of a Toys 'R Us sign. I recently read about this store in U. S. News & World Report. It is the first chain discount store that has been allowed in Japan. It has been heralded as a new breakthrough in trade relations with the Japanese, the beginning of a consumer upsurge that the Japanese government hopes will help pull its economy out of recession.

I'm focused on the store and its implications when one of the Japanese turns and points over my shoulder: "*Honcho-san* there is Camp Fuchinobe."

I turn to look and see nothing but homes scattered amidst some wooded areas. Nothing that I see outside the bus looks anything like I expected the old Army camp area to look. I was prepared to see houses and businesses standing where rice paddies once encircled the base, but not woods this dense. We had kept the areas around the perimeter of the base as open as possible. There had been some trees on the base, but not woods and park areas littered with trash and paper like I see alongside   the road we are travelling.

About a mile down the road, in the general area as I had remembered it, I see a sign over an intersection that reads "Fuchinobe Station." The arrow on the sign points north where the town's station is located. There used to be a few small houses, some bars and a soba shop here. It was a mile or so walk from the entrance to the base. There had been nothing between the base and the small town and railroad station in the '50s. It's wall-to-wall buildings, traffic and people now.

The Japanese travelling with us on the bus tell me I'll get a closer look at the camp later in the day although it doesn't appear on the schedule I have been given. But first we are going to stop for lunch with the Sagamihara Rotary clubs and then meet the Sagamihara mayor. We have a visit later this afternoon to the Japanese National Aerospace Center.

While we're looking at the latest in Japanese satellites and rockets, Rick Ramsay is slatted to spend the afternoon with the local fire department. It is the first individual vocational exchange privilege that anyone on the team has been allowed. It is encouraging. Maybe we're going to get a chance to look at our career counterparts in Japan like Rotary International had promised in the information they sent us about the trip. That opportunity was the No. 1 thing that attracted the other members of our Rotary team to the Japan visit.

When we pull up in front of Sagamihara's top restaurant I know instantly live fish is on the menu. I see them in the tanks as we enter the restaurant. I don't think the rest of the team is going to be ready for this one.

About 25 of us are seated on the floor around a rectangular table. I'm seated at the center of one end. Three of our team members are seated to my left around the corner of the table. The other two, plus our interpreter for the day, are seated to my right around the other corner of the table. A Japanese woman comes to the door of the upstairs dining room. She slips off her shoes at the sliding rice paper and wood door, drops to her knees on the *tatami* mat floor of the room, and leaning forward places a large wooden platter of *sushi* – sliced raw fish – in front of me. In the center of the platter, which is shaped like a Japanese fishing vessel, lies a large sea bream. The flesh from its fillets has been neatly cut into thin slices and arranged in tumbling domino order between its spine and dorsal fin. It is one of the most beautiful displays of Japanese food and garnish I have ever seen.

The tip of the tail of the fish is hanging over the edge of the platter on my side and is hidden from the view of the other team members. I watch it flick meekly. I take my chopsticks and reach for a piece of raw tuna off to the side of the sea bream. At about the same time Ron Pullman, seated to my right, asks, "Is that fish's eye moving?"

Paul White, seated to my left has his chopsticks in hand and touches the fish's eye with the tip of one. The fish flops on the platter. It's gills grab for air. Tim Wilson jumps to his feet with his video camera in hand and starts taping the experience. I pick up a slice of the meat from the fish, dip it in my soy sauce and eat it.

"That's fresh fish," I comment. Pullman moans. White draws back in disgust. Whitney Bain from the Bahamas cringes. Rick Ramsay, whose system doesn't tolerate raw fish under the best of circumstances, is dumbstruck.

Our Japanese hosts have been watching our reaction. They are amused at the customary Western reaction to one of the most honorable dishes they serve. Filleted live sea bream is the meal that was served Japanese Navy pilots just before they took off from their aircraft carriers to attack Pearl Harbor. It is reserved for special occasions.

Following the 10-course lunch, we ride to city hall where we meet with the Mayor of Sagamihara. By now the ritual of meeting mayors of the cities we visit is becoming routine. After being seated in the proper positions around a rectangular layout of tables or easy chairs, we wait for the mayor and his entourage to appear. It is my job to greet the mayor and introduce the members of my team to him. Business cards are exchanged, hands shaken, and bows made.

The mayor makes the first speech. Again today it starts with, "You are fortunate to be visiting Japan at the prettiest time of year. The cherry blossoms are in bloom."

My job is to thank the mayor for taking the time out of his busy schedule to meet with us. I tell the mayor of Sagamihara, like I have told the other mayors we have met, that it is indeed an honor. But today, I add a few extra comments beyond the normal polite exchanges that take place.

"It is a privilege for me to return to Sagamihara after 35 years. I do not recognize the city as the one I used to know. I miss the rice paddies and countryside that used to surround it. I miss not being able to see Mt. Fuji in the distance," I say pointing in the direction of the sacred mountain.

"*Ah so desaku*," the mayor replies. "Sagamihara has grown. Progress has been good for us. We have many factories and jobs now."

"Your city was written up in U.S. News & World Report a couple of weeks ago," I tell the mayor. "The new Toys 'R Us down the road is the first in Japan."

The mayor turns to his interpreter for a minute, then looks back at me. "We have made much progress," he says.

"The magazine story also said the Nissan plant in Zama will be closing next year. Will putting 6,500 people out of work have a bad economic effect on Sagamihara?" I ask.

Again he conferred with his interpreter, then turning back to me, said, "Only about 4,500 people will lose the jobs they now have when the auto plant closes. Nissan has a year to take care of them. We have other new businesses in the area. We have made much progress."

"I still miss the days when the city was surrounded by countryside," I reply. The mayor smiles. Several in his entourage nod their heads without making any comment. I sense they, too, miss the beauty of the countryside that in the 1950s had not changed much from what it must have been during feudal days.

Progress has claimed almost all of it today.

The customary gifts are presented to us by the mayor. As team leader I am given a large bound volume commemorating a major "Green" festival the city had several months ago. It is written entirely in Japanese, but the color photography is outstanding. I don't recognize any of the locations filmed.

The boulevard in front of city hall is lined on both sides and down the middle with cherry trees in full bloom. It is a colorful sight, but still all the buildings bear the marks left by years of acid rain. One of the features of Japan is its ability to be grey and colorful at the same time. It gives the country a strange, aged beauty.

We are riding our bus through city streets, packed with cars and people. Traffic, no matter what type of street we are travelling on, is politely slow. It gives us a chance to take in the surroundings. In this section of Sagamihara I guess the houses and shops were built sometime in the last 20 years. The major difference I find between old and newer construction, especially when it was been done as a city is built in concentric rings outward from its center, is the layout of the streets.

In the older sections of Sagamihara, or almost any Japanese city, the streets are narrow and sometimes twisting. It is almost impossible to get two cars side by side on some of these streets. High vehicles are forbidden. The height of buildings is not uniform. A one-story structure may find itself surrounded by two or three-story buildings. Shops line the streets, living quarters are behind the shops or on the floors above. Laundry flutters from the balconies. It hangs from bamboo poles inserted through the arms of shirts and sweaters so they hang to dry as if they were being worn.

Lower roof lines often extend into the street. Many of the roofs on the older buildings are rusting corrugated tin. Sidewalks are non-existent. Utility poles poke up through the pavement, standing in the street themselves. Sewers, which used to be open, run along the edge of the street. Now they are covered with concrete tiles separated by small open slits that provide the necessary ventilation that prevents a build-up of methane gases from decomposing human waste.

There is no clear debarkation line as we cross from the older to the newer sections of the city.

The first indication we get is that the streets are wider, less twisting, and the houses are more uniform. A little bit larger than the average old-style, one-story Japanese home. These are two stories high. Most are surrounded by some type of fence, usually concrete. They have very small yards, but there are a few trees. These are the houses I saw contractors building in the '80s on land that used to be rice paddies. They would be called tract homes in the U.S. Here in Japan they are simply a scaled down version, sans yards, with dull, repetitive grey-white exteriors, tile roofs, and an occasional sliding wood frame and rice paper door. This is the new Japanese suburbia.

Even though these homes were built one after the other in what used to be open country, the streets that run through this suburban area are hardly larger than the streets in the old section of town. A little bit wider and a little bit tidier maybe, but not the type of suburban street we are accustomed to. Utility poles still pop up through the street's surface. Sewers are buried instead of covered. Sidewalks are still non-existent. Instead people walk on areas inside a white line that separates walkers from the cars in the street.

When the bus meets an oncoming car one must pull over to the side to let the other pass. The most efficient use of space overrides comfort and convenience almost everywhere in Japan.

The street we are turning into is wider than the average Japanese suburban street. It has a line of trees along it and a sidewalk. One of the Japanese riding in a seat in front of me stands up, turns around, points down the street, and says to me: "We are coming to Camp Fuchinobe."

"Where?" I think to myself. Nothing in the area looks familiar. The last time I saw Camp Fuchinobe it sat in the center of open fields. The nearest town, Fuchinobe was a mile or so away. Here the street is lined with wooded areas on the right. We drive past one street that enters them. A quarter of a mile farther down the road, the bus slows to take a right turn on a street that goes into the woods. I see a sign that says "Aerospace Center."

The connection had never occurred to me. Maybe it was because the cab driver at Sagami-ono had told me back in the '80s

Camp Fuchinobe had been turned into a park that it never dawned on me it could be anything else. When I saw the aerospace center on our itinerary I assumed it was in Sagamihara, not Fuchinobe. But here it is – the Houston of Japan's space program – located on the grounds of what used to be my military home in Japan.

The bus pulls onto a circular drive in front of a modern office building. There are more buildings down a brick sidewalk to our right. Alongside the wide sidewalk sits several of the rocket models used by Japan to launch satellites. The woods between the building and the street are much thicker than any I remember in the area. They form a park for the local people, some of whom are picnicking across the fence from us. The park area is not well kept. Trash and litter are scattered throughout it.

I've seen this in other public areas in Japan. In spite of their personal penchant for cleanliness, the Japanese don't seem to mind trashing common areas.

When this was a military base, I remember the Japanese nationals that worked for us. If you dropped a cigarette butt, a man with a No. 2 tin can bucket would come along behind you and pick it up with his nail-in-a-broom-handle spear.

Camp Fuchinobe became a U.S. military base because it had once been a Japanese military base, a military hospital base far out in the country away from urban areas that were bombed incessantly in the last years of the war. It was out in the open, easy to defend, and isolated by its agrarian setting from spying eyes. That was probably the major reason we had chosen it for the location of a military intelligence unit.

The base had other units and together we shared two clubs, a gymnasium, a football field, tennis courts, motor pool, and an old metal incinerator that sat in the middle of the camp. Occasionally my number would come up and I would spend the whole day standing by the incinerator checking off classified documents as we burned them. I decide I'll see if I can find the incinerator, or at least where it was located, on our tour of the aerospace center today. But first, there are the usual formalities
to get out of the way.

We are taken to the large conference room on the ground floor of the main building of the aerospace center. Several Japanese from the center join us. Since Paul White has a degree in aerospace engineering, we have decided he should be the team leader for this portion of our trip. As the initial introductions are being made, I inform our Japanese hosts that Paul will be the *honcho* for the afternoon. I might as well have saved my words.

Although our hosts nod in agreement, they will not address Paul as our group leader. They direct the conversation to me and only acknowledge Paul's presence and knowledge of the aerospace industry when he is permitted to ask them a direct question.
This is becoming a pattern. The Japanese refuse to recognize our team members as specialists in their various fields, to accept them as our team leader when we were visiting in a area that pertains to their individual field of expertise.

There appear to be two reasons for this: (1) It is difficult for Japanese whose careers are built on the seniority system to accept anyone under 50 as being capable of providing leadership; and (2) almost all Japanese in business are generalists. It matters little what a Japanese receives a degree in. Once hired by a major corporation and started up the management career ladder, Japanese *sarariimen* are shifted from one area of their company to another every three years. They may start in personnel, move to research and development, and then on to accounting. They are not considered for top management positions until well into their 50s or 60s, so they have no frame of reference that allows them to accept the fact that members of my team in their 30s are business owners and managers. They automatically treat them as inferiors as if they were their subordinates at work.

During a film we are shown I realize that the Japanese launch their rockets and satellites from Kagoshima, an old airfield on the southern tip of the southernmost of the home islands, Kyushu. Kagoshima was a base we used to land at to refuel or get an engine repaired back in the '50s when I flew courier runs aboard Civil Air Transport – one of the CIA's covert airlines – C-47s from Okinawa to Tachikawa Air Force Base north of here. Tachikawa was returned to the Japanese years ago and has become a part of suburban Tokyo the Japanese tell me. Kagoshima, though, has survived to become the Cape Kennedy of Japan.

By comparison to our space program, the Japanese program is small. But Japanese technology has produced some serviceable rockets with commercial satellite applications. Their aerospace budget wouldn't pay the fuel bill for our space shuttle, but there is an air of confidence about those who work in Japan's space program that gives me the impression they are following a well-planned course. While we pour billions into the sky, the Japanese are working on sophisticated satellite delivery systems that can meet demands for putting hardware into orbit for other nations. The Japanese space program appears to be designed ultimately to pay its own way.

On a walk from the main center to the center's vertical assembly building – a miniature compared to the monster at Cape Kennedy – we get a close-up look at their primary rockets. In size they compare to our old Atlas boosters. In detail they are much more sophisticated.

I try to orient myself to the old layout of the base as we walk from one building to another. The feeling I get is that the small security building to the right of the circle in front of the main building is about where our old club used to be located. That would put the football field right behind the main building, the old gym where one of the more modern office buildings now sits, and the old metal incinerator behind that building.

It is evident to me that the road we came in on was not the main road into the camp when I lived here. While the others tour the vertical assembly building I slip out and visit with one of the Japanese who works at the center. I ask him if any of the buildings from the old Camp Fuchinobe are still standing.

"There were some still here when I came here about 10 years ago, but they were just shells," he says. "We tore them all down."

About the time I begin to think that there is nothing left from which I can identify the old base, I remember a street that ran in front of the building in which I lived. The building had been a combination barracks, administrative offices, and intelligence center. It had been the old Japanese military hospital. We slept four each in what had been at one time hospital wards on the second floor of the long, frame building. Each bay had its own coal-fired stove with a tall stove pipe that ran through the ceiling over our heads. I remembered being awakened by a mild earthquake early one morning when the stove pipe came toppling down sending soot shooting across my bunk like black snow. I jumped out of bed, and ran through the double swinging doors in the hallway, flew down the

stairs, out another set of doors to the area in front of the building where we were to
assemble in times of disaster.

That area was just above a slight "S" curve in the street that ran from the main gate west past our building. I wonder if the "S" curve still exists and decide to go looking for it.

If my orientation is correct and the old club where we drank, and ordered custom-tailored clothes from the Hong Kong tailor that came by every month, was located back by the security building, then the first street we passed on the way in should be the old main gate road to Camp Fuchinobe. I walk north along the brick sidewalk running past the vertical assembly building, on past the office building on the opposite side of the sidewalk and come to the street. Well beyond it, across several open athletic fields is a stadium.

I look east and sure enough the street runs through the wooded area to the main road. Thirty-five years of memories can distort distances, but if I am correct I can walk the opposite direction down the street, beyond the office building, and if the old "S" curve is still there I should find it in about a quarter of a mile. I turn and head in that direction. Just as I turn, one of our Japanese hosts comes down the sidewalk waving at me and saying, "It is time to get on the bus."

My fantasy of finding my old home fades. I rejoin the group. We walk back to the bus, bow our formal good-byes, and board. The bus driver pulls around the circle and heads back out the same road we came in. Then he turns north on the highway, goes to the next street, turns left and I find myself riding the bus down the street that I had wanted to walk in search of the old "S" curve a few minutes before.

As we pass the office building on the left and the open fields leading out to the stadium on the right, I see a relatively new brick building ahead. It looks like a gymnasium but it certainly isn't the old one we had. Just before we get to it, the road takes a small jog to the left and almost immediately another small jog to the right so we are heading in the same direction. That was the "S" curve. It remains in the road, right where it used to be. My old building sat directly where the public gymnasium is now located.

This area is definitely old Camp Fuchinobe.

We drive around the gymnasium and head out a road that used to be a back road out of the camp. Back in the '50s it was barely passable in anything but a four-wheel-drive vehicle. We used it sometimes as a back way through the rice paddies to a river valley in the distance where we could pick up another dirt road that wound through the countryside and eventually connected with another road that took us to Camp Zama. It was a desolate area.

I once watched the Japanese army on maneuvers in this area. The Japanese army did not disband after the war. It became the Japanese Ground Self Defense Force. The most impressive thing I remember about it was a set of maneuvers they were on in 1957. A group of army trucks had driven down this road, which then was flanked on both sides by rice paddies. They stopped and unloaded several platoons of Japanese soldiers armed with rifles. Then they drove on. By the time the empty troop trucks disappeared into the twilight down the road that led to the river valley every one of the Japanese soldiers had become invisible. They had simply faded into the rice paddies. It was one of the most fascinating exercises I had ever witnessed. No trees to hide behind. No major topographical features. Just rice paddies that swallowed up an entire Japanese infantry company in a matter of minutes.

We pass the large stadium on the right. On our left are homes and small businesses. We top the small ridge that leads to the river valley and spread before us is a large park with giant mosaic flower beds. It is the festival park featured in the book the mayor of Sagamihara gave me. Across the small river valley are several buildings that look like a college campus. I ask one of the Japanese and he tells me it is a local college. The main building is a nursing school.

We take the same turn in the road I used to take years ago.

The roads now are city streets, not dirt country roads. We head for Yamato where we are staying. Along the way, we see a few small produce fields, but for the most part this area is now suburban. The road is lined with homes, businesses and small factories. No more rice paddies.

Rick Ramsay has rejoined us. We get the Rotarians with us to make a stop at the McDonald's in Sagamihara so he can get some solid food in his stomach. Ramsay has brought with him some history of the fire department he visited. It's in English.

The Sagamihara-Fuchinobe Fire Department has nearly 650 fulltime firemen, and more than 650 volunteers.

It was founded in 1958 – the last year I lived in the area.

The city's first fire department had 12 volunteers. That's growth of more than a hundredfold. That's why there are no more rice paddies around here.

- Hai, so desu -

Today is one of those days that I have been looking forward to. We are going to visit a Nissan plant, attend a Rotary luncheon meeting, visit the *Asahi Shimbun* newspaper plant, and then tour Camp Zama, all in Zama, an area in which I spent a lot of time in the 1950s.

This Nissan plant is of particular interest. In 1981 when I was here as a visiting journalist, neither Nissan or Toyota would let us tour their plants. Instead we went out to Hiroshima where we were welcomed by Mazda. Now Japan is experiencing a recession, lagging one in the U.S. by at least a couple of years.

The big drawback to recovery in Japan appears to be a growing need to break with tradition – mainly an established system of lifetime employment – and shift its economy from big corporate business, that has traditionally been responsible for providing jobs but apparently is weakening in its ability to do so, to entrepreneurship and small business, that traditionally has been the generator of new jobs in the U.S. economy. At the Nissan plant in Zama we get the traditional factory tour of video, hand shaking, a walk through a section of the plant, and a question-and-answer period during which all our questions are answered in the most positive light in spite of the fact I have read about this plant's troubles in the American press before leaving for Japan, and I am sure our Japanese hosts at Nissan know, from some of the questions I ask, that I am aware of the predicament they are in.

This is the first auto plant to be forced to close down in Japan due to a decline in auto exports. The Japanese tell us that is not necessarily so, that the plant is closing because it is old. But, when I left Sagamihara in 1958 it was still a dream. It is one of the most automated automobile plants in Japan. It simply is not needed any longer.

The plant will close in 1995 and 6,000 workers will be displaced. Our hosts tell us the displaced workers will not suffer. Approximately 3,000 will be retrained and transferred to other Nissan plants in Japan. Early retirement will be offered to about 1,500. The remaining 1,500 will simply disappear because Nissan will not replace workers, who leave due to normal attrition, at this plant between now and when it is closed.

Other Japanese companies that have had to try such cut-back tactics on a smaller scale report they have not achieved good results. The early retirement program does not work as well as Japanese businesses had hoped. Many who could qualify do not opt for it simply because it is not Japanese not to work. *Sarariimen* cannot go home, or be at home, during normal work hours in Japan. It defies custom. It says to one's neighbors that the husband-father-breadwinner is not doing everything he can for his family.

Other slips backward are beginning to impact Japanese business. At Nissan today, like at Fuji Xerox and Mitsubishi a few days ago, we have seen a slow down in the pace of Japanese technological advances over that witnessed in the past two decades. What we have been seeing is technology that is a generation or so behind that which we are using in the U.S. This is just the opposite of what I saw in 1981 in computers and other high-tech work tools in Japan.

There seems to be more of a hold-on-at-any-cost attitude in Japan today than the traditional jump-out-in-front-and-grab-the-market attitudes that prevailed in the past four decades. Plants capable of running three shifts and churning out high-tech products are now operating on one shift and it appears they are running that shift at a minimum level.

Research and Development expenditures have increased to levels equal to about 8 percent of corporate revenues, but while the Japanese point out to us that this is an increase in percentages the decline in corporate income, and its subsequent lowering of money available to develop and build new products, means that the overall expenditure on R&D may not be sufficient to maintain the major advances the Japanese were able to make during the bubble economy of the '70s and '80s.

What we are being shown, although I doubt if the Japanese industries that we have been touring are showing us their latest technological developments, are more and more Japanese systems driven by American-made components such as Hewlett-Packard and Intel 386 processors for many computer devices. In fact, the 386 is one of the primary personal computers being produced in Japan today at a time when we are into the Intel 486 and the Pentium is about to be released in the U.S.

Japanese recover from what they call "shocks" differently than we do. The oil shocks of the '70s left the Japanese to cope with problems Americans have never faced so intently. Japan is 100 percent dependent upon outside sources for its oil.

Mazda's auto plant in Hiroshima that I visited in 1981 was at that time the Chrysler of Japan – the country's manufacturer of big cars. It had to redeploy its resources to the development of a small car that would sell both domestically and on foreign markets if it wanted to survive. To do so, the company simply asked for 5,000 "volunteers" from all parts of the company to go into sales. At that time car sales in Japan were done door-to-door.

Today there are more dealerships in the American style.

The volunteers moved out of corporate offices, off assembly lines, and into the streets. While new models were developed, the volunteer sales force sold cars in unprecedented numbers and Mazda made it.

National attitudes that have been adopted to conserve energy after the oil shocks of the '70s are still evident. Today Japanese may drive the must luxurious cars in the world, equipped with all the bells and whistles, but seldom do they turn on their air-conditioners even on warm or hot days when Americans would have the AC blasting away. In buildings they climb stairs rather than use elevators that require extra energy. Heating is used minimally. Air-conditioning in buildings is rarely set below 80 degrees when it is used at all. Mass transportation is used whenever possible.

A dozen years ago, the normal work week was six days in Japan. Since then it has been reduced to an average of 44 hours. Now there is a national movement to cut the work week back to 40 hours. Because of the current recession, overtime has been eliminated in most companies, so the strain on the family budget is growing.

Prices continue to rise, however.

The younger generation in Japan is no different than the younger generation in the U.S. with the exception that in Japan hiring is done by class. Annual hires traditionally begin to work for corporations around the first of April each year and their lifetime of employment with their corporation is based on the class in which they joined the company. Pay is based on seniority, not merit.

For the first time in Japanese history, which dates back more than 2,500 years as a nation, corporations – more than 400 of them this year – have canceled hiring contracts. That means that some college graduates who were contracted for hire by corporations will not be hired. Breaking of contracts is almost unheard of in Japan, a country in which lawyers are almost nonexistent compared to the over-proliferation of attorneys in the U.S.

Japan uses a 6-3-3 education system. Everything – every parent's desire – is aimed at getting young people through their college entrance exams. Middle and upper-class society is based on one's ability to gain entrance to a university in order to qualify for hiring by a major corporation or government agency.

That means *juku* – second schools – for students after regular school hours and hours of study at home each night under the mother's supervision while the husband stays at work or is out drinking with his boss.

Once a student gains entrance to a college he – the emphasis is on the male because few females in the past have been considered for college although there is now a growing number of female college students – goes off to university and enjoys four years of fun and games. All that is needed is graduation to qualify for hiring by a corporation.

Something different has begun to happen. Many college graduates are not taking the first opportunity they are offered to join a corporation. Instead they are shopping for the corporations that have the shortest work hours, the least overtime, and offer the highest hiring class salaries. No longer is it just sufficient to be offered a job with a Japanese corporation. Yet young Japanese show a propensity to shop the market at a time when the job market is shrinking.

And, layoffs have occurred – an unprecedented move in Japanese industry. The silk and fabric industries have been particularly hard hit. Stories of families who are having to cope with something that is contrary to their life experience in Japan appear in English-language publications. They are having to learn how to cope. Wives and children are taking jobs pumping gas – there are no self-service gas stations in Japan – working in markets and fast-food establishments, all of which is a new experience for many Japanese. Their parents suffer in silence.

I heard a rumor the other day that there might be a buyer for the Nissan plant. The buyer was supposedly China. They apparently want to buy, and move, the entire Zama Nissan plant to the Chinese mainland. After Korea's success at producing quality automobiles at cut-rate prices compared to Japanese autos in the world market, I doubt if Nissan is going to jump at helping the Chinese set up, especially with China's vast, untapped relatively inexpensive labor pool. No one around the Nissan plant today, or anyone in the Zama-Sagamihara area will discuss the question with me.

I ride away from the plant, in a Nissan van, pondering the issue, realizing that the whole experience is so far from the norm that has been established in post-war Japan that it is an embarrassment for business leaders to have to deal with it. Still, when this Nissan plant closes there will be people out of work, husbands-fathers-breadwinners disgraced by being seen in their neighborhoods when they should be off working, wives quietly taking menial jobs to help support the household, less family money for *juku*, more young people working at entry-level service jobs, fewer students qualifying for university, a loss of trust in corporate employment contracts, and over a period of time a smaller number of qualified *sarariimen* for corporations to draw from. Multiply this plant's closing by a few more around the country during this prolonged depression and you come up
with a significant shift in Japan's economic base.

The next time I come this way, Nissan in Zama will be history just like so many other elements that have made up the Zama area I have known in the past. Today I can find no traces that many of them ever existed.

- Hai, so desu -

Zama Rotary Club is a treat. It is held in a Western-style conference center. Of all the Rotary clubs we have visited in Japan, this one seems to be made up of younger businessmen, many entrepreneurs. Instead of the more rigid formality – seating from front to back by seniority at tables lined up in rows facing the head table – that we have seen in other clubs, the president of the Zama club rushes through the routines, introduces us to the members, and then makes sure one of us is seated at each of a half dozen round tables with a half dozen Japanese Rotarians at each of our tables.

Lunch is served while open dialog between each of us, and our Japanese hosts, is encouraged. It is the least formal setting we have seen, and the most comfortable.   Language seems to be no barrier in this setting. At each table there is at least one Japanese whose English is sufficient to help us, with our limited Japanese, communicate with the Japanese Rotarians.

I am at a table with the president of the Zama Rotary Club, a relatively young Japanese – in his mid-40s – to be the head of an organization. He is unconventional in his dress, an ascot instead of a tie, a tweed sport coat instead of the traditional business suit. He is outgoing, and handsome in a Western way.

During the conversation at our table, a couple of the Japanese ask me about South Florida and Miami. A quirk in the Japanese language sometimes makes it difficult to separate the city of Miami from the area of South Florida. In Japanese, *minami* means south. It is so close to Miami that with my southern accent it is difficult for me to pronounce the two differently enough for the Japanese to understand the difference.

Yet Miami is only a small portion of South Florida, which includes the Florida Keys where I live, the Everglades, an uninhabitable wilderness area larger than the Shonan area – Kanagawa Prefecture mainly – that we are visiting in Japan.

Of course, while we think the Miami-Fort Lauderdale-Palm Beach area of Florida is densely populated, it is no where as densely populated as the region we are visiting in Japan.

In the middle of this confusing conversation about Miami and *minami* Florida, the club president looks across the table at me, smiles, raises his arms off the table as if he was holding a machine gun, swings them from left to right and goes, "rat-a-tattat

... rat-a-tat-tat."

"*Ah so desu,*" I reply. "Don Johnson. Miami Vice."

He smiles, "*Hai,* much crime?"

"You remind me of Don Johnson," I tell him. "You look a lot like him."

He beams. From that point on, when we meet him several more times during our stay in Japan, we call him Johnson-san. He loves it.

The conversation at my table turns to crime in Miami. Crime, particularly as depicted on the television series Miami Vice, seems to be fascinating to the Japanese. They have a tendency to accept the television series as gospel. My attempts to explain that life in Miami and *minami* Florida is not like that depicted on Miami Vice, seems to fall a little short, especially when I tell them that an automobile, similar to one driven by the Florida Highway Patrol, that I once owned was shot at and hit one day when I was driving through one of the less-desirable neighborhoods on the north side of Miami. I was not hurt. In fact, I didn't even discover the bullet hole, right over my head, until I stopped for lunch with some friends at a hotel alongside Miami International Airport and the friends saw the hole.

The fact that we have guns fascinates the Japanese. The fact that after my car got shot, I applied for and received a permit to carry a concealed weapon, and do when I travel in my car in Miami, is even more fascinating.

"Would you use your gun?" One of the Japanese asked.

"*Hai,* if my life were threatened," I answer.

"Would you shoot another person?" Another one of the Japanese asked.

"If you are not prepared to shoot another person to save your own life when it is threatened, then you have no business carrying a gun," I reply.

"Doesn't it frighten you that you might shoot another person?" One of the Japanese at my table asks.

"I never want to be in a position where I have to make that decision," I said.

"Would you make the decision if you had to?"

"If I thought I could not make the decision, I would sell my guns and not carry one," I answer.

For the first time, I feel like I am an alien. With the cultural differences – in Japan guns are not owned or carried by private citizens – replying to these questions about guns in light of the distorted view my Japanese hosts have of crime in Miami, I feel like I have been put in the cowboy category rather than that of a person who owns guns mainly for hunting, although I have been trained in how to use them for self-protection. Ironically, some of that training in the use of weapons for self-protection took place 35 years ago within a few miles of where we are eating lunch with this Zama Rotary group.

Of hunting in the Everglades and other wilderness areas of Florida, the Japanese know, or can understand little about it when I try to explain it. Guns and hunting are so far out of their frame of experience that anyway I try to explain it, it seems to come back to their Miami Vice view of Miami and *minami* Florida.

When lunch is over, and the tables cleared, Johnson-san asks me if I will step to the podium and take questions from the club members. I agree.

There are some routine questions: How do you like Japan? How long have you been here? What have you seen? Then, one of the Japanese asks the question: "How did you chose your team members?"

No one has asked that question publicly of me yet, although, several older Japanese have asked it privately after seeing how young our team members are and seeing, from their biographical material that has been included in the information package sent each group we visit, that most of them hold responsible management positions in businesses in the U.S.

The question surprises me, coming from this group of Rotarians who appear to be younger, successful businessmen.

"This group study exchange was planned a year or so ago, and as we set out to recruit team members, the Rotary district we come from began searching throughout south Florida and in the Bahama Islands for a select group of people who would best represent the various segments of the business community that make up our district.

"And then, just as the selection process was getting under way Hurricane Andrew came along and blew away a big part of our district on the Florida mainland. People who might have been chosen to make the trip found themselves too busy trying to rebuild from Hurricane Andrew, or having to move out of the district because their homes and businesses were destroyed by the Hurricane and the selection list began to shrink.

"Other people here in Japan have asked me why none of the team members are from Miami. Why all of us are from the islands off Florida – the Florida Keys and the Bahamas. The answer to that is that people who took the biggest hit from Hurricane Andrew on the mainland of Florida could not take the time from their rebuilding efforts to make the trip.

"The job fell to our district governor, our Group Study Exchange chairman, and myself as team leader to put together – on rather short notice – a team that would be representative of our district. We are all from the islands, five of us from the Florida Keys, and Whitney Bain from the Bahamas.

"And, unlike the Group Study Exchange team you sent to our district last year, we do not represent the similarities, the commonalties, of our culture. We represent the differences. We are of different races, nationalities, educational backgrounds, business backgrounds, and still can come together as a team.

"I was chosen for team leader because the person who had first been picked, who was more fluent in Japanese, and who works for what would be a chamber of commerce and industry here in Japan, could not come after the hurricane. I was the second choice because I have spent time in Japan before, and although my proficiency in the Japanese language leaves something to be desired, I do have a fairly broad knowledge of Japanese culture and history.

"To a large degree I influenced the choice of team members by insisting that they have one trait in common – that they be successful young businessmen who would, after given the opportunity to see and experience Japan, most likely return several times during their lifetime and strengthen better relations between our countries.

"That was the overriding factor in the choice of our team members, and that is why you see the ones that are here. They are extraordinary people, and look forward to gaining first-hand knowledge of your culture. Each has been exceptional in his field of study or business, and each has a lot to offer in bettering relations between our counties," I told them.

There were no more questions. I don't know if what I said got around to other clubs and other Rotarians, but never again during our trip did anyone ask me how we picked our team members. Never again did anyone try to take me aside as the "older" member of the team and insinuate that my team members were too young to hold responsible positions in business.

In Japan, they certainly would have been. But in the U.S., they are exactly what their bios showed – owners, officers, and managers of their own businesses or divisions of fairly good-sized firms. They are young, but proven and responsible people, something
that is difficult for the average Japanese who spends his lifetime in the corporate ranks, where seniority rules, to understand.

- Hai, so desu -

After Rotary we loaded into our vans and head for the *Asahi Shimbun* plant. The Asahi is one of the largest newspapers in Japan – a national daily with millions in circulation, at least 10 times larger than any newspaper we have in the United States.

Driving up to the plant, I could see the old Japanese battle flag flying – the red meatball in the center with red rays flowing outward on a field of white to the edge of the flag. Although this flag seldom has been seen since the end of the war, it is still flown with pride at *Asahi* because it is part of the *Asahi* banner or trademark. It appears every day, in black and white, on their masthead.

This is a large printing plant. There are no editorial offices here, only printing and production facilities. The main editorial offices of Asahi, and other mega-dailies are in Tokyo. In the early '80s I visited the Tokyo editorial offices of the *Mianichi Daily News*, another of Japan's large national newspapers.

Although we had computers – main frames with terminals for each writer and editor to work on – in our news rooms in the U.S., it was at the *Mianichi* that I first saw pagination – the ability to show a whole page of a newspaper on the computer monitor and manipulate the type and pictures onto the page for output as a single element ready for the press.

I'm hoping today, although I realize that this is probably a regional printing plant like the *New York Times* and *USA Today* have around the U.S., to see how far the Japanese have come in their development of their editorial and production computer systems. They do, I know from having seen many publications in the U.S. that were printed in Japan, produce some of the best four-color process printing in the world.

Riding up to the plant, I wonder if they have miniaturized their graphics capabilities to the degree that we have. With Apple's introduction of the Macintosh in 1984, and its GUI – gooey, or graphics user interface – we have been producing newspapers like my weekly in the Florida Keys with our desktop PCs, and now with our portables and laptops.

As we are getting out of the vans, I am introduced to a production manager who tells me we must hurry, that our tour will be short because plant employees are going on strike. We go in a side entrance, walk through the distribution room, up some stairs, walk the length of second floor to some machines that make negatives where the manager fields a couple of quick questions, and then are out of the building with an apology from the manager, who says he must join the striking employees.

We find ourselves in the parking lot, ready to load back on our vans. The employees are donning red head bands and forming up in a military-style block formation at the far end of the parking lot.

Strikes are different in Japan, as are unions. Instead of a union for all similar tradesmen in all companies in Japan, each company has its own union for all workers regardless of their trade. Strikes are scheduled for times when production is down at the plants – lunch, afternoon break, etc. It's not unusual to hold a 10-minute strike and then have every one go quietly back to work.

As we drive away from *Asahi* the employees, and our production manager-tour guide, are wearing their red head bands and doing the wave in unison from their block formation.

I get the feeling that I have just had my vocational exchange experience that was the big part of this Rotary Group Study Exchange program that attracted many of us. The Japanese have, to their way of thinking, just shown me a newspaper plant. That about covers it.

I had hoped for at least a day a week, as Rotary International had proposed in their planning guide for Group Study Exchange programs, at a Japanese newspaper studying their editorial operations. It ain't gonna happen, I now realize.

Nearly two weeks into this trip, and the best they have shown me is a newspaper plant strike today. Maybe we should start looking for some red head bands if our Japanese hosts are not going to deliver on the vocational exchange portion of the program.

The fallacy in this reasoning is that the Japanese believe they have fulfilled their vocational obligations to me by taking me on this plant tour today, and another tour of another newspaper production plant scheduled for next week. Never mind that the other five people with me have no real interest in newspapers.

The Japanese will balance it all out, to their way of thinking, by making me do a factory tour of something in each of their fields of interest.

- Hai, so desu -

Chinami Hopson has been my interpreter for the last couple of days. Chinami is married to an American sailor named Bart Hopson, who serves on American destroyers out of Japan. He is at sea for three months, and then spends three months on shore duty in Japan. Chinami, and their daughter Eliscia, live at Atsugi.

The Hopsons are due to go to the U.S. next Spring, and Chinami is trying to figure out a business she can get into in America. Her mother is a businesswoman in Japan. She owns and operates entertainment clubs. Many of the Japanese Rotarians we meet here in Zama know Chinami's mother and entertain at her clubs.

We have just arrived a little early at Camp Zama, so Chinami and I are standing in the parking lot smoking cigarettes.

She points to a church up the hill just a little way from the entrance gate to the camp. "That's where I was married," she says. "Have you ever seen the chapel?"

"Yes," I tell her. "The few times I went to church in the '50s when I was here was to the non-denominational services they held there."

"It's a pretty church," she says.

I agree. Maybe the trees around the church are a little bigger than they used to be, but other than that the chapel seems not to have changed in the 35 years since I was last stationed here. I can't say that for the rest of Zama Camp. Just from what I can see from the gate area, there have been a lot of changes, many of them since I was last here a dozen years ago.

The most noticeable thing is that there appear to be more Japanese soldiers than American on the base. Guard duty is all done by Japanese. There are more women on the base these days, most of them Japanese women.

"I wonder what is taking them so long to get us on the base?" I ask Chinami.

"They have to do everything just right. We are a little early," she says.

"I'm about to run out of cigarettes. Can we get some around here? At the Post Exchange, maybe?" I ask her.

"No problem, I have PX privileges," she says. "I do a lot of shopping at the exchange and the commissary."

That's coming full circle for me. I have to ask a Japanese woman to buy me a pack of cigarettes at the Post Exchange. Back when I was stationed here, we used to buy the cigarettes and share them with our Japanese friends who did not have top-quality tobacco, or the money to buy it with, in the '50s. Some of those cigarettes I bought and shared with Japanese friends came right out of this same PX. Today, I am on the outside and Chinami, my Japanese translator, is on the inside. I explain the situation to her. We both get a laugh out of it.

Finally, the Japanese get us checked onto the base and we load back aboard our vans for a tour of the base. We start up across the base past the athletic fields. I notice the old Post Office building, part of the original contingent of buildings built and used by the Japanese at Zama as part of their army military academy up through World War II, still appears to be in use. But for the most part, the buildings on this section of the base are relatively new.

As we pass the football field, and its bank of bleachers built into a small hillside, we make the turn to one of the higher spots on the base. Atop the hill is the clubhouse for the Zama Golf Course, one of the finest courses in Japan. It is still well maintained, and we pass golfers playing it on the perimeter road.

I made this same loop with a lieutenant colonel in public information when I visited the base in 1981, and what astounded me at that time was the fact the Japanese had been permitted to build apartment buildings right up to the perimeter fence. In the '50s we had maintained a wide, cleared defensive perimeter around the base. In 1981 the apartments were so close to the fence, anyone could have jumped from one of their balconies, across the fence, and into the base.

Today I notice a line of large concrete poles on the base side of the perimeter road and fence, along one of the fairways of the golf course. As we approach them I can see they are poles to hold nets, maybe 50-75 feet high, along the rough off the fairway.

"Do they have to protect the apartments outside the base from flying golf balls now?" I ask one of the Japanese tour guides on our van.

"*Hai*, the neighbors complained so the nets were put there," he said.

Our motor tour of the base ends at the "Little Pentagon." The five-sided, two-storied headquarters for the U.S. Army Far East Command, or USAFE, had been completed at Camp Zama the year before I arrived. In the '50s it housed 23 generals. So many, in fact, that a general would often hold the door when one of us from intelligence was trying to enter our office off one of the corridors in the building. I suspect their generosity was because they were never quite sure what we were up to.

Today there is only one American general at Camp Zama these days. The one-star brigadier is assigned here so the U.S. has a commander of near-equal rank to his Japanese counterpart on the base as we continue to turn more and more of our facilities over to the Japanese, according to Col. Gordon H. Call, U.S. Army Japan deputy chief of staff for information management on the base. Hall tells us, as we stand packed in his
Little Pentagon office, that the U.S. Army has less than 3,000 troops left in Japan. Their mission today is mainly public relations.

The old Zama base is less than half its original size and no longer has a defensive perimeter. There are more Japanese soldiers based at Zama than American now. Hall refers to the base as "the community." Even though the base golf course we have just driven around is still there, it belongs to "the community." It brings in a million dollars a year to help finance other things for the community such as new recreational facilities.   "The community" is basically Japanese these days. They pay for almost everything on the base, according to Col. Hall.

We leave the Little Pentagon, and have an hour or so to kill before we are scheduled to eat dinner at the Zama Community Club, a building left over from the past that is due to be replaced by a new club in a month. The vans take us back across the
bridge over the highway into Zama town connecting the Little Pentagon side of the base with the side that includes the clubs, barracks, and other base operations. They leave us in the parking lot at the PX and club.

The old recreation club, a fine example of Japanese-built, Western architecture still sits up the hill above the club. Some of the guys decide to go up to the two-story building, whose long porch looks out through the trees and across the main body of the camp, and shoot some pool. Chinami and I go into the PX to get some cigarettes.

Inside, I am restricted to the fast-food section since I do not have a commissary card. I am not allowed to go over into the section that resembles a medium-sized department store in any American shopping mall. Chinami flashes her card and is admitted. She comes back with my brand of American cigarettes, the first of them that I have smoked in nearly two weeks. Once I finished the pack I arrived with I switched to Lucky Sevens, a Japanese brand that I discovered on my trip in 1981. They are similar to the cigarettes I smoke back home.

"Do you want to see the club?" She asks.

"Sure, I haven't been in it since the 1950s, and then only to play in a band now and then. Back then it was the Zama Officers Club. Over there where they are building the new building was where the NCO and enlisted men's club used to be. It was called just the Zama Club and was an infamous watering hole for Army guys back then," I tell her.

"Now we just have the one club," Chinami reminds me. "It is open to all the people who work on the base, and their families."

We walk around to the club. It looks pretty much like it used to, a little long of tooth, but still usable considering it will go under the wrecker's ball in a month or so. This will definitely be my last supper in the old Zama Club. When it is gone, the last social traces of its American heritage will have been removed. The Japanese Yen, not American Dollars, is paying for the new Zama Community Club.

Inside the old club smoking is limited to the vestibule area, the slot machine room, and a bar off to the side that is more intimate than the main ballroom-dining room-restaurant area. We stop in the front room for a smoke and watch the people come and go. Again, there are more Japanese than Americans.

"What kind of a business do you think I should open when I get to America?" Chinami asks.

"Retail is where the money is if you have a product that you can buy inexpensively and sell at a decent price," I say.

"What about silk? Are there a lot of silk shops?" She asks.

"What kind of silk? Material? Clothes?"

"I can buy good silk clothes from sources here," she says.

"Do you think they would sell well in the U.S.?"

"Good silk clothing should always sell," I tell her, "but I am no expert in retail, so you need to check it out before you invest a lot in it."

"Oh, I will," Chinami says. "I have been thinking a lot about the silk business lately. I like the idea."

A couple of the guys, and their Japanese Rotarian friends, come back from the recreation club and see us sitting in the vestibule of the club.

"Want to play some slot machines?" One of them asks.

"Yeah, why not. I had forgotten all about them," I answer.

Chinami excuses herself. It's time for her to go home to Atsugi. I join the others and head for the slot machine room. I had really forgotten about slot machines on bases in Japan. They were there back in the '50s, but I had totally forgotten about them. In the slot machine room, we found most of the machines taken. There is a mixture of players, Japanese and American, but mostly Japanese – a lot of women, most of whom seem to smoke, something you don't usually see a Japanese woman do in public. I still have some greenbacks in my wallet, so I buy $20 worth of quarters and try a couple of machines. They last about 15 minutes. Now I remember why slot machines are easy to forget.

Dinner is being served buffet style in the main ballroom-restaurant area of the club. I walk down the hall, through the door into the main room of the club, past the stage where I pause for a moment. Thirty-five years ago I played acoustic bass for a couple of groups – one jazz, the other country – on this stage. I wait for some feeling of familiarity to come over me. It doesn't.

It is the same elevated stage facing a hardwood dance floor surrounded by tables and chairs, and as far as I can recall, the same drab curtains for a backdrop. I get no feeling from it. I guess I didn't leave anything here.

It's fun to watch the different items our team and the Japanese Rotarians pick from the buffet. Our guys have had a deficiency of mashed potatoes, gravy, beef and cooked vegetables in their diet since they arrived in Japan. The pile their plates high with them. I go for a pile of mashed potatoes, gravy, cooked corn, green beans, and a slice of beef.

The Japanese seated across the long table from me go for the beef. They enjoy
hearty slices of it, but shy away from the starches that we crave. I finish my meal and head back up the hall to the front room for a cigarette. As I am passing one of the tables – actually two long folding ones put together end to end just off the dance floor – some one drops a piece of paper. I bend over, pick it up, and turn to hand it to an American who is seated at the table with two or three other Americans and several Japanese, both men and
women. The paper looks like a score sheet. I hand it to the man, and ask, "Bowling league?"

"Oh, no," he says in a midwestern non-accent. "We've got a small investment club and are just having a meeting."

Capitalism is alive and well at Camp Zama.

- Hai, so desu -

Dinner is over and it is time for us to go back to our hotel at Yamato. Four of us load into one of the vans. Our driver asks me if it is okay if he makes a stop to see his family on the way. I assure him it would be okay, looking forward to seeing a present-day Japanese neighborhood up close.

Apparently I misunderstood him. He leaves the main Zama gate, turns right down the highway to Zama town, under the bridge that connects the two sections of the camp. As he approaches the perimeter fence of the camp, he slows and turns off onto a road that leads back up the hill on which the camp sits overlooking the valley below and Zama town.

He pushes the van up the steep grade, winding skillfully along a path through the trees. As we near the ridge, the head lights shine on cherry trees in full bloom. The driver makes a sharp turn around a couple of trees, the headlights flash along the wire of Camp Zama's perimeter fence and come to rest on a group of Japanese seated on their legs on plastic ground clothes spread out beneath the falling cherry blossoms.

The driver stops. "Come meet my family," he says. "It is the custom each year when the cherry blossoms begin to fall to bring the family together under the cherry blossoms, cook noodles and tea, and wish each other well."

We get out of the van and he leads us over to his family's ground cloth. Along one edge of it, their shoes are lined up neatly in a row, just as you find them in the *genkan* in Japanese homes. We are invited to join them in their noodles and tea.

I am more intrigued by the Coleman stove on which they are cooking their noodles. It is set up on folding legs with a pot of water boiling for noodles and tea. It is a genuine Coleman, white gas camp stove, complete with stand, from the Coleman people in Wichita, Kan. To an American who has spent a lot of time in the outdoors world, it is completely out of context with the rest of the evening.

But then, as I get my camera out of the van and am taking a picture of the setup, I wonder to myself: "Is it really?"

- *Hai, so desu* -

The Japanese media says it is going to loosen its stranglehold on Japanese government news and let outsiders get a closer look.

For nearly a century Japanese government and business news has been dispensed through a club system that links Japanese newspaper writers and broadcasters with the various agencies they are assigned to cover. If you are not a member of the club, you don't get access to whatever news or information they are about to release.

No foreigners, or *gaijin*, were permitted to join the exclusive Japanese press clubs until *The Associated Press* and *Reuters* were admitted to the Foreign Ministry Press Club in 1992.

This trip is no press trip for me. Instead I'm the leader of a team made up of five young businessmen who thought they were coming to Japan to visit their counterparts in Japanese commerce. I've been here before and I find little has changed in the way Japanese treat *gaijin*. As tourists we are treated like kings until we try to exercise the study exchange opportunities that we had been led to believe were the main reason for our visit.

When it comes to getting down to business – to finding out how the Japanese perform their daily work tasks – the doors are closed. We are being given factory tours and having our pictures taken with innumerable managing directors under the cherry blossoms, but we are not allowed access to even the more mundane business routines of our Japanese hosts.

My last visit to Japan, in 1981, was under somewhat different conditions. I was travelling on a fellowship from the International Press Institute and my *sensei* - teacher or sponsor - Masaru Ogawa, was the editor-in-chief emeritus of the *Japan Times*. With a sponsor of that stature I had access to almost any agency or government body I wanted. I had both Japanese and American interpreters and could ask any question I wanted.

What I learned quickly, since my field of study was economics, was that the Japanese could stymie any question I asked by simply informing the interpreters to tell me that it didn't translate into anything in their language.

The kicker was that I had lived in Japan from 1956 to 1958 and knew a little of their language. While it's not a language I'll ever be fluent in, I do know enough of it to understand what is being said much of the time. That has led to many interesting encounters during my trips to Japan, none of which have ever fully produced the information I was seeking.

Japanese play it close to the chest. They don't tell you anything they don't want you to know. They follow the same rule with their journalists. They hand feed them. The Japanese press clubs are the feeding trough. If you're not a member of them than you have to dig out anything you want to write about the Japan and the Japanese on your own. It takes a mountain of research to write a short story about Japan.

Japanese journalists don't see anything wrong with this arrangement. The truth is they enjoy the drinking and elbow rubbing that is associated with the press club setup and since it's never been any other way they don't know the difference.

I've entertained several groups of them when they have toured the U.S. and Japanese journalists have little in common with those of us who practice journalism in the States.

The first thing I always notice about Japanese journalists is that they are generally older – often much older – than their American counterparts. They aren't even allowed to travel outside Japan until they are 20 years or more into their careers. And, their journalism careers are limited to whatever publication they start with. They are astounded that American journalists can move from one job to another.

They are even more astounded that we openly question our politicians. More than once I have been the host of Japanese journalists when I have been interviewing political candidates or politicians.

During my 1981 visit to Japan I attended a press conference for Jimmy Carter, who had just been replaced by Ronald Reagan as president. The Japanese journalists would ask Carter a single question and accept whatever answer he gave them. There were no follow-ups, no tough questions.

Some of the Americans travelling with Carter knew me from my days in Washington and Jacksonville. When they saw me sitting in the front row of reporters at the Tokyo press conference they appeared apprehensive about me asking a question. I just grinned and kept my mouth shut. They gave me an approving smile as the press conference ended. I behaved like a good Japanese journalist would since this was a Japanese-sponsored press conference.

I really wanted to ask Carter how much the Japanese paid him to make the visit, but knew such a question would be out of line by Japanese media protocol. I learned later, however, that Carter received a couple million dollars to make the trip – something that Reagan caught hell for from the media eight years later but no one that I know of, except me in one of my *Florida Times-Union* columns, ever reported about Carter's payola.

The best example I can recall of how controlled the Japanese press is through its cozy press club relationships happened last night when I was having dinner with several Japanese businessmen and they asked me what I thought of Japan.

"I can't understand why I can buy Japanese cameras and Japanese automobiles in the U.S. for half the price you pay for them here in Japan," I said.

One of the Japanese replied: "That can't be so."

"*Hontoo ni*, really," I said.

"If that were true," he answered, "we would read about it in our newspapers."

"But you don't have a free press," I countered.

"Do you?" He asked.

"*Hai*, yes," was my reply.

He shrugged his shoulders.

No matter how much the Japanese try to open their exclusive press clubs to foreigners no *gaijin* will ever rise to the leadership of one. No *gaijin* will ever gain direct access to any information the Japanese government agency sponsoring the press club doesn't want him to have. By our standards there is no real freedom of information in Japan.

Even Japan's current constitution places some restraint on the free exchange of information when it is in the national interest. Ogawa-san confirmed that for me during my 1981 press visit to Japan.

That is "The Japanese Way."

- *Hai, so desu -*

Yokohama has always been Japan's "Foreigner's City." It even contains the island nation's Foreigner's Cemetery. When I first arrived in Yokohama aboard the *MSTS Mitchell* in 1956 the city was still recovering from the devastating bomb raids of World War II. Falling in at dockside with my duffel bag, I marched to some nearby buses and headed for Tokyo 40 miles to the north. Between Yokohama and Tokyo there were still many bombed out areas.

In the '50s I spent a lot of off-duty time in Yokohama. When I returned to Japan in 1981 I found virtually a new city where the old Yokohama had stood. But, I wasn't prepared for what I was heading into town to see today.

Our schedule had originally said we would go for a boat ride today, but about three days into our visit one of the Rotary governor's top assistants came up to me and said, "Since all of you live around boats, you won't mind if we don't take you on a boat ride we have scheduled, will you?"

It sounded good to me, especially since a boat ride was all that we had on our schedule for today. Once it was removed I was led to believe we would have the day off – our first in two weeks. My guys were certainly looking forward to it, especially after being crammed last night into the smallest business hotel we have yet run across. I almost had a revolt on my hands when I told them after dinner our Japanese hosts had told me to have them ready to board the bus at eight o'clock this morning for a ride to Yokohama.

Tomorrow is Easter Sunday and many of them had been looking for phones to call home. The ones in the hotel weren't handling international calls last night, and when I mentioned it to our hosts they said the hotel we would end up in tonight would have good phones.

So, here we are on the bus. The guys are in a sour mood. I am tired, but the leader of today's Rotary hosts is a younger-than-usual Japanese and interested in showing us a good time.

It seems every time our schedule says we have free time, the Rotarians fill it with some activity that keeps us on the move.

We've been promised today's outing to Yokohama won't be a tiring, or a particularly long one. I've got my fingers crossed, knowing it probably won't do any good.

As we ride along the Japanese turnpike heading forYokohama I marvel at how each driver seems to obey traffic laws, including speed. Of course, this is not a full work day for many Japanese so the traffic in the area is not as heavy as during the week. The politeness of Japanese drivers is something that has always amazed me, particularly after the years that I rode in the *kamikaze* taxi cabs of the '50s when ¥70 would keep you going forever and drivers only had one speed – wide open – driving constantly with one hand on the horn.

Those old cabbies must have all been killed in horrendous accidents, or the government forced them all to retire and sent them off to the mountains. Traffic, even though it travels on the wrong side of the road for us, is simply too polite in modern-day Japan.

Mulling over this my mind drifts back to a conversation I had with one of our Japanese hosts while riding on the bus yesterday. He was a successful importer of American camping equipment and other outdoors items, but sold the business a couple of years ago. After selling that business, he went to the U.S. and bought all the molds for a popular sailboat that the U.S. manufacturer had gone broke trying to build and market in the States.

I am familiar with the American version of the boat. It is an excellent sailing craft. Add a little Japanese handcrafting to it and you have one of the best 26 footers that can be found anywhere. The price is right for Japan, too. But the boats are difficult to sell.

Keeping a boat in the water is almost an impossibility in Japan. There just aren't enough docks available. So, almost everyone who owns a boat in Japan tows it to and from the water. That means they must have some place to keep it. My guess was that since most Japanese don't have yards like we are used to around our homes in the U.S., they have difficulty finding a place to keep their boat.

My Japanese friend said that had some effect on his boat sales, but the real problem was that people were too polite to take to the highways with a car and a boat.

"The typical Japanese fears he will be considered rude if he takes up too much room on the highway, especially when traffic is bumper to bumper as it is in areas where enough water is available to sail a boat this size. To take up extra room on the highway is bad enough, but the thought of having a breakdown while pulling a boat is just unbearable. To be the one responsible for holding up traffic while pulling a boat is the biggest obstacle I have to overcome in selling them," he said.

As the turnpike cuts through the not-so-tall mountains that form a ridge line behind Yokohama I study the waffled hillsides where the highway has been cut through the hills. I have noticed more of this on this trip than on any previous visit to Japan. Maybe waffled is not the right word, but I'm no engineer. What I am talking about is the stabilization of hillsides by pouring what appear to be concrete footers in a grid up and down the hillside.

As the Japanese search for more living space, more and more hillsides have been shaved back to open up flatter surfaces, and more and more hillsides have been waffled to keep them from coming unglued in a rain storm or snow melt and wiping out the houses below them.

We arrive at a toll gate, not much different than the toll gates on the Florida Turnpike. It snaps me out of my daydreams. As we pull out of the toll gate, make a slight turn towards Yokohama Harbor, I get my first glimpse of modern Yokohama. The new bay bridge is awesome.

When Commodore Perry sailed into Tokyo-*Wan* in 1854 to force Japan to open its doors to the world, this was a dirty little seaside town far enough away from Tokyo that the powers-to-be in Japan felt foreigners restricted to this area could not launch an attack on the capital city without being observed. For most of the last century and a half, the Japanese have tried to steer foreigners to Yokohama rather than Tokyo, especially those who arrive by ship.

Yokohama today has a population of more than three million people.

When I catch a glimpse of the downtown waterfront area I realize just what a new town this Yokohama is. The harbor, where I first arrived in 1956 and disembarked at the North Pier, is much smaller than it was back then. I learned in the '50s that much of the bayfront in Yokohama was fill – land and rubble from the big 1923 Tokyo earthquake that had been pushed into the water to make what the Japanese call "reclaimed land."

But today I see something I had only heard about in recent years. It is an additional 450 acres of reclaimed land that fills the harbor from what used to be the bayfront out about a half mile.

It's called *Minato Mirai 21*, literally a city of the future for the 21st Century. It is a new city being developed as a joint public-private project aimed at relieving some of the pressures of having to do business in nearby Tokyo, itself congested almost beyond its capacity to expand.

This new city business district is, other than the land that has been reclaimed, maybe 20-25 percent complete at this point. A new international hotel-conference center rises from its bayside shore. A couple of taller business-office buildings have been built on the new land. Parks and a marina have been installed.

The biggest sign that things have slowed economically in Japan is one tall office building that remains unfinished, work having slowed to a crawl. Still, that has not dampened the Japanese spirit. Our hosts take us to a new exhibition center that has been built on the waterfront. We get a tour of the Yokohama Pavilion, including an exclusive visit to a part of it that is being completed for use primarily when the emperor and his entourage visit the area.

The Pavilion contains many displays, most high-tech based and oriented towards expanding the adaptation of Japanese of all ages to the new age of advanced electronics.
Yokohama Gulliver Land gets the majority of my attention. I have been walking back and forth through this miniature exhibit of the whole city of Yokohama for at least a half hour and I am absolutely fascinated by the attention to detail the modelers have demonstrated. I have no idea of what the scale of this is, but it has to be something close to that of an HO railroad layout. Over there, on the hill, is the Foreigners Cemetery, a place I've visited a couple of times in the past. It's simply where foreigners – *gaijin* – get buried in this part of Japan. It sits up on a hill in the southwest section of the city overlooking the bay.

I'm enjoying this huge scale model of Yokohama when one of the hosts comes up to me: "We are going for a gondola ride. It is time to leave."

"Ah," I think to myself, "here comes the boat ride." I just assumed a "gondola" was a Japanese version of an Italian tourist boat.

We leave the building, board our bus, and drive across the new reclaimed 21st Century city, stopping in front of a giant ferris wheel – at least 300-400 feet in height. I've never seen one this large before. It apparently appeals to the Japanese. They are lined up waiting to get one it.

"This is the gondola," my host says.

I look puzzled.

"You can see downtown Tokyo and Mount Fuji from the gondola cars when they get to the top," he says. So "gondola" to the Japanese means ferris wheel cars? Maybe we've really escaped a boat ride for today. It doesn't look like we're going to escape a ferris wheel ride, though.

Once inside the ferris wheel car, with three other people, I finally realize what they mean by "gondola." The cars, instead of seats, on this giant ferris wheel are like gondola cars on a cable car system running between two mountain peaks. It is a big ferris wheel. The biggest in the world I am told. It is called "Cosmos Clock 21."

You can see from up here. Haneda Airport, on Tokyo Bay, can be easily spotted. I haven't been able to find Mount Fuji. It remains hidden behind the permanent haze that engulfs the densely populated Kanto Plain of Yokohama-Kawasaki-Tokyo.
But, from up here I can see the park where the *Nippon Maru* – the last of the Japanese tall sailing ships, used to train Navy midshipmen up until 1984 – is anchored near the new Yokohama Maritime Museum.

Nearby, at the base of a new 70-story building, I can see one of the old Yokohama dry docks built back before the turn of the century. It is nowhere near the water today. It sits at the foot of the new skyscraper and is being developed into a dockyard garden, according to the literature I picked up as we were boarding the gondola. The dry dock is located about a half-mile in land today and will be preserved for its historical usefulness.   That could be interpreted a lot of ways.

As we descend from the top on the ferris wheel, I sweep the area of downtown Yokohama that used to be the old waterfront when I hung out here in the '50s. It is barely recognizable, but I do spot the old Grand Hotel, built back in 1929 if I remember correctly, and left unharmed by the war. General Douglas MacArthur stayed here when he first arrived in Japan following the Japanese surrender.

Next door to it has been built the New Grand Hotel, a more modern structure reaching high into the sky. The old Grand was a fine western-style hotel in the best tradition.

One reason the dry dock that is being preserved and the old Grand Hotel are still here to be preserved today is that they were near a portion of the old Yokohama Bay waterfront that escaped the saturation bombings that destroyed most Japanese metropolitan areas in this part of the country towards the end of World War II. The dry dock, like those down at Yokosuka Naval Station south of here, were spared bombing because U.S. forces thought they might need them to repair American ships when we invaded. The necessity to destroy the dry docks never arose because the war ended before the invasion was scheduled to get under way,

The old Grand Hotel survived, not because we wanted to use it if we had to invade Japan, but rather because it was too close to the Yokohama waterfront where U.S. prisoners of war were impounded and used as slave labor to load and unload Japanese shipping. This was a brutal waterfront during the war. American prisoners were worked, starved and beaten to death with regularity along this waterfront.

Much of the shipping, and some of it was still around in the '50s, consisted of smaller vessels – more like coastal transports – on which the skippers, crews and their families lived on them full time. The women wore nothing but a skirt in warmer weather, their weathered breasts swinging in the breeze. Their only toilet facilities were a railing hung over the side of the boat. One of their great sports was taking a crap, or pissing, on a passing *gaijin*. So much for the hospitality in the Foreigner's City in those days.

Actually Yokohama is an enigma of a town. It was the main headquarters for the Japanese Thought Police during World War II. In its jails people were hauled and beaten for not toeing the party propaganda line. Many intellectuals found themselves locked up in jails in Yokohama for the duration of the war.

Japan's *Kempei Tai* – its greatly feared military secret police – also had a major presence in Yokohama during the war. I've often wondered whether the *Tokumu Kikan* – Japan's civilian international intelligence network – wasn't headquartered, or didn't have a major presence in the so-called "Foreigner's City," too. But no one has ever wanted to talk, or for that matter acknowledge, that the *Tokumu*

Kikan even existed. The one or two references I have found to the *Tokumu Kikan* indicated it was headquartered in Tokyo, but with the steady commerce in war material and manpower between Tokyo and Yokohama, and with Yokohama's propensity towards things foreign I have to continue to suspect the *Tokumu Kikan* played some role in wartime Yokohama.

We get off the gondola and back on our bus. We drive back across the new city around Yokohama Harbor and unload in a waterfront park where a long, passenger boat is tied to the seawall.

"We're going to ride the boat across the bay," our hosts' leader says smiling. So, we get the boat ride that none of us are looking forward to after all. It takes about a half an hour to cruise around the new city, past an old light house that used to mark the entrance to the harbor, and then into a notch between two of the old piers where we finally tie up and disembark.

I can tell the guys are getting hungry. They're checking out the food places. Ramsay is looking for a McDonalds or some other place that serves American-style food. There wasn't much for breakfast at the little business hotel we stayed in last night. Our hosts tell us we are going to China Town for lunch. It's up the street a ways. We head for it on foot.

On the way to China Town we pass a car dealership that sells both Japanese and American cars. It's not like an American dealership. There's no lot full of cars outside. Instead it is a corner building with large display windows. Inside, parked on a showroom floor is a Suzuki utility vehicle similar to the Suzuki *Samauri* sold in the United States. The price listed for it is just about twice that charged in the U.S. Next to it is parked a
Pontiac Gran Prix. It's price, too, is double what it would sell for in the United States.

I mention to one of our hosts that it appears Japan is charging its own people more for their Japanese cars than we have to pay for them in the U.S. He doesn't want to believe it. I get the standard Japanese line, "Cars cost more here because we have an expensive distribution system."

Sure.

The red gates to China Town are just up the street from the auto dealership. They don't appear to have changed in since I first saw them nearly four decades ago. There are a lot more people coming through them than I remember in the past, but then this is a Saturday and more and more Japanese are beginning to work a five-day week with Saturdays and Sundays off. Once through the gate, I realize just how little China Town has really changed. It's like turning back the clock.

We take a turn down one of the many side streets off the main drag and are led into a fair-sized restaurant. They take us to our own room where we sit cross-legged on the *tatami* mats while piles of Chinese food are brought to us in constant waves.

A lazy susan in the center of the large table around which we sit makes it easy for everyone to get what he wants. We spend at least two hours on lunch. There is plenty of beer, plenty of food, but it's difficult to get water.

It's now mid-afternoon. We have been bussed, walked, toured, ridden, fed and watered well. The whole group, after nearly two weeks of being dragged around Japan from sunrise to late at night are exhausted. They would all settle for a nap right now, but really want to know where we are going to spend the night. This was to have been their day off, or so they thought after we originally convinced the Japanese we didn't need a boat ride – the only thing that had been scheduled for today. Now my crew's big question is: "Where's our next hotel?"

The only thing I have on my schedule – given to me when we first arrived in Japan – is the Hotel Otowano-Mori and I have no idea of where that is. I ask one of our Japanese hosts. He replies, "Hayama."

Hayama is over the hills behind Yokohama and down on the southern coast of Japan. It is the seaside town in which Emperor Hirohito used to maintain a private residential compound so he could conduct his marine biology experiments. After World War II, the Hayama beach area became a seaside resort for the American occupation troops. From the past hotels we stayed in, I doubt if we are going to have a seaside one tonight, but nowhere in Hayama is more than a short walk to the beach so the guys will have a chance to do at least a little communing with nature.

What they are more interested in are telephones so they can call home for Easter. By the time we get situated at the hotel it will already be Easter Sunday in the U.S. Most of them are looking forward to placing a call home. They have had all the touring they want for today and are ready to head for the hotel.

It's a good 45-minute bus ride down to Hayama and we end up at another small business hotel. I'm assigned a Japanese-style room while the rest of the crew has to double up in small Western-style rooms. While they are putting their gear away, the leader of a new group of local Rotarians shows up. "We'll have dinner at six here," he says. "My Rotary friends are anxious to meet your group."

Again, it's something that wasn't on the schedule – at least the schedule I was given. It's not going to go down well with my guys. They are planning to head down to the beach, grab something to eat, and then come back to the hotel and call home for Easter.

"Look," I tell the local Rotarian. "My people have not had any time off in more than two weeks. They were told today was a free day in which they could do what they want. Instead we've been touring Yokohama all day and they would like to have the evening to themselves."

"*Ah so desu*," is the reply. "We have ordered dinner for you here at the hotel. Some of our people are coming to eat with you. It is almost ready. You must join us."

"Talk to the hotel people," I suggest. "Tell them that five of us will not be eating dinner here. I am going to let my people have the evening off. They have earned it. I will join your people for dinner, *daijóobu*."

"The plan is for all of you to have dinner with us," the Japanese Rotarian, a younger one for a change and quite fluent in English, says. "Why do your people not want to eat dinner with us?"

"It is not that they don't want to eat dinner with you specifically. It's that they want to go out on the town and have something to eat on their own. They want the free time that the schedule says they were going to get today," I say showing him the schedule I was originally given.

"*Hai so, desu*," he replies. "But it is the responsibility of our Rotary club to see that you are fed and taken care of here in Hayama and then taken to Kamakura for the big festival in the morning."

"That's fine," I reply. "Just let my people have the evening off here in Hayama. I am the only Rotarian in the group, so I will have dinner with your fellow Rotarians."

The conversation goes on for at least another 15 minutes. A couple of other local Rotarians show up for dinner. A couple of my people show up in the lobby and I introduce them to the local Rotarians. There is much chatter back and forth among the Japanese, trips to the dining room, conversations with the hotel management.

As more local Rotarians show up the rest of my crew appear in the lobby. They are ready for a night on the town. Introductions are made around the lobby and my guys wish the Japanese well and head for the door to the street.

"Where are they going?" A new leader of the Japanese Rotarians asks.

"They are off for a night on the town. This is their free night, according to my schedule," I say. "I am the only Rotarian on the team and I am going to have dinner with you. My people are taking their free night off."

Again much chatter back and forth among the Japanese. I even think I hear "*dadákko*" once or twice in their conversation. "*Dadákko*" is the equivalent of "spoiled child" in English. I chuckle under my breath. I have upset the "*Wa*" by letting my gang have the night off. So be it.

Actually dinner goes very well. I still enjoy jawboning with the average Japanese. They ask the same questions other groups do, and I give the same answers I have been giving for the past two weeks. Actually it is a no-brainer for me and I am happy the guys got their night off.

After dinner I say "good night" to the Japanese and retire to my Japanese-style room after they make sure I understand they will be here at 7:30 a.m. to pick us up and take us to Kamakura.

Sitting cross-legged on the *tatami* mats, dressed in the sleeping *kimono* provided by the hotel, I enjoy looking out the window I have slid open at the tiny Japanese garden in the rear of the hotel. It is getting cool outside. I unpack my portable computer and sit it on the low table in front of me, pour myself a cup of hot green tea I have made on the hot plate in the entrance alcove to the room, and begin entering the notes from which this is being written.

It is a pleasant evening, an enjoyable respite from the constant grind we have been through. I hope the guys are enjoying their night on the town. (I find out later they had a great time enjoying sunset on the beach. They video tape it and part of it comes through in the video Tim Wilson made as our final report of our trip to Rotary International. They guys look like a bunch of nymphs skipping and jogging up and down the Hayama beach silhouetted in the setting sun. They apparently enjoyed the brief break they got.)

When I finish the notes I drag the telephone over from the wall and decide I will call home for Easter. It is now Easter Sunday in the States. I try to dial the usual long-distance combination and nothing happens. I try again. Nothing. Again. Nothing.

So, I get up, leave the room in my sleeping *kimono* and go down to the desk. There is no one there. I look around and find one of the hotel staff cleaning up in the dining room. I ask him why I am having trouble with the telephone.

"*Denwa* no work at night," he says in broken English.

It's true, when they close the front desk after dinner, the hotel shuts down the switchboard. There are no outside calls. I am in deep doo-doo. When the guys get back and try to call home for Easter, they are going to be mad as hell and I can't blame them.   The Yokohama Rotarians had promised them all day long they would have telephones in their hotel tonight so they could call home. They aren't going to be happy about this!

- Hia, so desu -

Maybe it is all the cans of Boss and Georgia coffee that I drank today walking up and down the streets of Yokohama and China Town. I'm sitting bowlegged on a pillow on the floor of a Japanese-style hotel room in Hayama – the home of the Emperor's summer palace on the southern coast of Japan – flipping through the television channels because I can't get to sleep on the futon I have rolled out across the tatami mats.

Four of the other five team members are doubled up in small Western-style rooms in the hotel. One has a Western-style room to himself. The phones were shut off after dinner, so there's no way to fax any data from the computer to the States. I've killed a couple hours writing, but am now brain dead wishing the body would give up the ghost soon.

Television is the only distraction left and I can't find a bilingual button on the remote control so whatever I find is going to be in Japanese. It is now 12:30 a.m. There's nothing I understand on any of the regular channels, and none of the pay channels seem to be working. I run through the national and commercial channels one more time since it's the half hour and maybe something new – maybe reruns of the national high school baseball tournaments now being held – will come up.

Half way through the channels I run across the title of a program I haven't seen before. It's "TIT•TIT•TAK" with the TAK written in calligraphy characters – "TIT•TIT• たk.". The announcer that follows the title panel leaves no doubt about the content of the show. Standing on each side of him are two giggling Japanese girls – one in a bra with everything cut out except the frame work, the other wearing two small megaphones for a bra with the camera aimed up the small end of one megaphone so her nipple is exposed.

The announcer, or emcee since this appears to be a game show, chatters on so rapidly it is impossible for me to pick up what he is saying. The girls answer in the high-pitched female voices that are considered sexy by Japanese men who put the emphasis on "cute" more than anything else when they think female. Japanese cute is high-school silly in the U.S., and difficult to translate.

A second male participant joins the trio and they sit down at a console that resembles an American television news set. Questions, and apparently answers, fly back and forth in hyperspeed Japanese.

The girls scream and giggle and the cameras zoom in on their TIT, TIT and eventually their たk.

I watch it for about five minutes and cannot come up with any sensible explanation of what is going on. It's apparently just one of the crazy game shows that the Japanese love, albeit a bit risque by American commercial television standards. It is more like something you might expect to rent in the backroom of a video shop and take home to watch on the VCR.

- Hai, so desu -

It is Easter Sunday morning. I am up early, packed and in the lobby of the hotel when the local Rotarians arrive to pick us up for our trip to Kamakura for the day. The leader of the Rotary group is at the counter checking us out.

I mention that I'm going to have some upset people on my team this morning because the phones in the hotel didn't work last night. The concept of Easter is difficult for the Japanese to understand. Don't even try to explain why it is important for Americans to make contact with their families on this Christian holiday. Only around 5 percent of Japan is Christian. Besides that this is another more important holiday in Japan, especially in Kamakura where we are headed for the day.

As the Rotarian checks us out, I notice he asks the clerk for the phone charges. She gives him the bill, and then hands him a printed out report of every phone call that our group made, including the numbers to which the calls were made.

I notice Tim Wilson was smart and called his wife, Nora, in the States before the phones were unhooked for the night. The Rotarian tucks the bills in his pocket. They will be turned in to the Rotary headquarters, adding to the pile of intelligence they have gathered on our every move in Japan. For what purposes, I do not know. It is just the Japanese way, but it certainly upsets our guys when they discover they are being tracked so closely.

One by one my gang starts showing up. With the exception of Tim Wilson, they are upset they couldn't get phone calls out of the hotel last night, especially after they had been told they could. I have no explanation. They are not happy. Our Japanese hosts do not understand. I have no logical explanation. Everyone is a bit on edge.

Outside the local Rotarians have come in several cars to take us to Kamakura, I think. I am wrong again. We load our luggage into the trunks of the cars and climb in for the ride. It is a short one. We pull up in front of the Hayama train station. Our Japanese hosts get out and start unloading our luggage.

"Are we going to take a train to Kamakura?" I ask.

"*Hai*," the local leader says. "There will be a million people in Kamakura for the festival today. It is impossible to drive there so we will put you on the train. It is only two stops down the line. You will be met at the Kamakura station."

They proceed not to carry our luggage into the station but rather throw it over the fence from the street into the station. We are led in by one of the local Rotarians who purchases us tickets for the ride to Kamakura. All our luggage is carried over to the side of the track where the train will arrive. We sort it out, strap on as much of it as we can, and arrange the rest so we can pick it up quickly and board the train when it pulls in.

A train approaches the station. Our hosts tell us this is the one we are to take and we load up our gear. We look like a bunch of traveling gypsies as we stand on the platform waiting to board the train. The local Rotarians line up and give us the obligatory bow. We don't do very well returning it. We are simply too loaded down to bow too low.

Somehow we get all our stuff together in the corner of one of the train cars and settle in for the short ride to Kamakura. The train is packed. It is Kamakura-*matsuri* day – the day of the largest town festival of the year. The Hayama Rotarian was correct. There will literally be a million or more people on hand for the big affair. Where they are going to put them all in the Kamakura I remember from the '50s is beyond me. I remember the town as a small resort village down on the coast.

Kamakura is one of the great historical treasures of Japan. It was the eastern capital of the *shogunate* for some four centuries from the late 1100s to the late 1300s by our calendar. It used to be a village of shrines and temples and small resort hotels.

As the train approaches Kamakura I begin to get an idea of what has taken place here in the past 40 years. Kamakura has become a bedroom city for Yokohama and Tokyo and the large, heavily populated industrial plain to the north of it. Every nook and cranny of the hillsides surrounding the city is now packed with houses.

At the Kamakura station, in the heart of the city, we are met by "Roger," one of the regular Japanese Rotarians who have appeared to translate for us since our arrival. "Roger" gets his nickname, which he prefers to his Japanese name, from having once been a pilot. He also is a Harley-Davidson addict. He'll stop at the drop of a ¥50 piece and talk motorcycles with you. His dream is to come to America, buy a Harley, and travel the country visiting friends he has made by translating for them when they have visited

Japan. At last count he had something like 66 or 67 stops lined up on his dream trip.

There are no porters or handcarts in Japanese railroad stations. Everyone carries they own gear, and that goes for us. This morning the station is packed and we are loaded down with everything we own except the few things we left in the storage room back at the Fujisawa hotel.

Roger leads us, loaded down with our gear, out of the station, across the large paved traffic circle in front of the station, up a street packed with a zillion festival visitors to the main drag – *Wakamiya-Oji* – that runs from the ocean a couple of miles through Kamakura up to the *Tsurugaoka-Hachiman* Shrine and the 700-year-old tree the Japanese revere as the site where the third Kamakura *shogun*, Sanetomo, was murdered by his nephew Kugyo in 1219. Why this is such a revered spot I have never figured out, but it will be the focal point of many of the celebrations that will take place on this high festival day today in Kamakura.

We are led across the street to the Kamakura City Hall and taken to an empty room in the police area where we are told to leave our luggage. We will come back later and meet the mayor of Kamakura and pick up our things for home visits tonight.

Another group of Rotarians from Kamakura meets us here and leads us back out on the street and we head, walking, down the main drag towards the ocean. I assume we are going to take a few minutes before the major festivities of the day get started to see the ocean and the beautiful waterfront area of Yuigahama and Zaimokuza beaches that have made Kamakura the famous resort area that it has become over the years.

Wrong again. About a mile up the street we stop at a fire station. Rick Ramsay is a member of the volunteer fire department in Marathon where he lives back in the Florida Keys as well as being a deputy sheriff. The local Rotarians have arranged for all of us to tour this three-story fire department as part of Ramsay's vocational exchange visit.

We spend a quick 15 minutes looking at the Japanese fire equipment, not much different than what we have back home, and touring their dispatch facilities. The one thing that stands out is the dispatch board, a large one displaying in digital format the locations of fire and other emergency assignments that are being handled. I have seen some of the equipment used in similar setups back in the States and it is electronically digitalized and broadcast on video monitors or projected onto large video screens. Undoubtedly, since it involves micro chips and miniaturization some of it comes from here in Japan. But, the Japanese do not use it in this modern fire station. Instead, their digitalized board is a mechanical one, the numbers being changed much like the ones you used to see on the old scoreboards at football and baseball games in the days before micro chips.

After the tour of the fire station we are led back up the main drag by the Rotarians. They are a somber group. Somewhere Roger our interpreter has gotten lost. These local Rotarians are not very talkative. Their English is about as good as my Japanese so all I get out of them is that we are going somewhere to watch the big parade. Somewhere turns out to be a second-story restaurant along the parade route. We get window seats overlooking the street.

The Rotarians take seats along an opposite wall and keep pretty well to themselves, gathered around one Rotarian who is dressed in a black suit wearing a black fedora he never takes off.

The parade starts. It is one band of musicians, much like our college and high school bands back home, interspersed with men carrying the inner shrines from local religious places, then another band, and then another shrine ad infinitum. The men, dressed in gaily colored short kimonos chant in rhythm as they dance down the street with the gaily festooned small shrines that are decorated in gold and other highly valued artifacts.

Another Japanese Rotarian shows up and I recognize him from having met him when he visited to U.S. last year. I ask him about the carrying of the small shrines through the street.

"It's a Spring cleaning of the spirits from the temples and shrines," he replies. "The men get together and carry the spirits out into the clean Spring air today. It is done every Spring."

I don't know if he knew about Spring cleaning in the U.S., but I guess cleaning out the attic at home and cleaning out the spiritual attics of Japanese shrines and temples is equally as important to each culture.

About midway through the parade we see the marching band from Yokosuka Naval Station coming down the street. Guess who is

marching at the head of it? Our friend "Roger." Roger evidently has a whole network of organizations and individuals
he for which he interprets. My guess is that by the end of the day he will have added No. 68 to the number of stops he has planned on his Harley ride across the U.S.

Behind the Navy band is the mayor of Kamakura riding in a top-down convertible with young Japanese girls on each arm.

When the parade ends we march back to Kamakura City Hall and are taken to the mayor's office where we wait to meet him and anticipate the ritual we have become accustomed to from city to city during our visit. We will be introduced to the local mayor, presented with a gift from the city, exchange pleasantries with the mayor – trying not to ask him any difficult questions – and then go our way.

As usual we sit in the formal meeting room outside the mayor's office for about a half hour sipping tea and waiting on him. Finally he arrives and the exchange of pleasantries begins.

"It is an honor to have you in our city," the mayor says through his interpreter.

Not particularly being in the mood for the whole exchange of pleasantries I have become accustomed to as the group leader, I cut right to the chase.

"It is indeed a pleasant adventure to visit Kamakura," I say, "but it looks like you have a much better job than I do riding around all day in a convertible with the top down and a lot of beautiful young ladies on your arm."

The mayor's translator looks at me. I nod, "Go ahead and translate it just like I said it." He hesitantly starts in and we all watch as a big grin starts to stretch across the mayor's face.

"*Hai, so desu*," the mayor says bowing to me from his chair.

It is the first time I have been able to break through the formal starchiness of any of the Japanese politicians we have met. And, I did it only because I was aware of the fascination of the Japanese male for young Japanese women. It is almost a fetish. The ideal woman to a Japanese male in no way resembles the big-boobed blond bombshells that are American icons. Instead the Japanese dream of young, nubile girls whose teeth are not particularly straight and who talk in the high-pitched voice of a high school sophomore. It doesn't really calculate in our minds, but it is very real to the

Japanese and I have just caught the mayor of Kamakura indulging in a little dirty-old-man fantasizing. It makes my day.

That feeling of finally sneaking one by the Japanese does not last for long. When we leave the mayor's office, Roger meets us in the lobby of the City Hall.

"We are going to the *Hachiman* Shrine for the big festival next, then lunch, and then to see the *Daibutsu* and have tea with the Buddhist priest there. And then we have home visits tonight,"

Roger says. "I'm going to have all your luggage put on a friend's truck and we'll haul it around today and deliver it to you when you get ready to go on your home visits tonight."

"*Gomen nasai, wakarimasen* - literally hang on there a minute," I say. "What kind of a truck are we talking about?"

"A pickup truck," Roger says.

"An open pickup truck? Are you going to pile our luggage, camera equipment, and computer in an open pickup truck and haul it around town in the middle of all these tourists?"

"*Hai*," Roger reverts to the Japanese for a brief moment, and finally the Japanese party line. "It will be okay. No one steals anything in Japan."

"That's what they keep telling us, but we've already had an expensive set of batteries for our video equipment disappear. We're not going to put our things on an open truck and let you haul it around town all day. No way. *Sumimasen*."

"But that's the plan," Roger counters.

"Change the plan," I retort, getting frustrated again by the Japanese Way.

A conference ensues. Evidently the restaurant where we are going to eat lunch is expecting us and we are falling behind schedule, a no-no to The Japanese Way. They are caught between being late for lunch and letting us leave our luggage in the police property room in City Hall until we decide to come back and get it. Lunch wins.

You can tell the stress is building between the Japanese and us. Stress is easy to understand in both the Japanese and our gang. The Japanese spend their whole lives stressed out from lack of space, being driven to pass their university exams, and from "The Japanese Way" as they describe it.

The Japanese Way is a society build on seniority. No young person is allowed to make a decision. That is left to the elders. It is impossible for the Japanese to understand that the members of the Group Study Exchange, all under 33, are owners and managers of businesses. To our hosts, GSE team members are about equivalent to advanced students – or young salarymen as they call white collar workers – in Japanese society. They are sheep, not shepherds.

Our team is made up of strong individuals, each successful at fairly young ages in their own businesses. All basically entrepreneurs who make their own decisions, pay their own prices for their mistakes, and don't look at failure as a bad thing but rather an opportunity to learn a valuable lesson that will help them become more successful in their endeavors.

This is as foreign to the Japanese as their decision by consensus and leadership by seniority is to us. After nearly two weeks of being treated this way, our team has pretty well decided they are not going to put up with it for a whole month. You can sense a revolt smoldering.

We are lead up a side street towards the restaurant at which we are going to have lunch. Unfortunately for our Japanese hosts the street passes a small Christian Church of some denomination I don't recognize. Church is just letting out. Small Japanese children are in the church yard in their gaily colored Easter finery. The Japanese are totally oblivious to the effect of this on those in our party who have been trying to find an opportunity to call home for Easter since yesterday. The team members don't miss it, though. There are mumbles about when we are going to stop and get a chance to make some phone calls.

We find ourselves at an Italian restaurant where we are joined for lunch seated at several long tables in a private dining room by several more local Rotarians. They enjoy the pastas and sauces, the beer and wines, and the conversation is cordial. What they don't catch are the sly comments among the team members around the table about the things they are really used to for Easter dinner at home. There's not much mention of Italian.

After another two-hour umpteen course lunch with plenty of beer for the Japanese and mostly soft drinks for us, we are marched back out on the street, down to the main drag again, and head up hill to the *Hachiman* Shrine where the major festivities of the day will take place.

This has to be one of the most beautiful urban walkways, especially at this time of year, anywhere in the world. Of course, on high festival day it is packed with shoulder-to-shoulder crowds of people. Still the cherry blossoms are in full bloom and the center of the boulevard is lined with cherry trees that stretch from one *torii* to another along the route. As you near the large shrine at the head of the street you get the feeling that all roads in Japan lead to this point on this day.

The street, or boulevard, was designed centuries ago to give you that impression. From its beginning two or three miles back on the ocean shore, the street gradually narrows – so slightly it is hardly noticeable to the eye – until it reaches the shrine and the 700-year-old tree behind it. The design accomplishes the exact hidden perspective the ancient designers wanted to achieve.

As we near the shrine there is but a narrow path. No more than one or two people can pass through the packed crowd surrounding the huge red and gold shrine. Roger is standing in the narrow opening motioning for us to come on through. He leads us across the open space surrounding the shrine, where the crowds are cordoned off at a distance, to a row of folding chairs near the stage center portion of the large open shrine. We are given the seats of honor in the center of this crowd of at least a million people that pack the grand boulevard leading through the center of Kamakura up to the shrine.

As the ceremonies get under way, Roger steps to the microphone near us and begins reading in English to the crowd. He tells the story of the festivities about to take place. For him, it is a great honor to be the translator for this grand event. Maybe a chance to add another stop or two on his dream trip, too.

We are about to see one of the most revered performances put on each year as part of this Kamakura Spring Festival – the dance performed by the legendary Shizuka who was the beloved of one 12th Century literary dignitary, Minamoto Yoshitune who was being sought by his brother Yoritome. Evidently Yoritome forced Shizuka to perform her dance as a way of getting her to reveal the hiding place of her beloved Yoshitune.

The performance is a beautiful recreation of what must have been a torrid dance during a torrid period of Japanese history. It brings tears to the eyes of the Japanese who witness it. It doesn't move they guys on our team much. They are tired, worn out, and getting fed up with the torrid Japanese pace they are being forced to maintain.

As soon as the festivities end, we are led back down the street. I am walking shoulder to shoulder among the million of Japanese who are packed into the boulevard. As I am privately marveling at the beauty of the cherry blossoms as they fall onto the shoulders of people who are passing beneath them I hear a familiar voice behind me.

"Dave-*san*. How is it going?" It's Shimizu walking slowly along through the crowd. He is wearing his sunglasses, something only members of the Japanese mobs or foreign tourists, normally do. Shimizu is anything but a mobster. He is simply one of those rare Japanese who is comfortable with himself and his successes as an entrepreneur in a nation of corporate conformists. If he wants to wear sunglasses he does. If he wants to drive a five-year-old car with 300,000 kilometers on it he does. He is great bridge between our culture and the Japanese.

Thank God for Shimizu.

He is the only thing that keeps me from going completely berserk some days. Religiously he checks in with me by phone every other morning at 8 a.m. no matter where I am on this trip. Today he is a little late, but it's not the day he normally checks in with me. Today he is joining us because we are going to visit the Great Buddha – *Daibutsu* – near Kamakura this afternoon and have tea with the head priest who is a friend of Shimizu's. Shimizu is a devote Buddhist. His brother is a Buddhist priest, but not at the *Daibutsu*.

"I've got problems," I tell Shimizu as we walk under the cherry blossoms on our way back to the train station to catch the spur railroad that runs out to the *Daibutsu*. "My guys are tired and they are upset. It is Easter and they haven't been able to call home. They were told they would have phones at the hotel in Hayama last night and they didn't. They were told that yesterday was to be a free day and instead spent the whole day touring Yokohama. They are tired. They want some time off. They want to call home."

"*Ah so desu*," Shimizu said. "We cannot do anything about it until tomorrow, but we will discuss it then. I will try to help."

Nothing ever seems to bother Shimizu. He takes good news and bad news all in the same stride. He may tend to seem like he is putting off bad news like the Japanese always seem to prefer to do, but he actually is mulling over the situation. If he says he'll help me solve the problems tomorrow, I know him well enough by now to know that he will.

"Good, we have a revolt brewing here if we don't let these guys have some time off - take a break," I say.

"*Hai, so desu*," Shimizu nods and we continue in quiet down the street to the train station.

- Hai, so desu -

For some reason the community outside Kamakura in which the *Daibutsu* is located is one of my favorite spots in all Japan. It never seems to change that much. The street from the train station down to Kotokuin Temple where the Great Buddha sits is narrow and lined with small Japanese shops. Like any other tourist area, it is packed with shops selling souvenirs, but for some reason in this town they do not look harsh or out of place.

It is a pleasant walk from the station to the temple. *Daibutsu*, or the Great Buddha, is the second largest statue in Japan. It is a seated bronze statue of Buddha that is 37 feet high. It weighs 93 tons and was cast in 1252. Originally it sat inside a huge building but the building was destroyed by a flood in 1495 and since then *Daibutsu* has sat outside in the weather.

He is garbed in a beautiful green patina that has developed over the centuries in the open air.

I am a Unitarian-Universalist. I suppose, depending upon how one wants to interpret their particular chosen version of Unitarian-Universalist philosophy, my beliefs fall somewhat in synch with those of some of the Buddha sects. From a spiritual standpoint a visit to the Great Buddha is always a moving experience for me. Especially when I make such a visit with someone like Shimizu to whom it means so much. It is an honor to pick up the metal dipper at the fountain at the entrance to the temple and share the cool water with him as we wash our hands as part of the ritual of entering the temple grounds.

Shimizu walks with me to the foot of the Great Buddha and we silently say whatever prayers we feel are warranted for the day. I thank God that I am alive, that I have been allowed to make this visit once again, and pray for guidance in working my way through what looks like a rough day or two ahead as I try to get my team members settled in a little more comfortably.

When we are done, Shimizu and I look at each other and bow slightly in quiet recognition of the fact that we have each made our own inner peace in our own way on this common ground.

After we have all had a chance to tour the museum on the grounds we are led around one side of it to a Japanese-style home from which the sliding doors open onto an immaculately manicured

Japanese lawn festooned with stone gardens. It is the priest's home and we are invited in for tea that is served by his wife.

The conversation over tea turns to the priest's many involvements in the various facets of Japanese life. He has, in the past, served as mayor of Kamakura, a fact that I find enlightening.

"There is no separation of church and state in Japan," I note in conversation with him.

"*Hai, so desu*," he replies, meaning not "yes" but that he understands what I am saying and that indeed there is no separation of church and state in Japan. It is a concept they do not understand very well, if at all, in spite of the fact their "MacArthur" Constitution provides for religious freedom in modern-day Japan.

After a delightful couple of hours at the temple Shimizu and I say our respective farewells to *Daibutsu*, again in our own ways with silent recognition to each other of what we have done. We gather up the gang and head back for the short train ride into Kamakura where we will pick up our luggage at City Hall and send everyone off on their respective home visits with local Rotarians for the night.

Everyone but Pullman and I will make home visits. Pullman and I will stay in a luxurious little hotel down in the Yuigahama district by the seashore. Pullman has been sick all day. He definitely cannot handle anymore Japanese food, but his sickness goes beyond that of the stomach. It has traveled to his heart. Back in Pittsburgh he has left a lady friend that he is head over heels in love with and they apparently are struggling with their relationship. The long distance, and the lack of readily accessible telephones, has not helped. Pullman definitely needs a night off, away from the rest of us. When we get to the hotel, he has a cup of tea with us then heads for the bathroom and disappears for the remainder of the night.

This is one of those small, private luxury hotels that foreigners seldom get a chance to see. My room here is the epitome of luxury. It is a good 15 by 25 feet, not counting the bathroom complete with whirlpools and saunas. It has rich paneling and hardwood floors. The closets are floor-to-ceiling solid walnut. I wouldn't dare ask what the bill for this one is going to be. Thank God someone else is paying for it.

In half an hour I am supposed to meet Shimizu-san and a handful of Rotary higher-ups for a Japanese-style dinner in one of the private dining rooms of the hotel. While I'm waiting, I'm flipping through the television channels, looking for the bilingual button on the remote when I come across a program in Japanese where a girl – with her panties on – is standing astride the cameraman who has his lens pointed directly into her crotch.

The announcer is rattling along in Japanese at warp speed, so I can't make out what he's saying. The girl is giggling like a "cute" little Japanese female is supposed to. She steps off the camera lens, the cameraman stands up, steps back and then zooms his lens down the sleeve slot in her sleeveless blouse and homes in on her left breast. All the time the announcer rattles on and the girl giggles.

I have no idea what this program is. It doesn't appear to be a game show like *TIT•TIT•たk*. It certainly isn't a news show. It may be an interview show, but I can't tell. Risque it certainly is, but how risque I can't tell, either.

Shimizu and four other Japanese gentleman have arranged for a fine Japanese dinner in my honor in a private dining room in the hotel. I join them, sitting cross-legged on the floor, and matching them orange juice for sake on every drink.

Roger shows up to join us and act as interpreter. The men are all my age and we drift into interesting conversations comparing things I have seen in my four decades of visiting Japan, things like the disappearance of eternally hungry children, Japanese war veterans begging on the street, and the domination of the U.S. military in everything Japanese.

Eventually the conversation turns to economics, money, how we make it and how we live. Again I am asked what I think about Japan's economic dominance of Asia and much of the world.

"Japan is the No. 2 economy in the world. The U.S. is No. 1," I say. "What we need to do is quit competing with each other to be No. 1 and join in efforts to capture the enormous markets for our goods that are opening in places like China and India."

"Japan will be No. 1," one of the gentlemen says. "We will continue to compete for the No. 1 economy in the world."

I'm afraid that's so. The Japanese do not easily tolerate being subordinate to anyone. It is just not in their make-up.

The conversation centers on economics for quite a while. All of sudden Roger notes that I am answering questions in Japanese without waiting for him to interpret. Caught again. After a couple of weeks in Japan I somehow or other begin to pick up on the language again. It makes for an enjoyable evening.

When the conversation turns to what I do for a living, some of the Japanese have a difficult time understanding the concept of a community newspaper. They are used to the millions-a-day circulations of the giant Japanese dailies.

"Can you make a living?" I am asked.

"Yes," I reply. "My wife works, also."

"Your wife works?" It's a question echoed by two or three of the men around the table. Wives do not generally work in Japan, especially wives of men of this age group.

"Yes, my wife works."

"What does she do?"

"She's a surgical recovery nurse who works on call at a hospital not far from our house."

"What's 'On Call'?" One of the Japanese asks.

I explain to him that she spends her time at home and goes to work only when they need her. They "call" her on the phone when she is needed to recover a surgery patient.

That brings a chuckle or two from around the table.

"What's so funny about that?" I ask Roger.

"Nothing," he replies, but a couple of the men chuckle again.

"Oh, come on, Roger, tell me what's so funny."

"Eh, uh," he stutters. "They wonder how you have sex if you are always waiting for the phone to ring."

I launch into my not-good Japanese, imitating at first the ring of a telephone and then miming picking up the receiver and placing it to my ear.

"*Mushi, Mushi!*" I pause, lowering the imaginary phone from my ear and looking at where my Japanese friends might imagine my wife to be. "*Denwa dozo,*" I say handing the imaginary phone to my imaginary wife.

"*Mushi, Mushi!*" I say in a female's pitch. "*Hai, Hai!*" I continue in the female pitch. "*Háyaku kudasai, dozo,*" I say, still in the female pitch, looking up and extending my arm to replace the receiver on the telephone. "*Kyúyó desu! Háyaku! Háyaku!*"

"*Chotto matte kudasai.*" I say in my own voice, giving just the hint of a pant.

"*Háyaku! Háyaku!*" I repeat in the female pitch, adding a pant to it and then adding, "*Ima!*"

"*Hai, so desu,*" I return to the male pitch. "*Ima.*"

"*Eeeeeeeeeeeow!*" I utter in a combination of the two pitches.

"*Gomennasai,*" I say in the female pitch. "*Taisetsu desu! Sayónara!*"

"*Dó itashimashite!*" I say in my own voice, throwing up both arms in a gesture of frustration.

That brings down the house. It has been an *utsukushii* evening.

- *Hai, so desu* -

Did you ever get up with the feeling that you were going to face a difficult day? I did this morning. It was fortified at breakfast. I was eating some English-style pastries in the neat little Western-style lounge at the hotel and waiting on some of the local Japanese Rotarians to show up to get the day rolling.

Ron Pullman walked in with a distraught look on his face. "They said we could make long distance calls from here last night and I haven't been able to. I can't get a dial tone out of here to the States."

"I don't know why not," I said. "I called home last night and then faxed a story to the paper in the Keys. I didn't have any trouble."

"What are you dialing?" He asked.

"The prefix for getting out of the hotel. It's on the phone. And then just the country code, area code and phone number. It's worked every time for me."

"Have I still got time to try it?" Pullman asked.

"Sure. I'm waiting on the Japanese to show up so don't take too long. We're due to meet the rest of the crew coming in from home visits in about a half hour at the Kamakura train station."

Without a word, Pullman is off. For some reason I knew when I said it that this phone call might be trouble.

One of the men from dinner last night comes in with another Japanese. They introduce themselves and ask if we – Pullman and myself – are ready to ride down to the train station and meet the others. We're to gather at the Kamakura train station, then load on a bus for a ride west to Chigasaki and the Matsushita (National/Panasonic) Institute of Government and Management.

I excuse myself and go up to my room and get my bags. On the way back down I go by Pullman's room. He is on the phone. I tell him to hurry it up and meet us down stairs with his luggage. The Japanese are here to give us a ride back to the train station.

Downstairs I drop my bags by the front door of the hotel and go back into the lounge where the two Japanese are drinking coffee. As soon as I come in they stand up. They are ready to go.

"Where is you friend?" Asks the one who was at the dinner the night before.

"He's on the phone, but he'll be right down," I say.

We pick up my bags at the door and walk out to his car parked on the brick-paved circle in front. He puts my bags in the trunk and we stand around waiting for Pullman to show.

Shimizu drives up and pulls in behind us. "They are starting to show up down at the train station. Are you and Ron-*san* ready to go?"

"Ron's on the phone. He should be down in a minute." I light a cigarette.

We stand around and visit. I finish one Japanese Lucky Seven cigarette and light another. Pullman still hasn't shown.

The Japanese are getting uneasy.

"You want me to go on down to the station and you wait on Pullman?" I ask Shimizu.

"That may be better," he says. "I'll bring him when he gets off the phone."

"Okay," I say, "I'll ride down with these two gentlemen."

We get in the car. I'm sitting up front with the driver, the man from last night's dinner. He's telling the other man in Japanese the story I told last night about trying to make love when the phone is ringing and my wife is being called to work.

"*Ah so desu*," the other man says, slapping me on the shoulder. They both have a good laugh. It is one of the few times this whole trip I have seen any levity from the Japanese.

When we arrive at the traffic circle in front of the Kamakura train station our bus is already there and Rick Ramsay, Paul White and Tim Wilson have loaded their gear aboard. They all had a good time on their home visits last night. A car pulls up and Whitney Bain gets out. He spends a minute or so saying good-bye to the middle-aged Japanese gentleman with whose family Bain spent the night last night. They bring his bags over to the bus and Bain is all smiles.

"Have a good time last night, Whitney-*san*," someone asks.

Bain grins. "You wouldn't believe it."

"What?" We ask as a group.

"That man really treated me nice. He took me into Tokyo to his hotel. We had a big dinner that must have cost at least a thousand dollars. He showed me the whole operation. Then he put me up in a nice room. I was just laying there relaxing and there was a knock on the door. I got up, in my shorts, and went to the door. It was two beautiful Japanese women. They had been sent up to give me a massage,' Bain grinned.

Bain is assistant food and beverage director of the Princess Resort and Casino on Grand Bahama Island. He finally got his vocational exchange the Rotarians had promised him. He also probably got the best massage he had ever had and my guess is that is all he got. Whitney has a beautiful wife in Freeport with whom he is head over heels in love. He also is a deeply religious person. I'd bet my last yen that he went strictly for the massage.

We've been standing by the bus talking for at least a half hour and Pullman still hasn't shown. The Japanese Rotarians who have gathered are getting nervous. We are behind schedule already. One of them goes and makes a phone call.

"Your man is still on the phone. He is talking to a woman in the States," he says. The only way they would know that is that the operator at the hotel must be listening in on the conversation.

"What can we do?"

"I guess we can wait," I say.

"Can we have the hotel cut off the telephone?" The Japanese asks me.

"That's your call, not mine," I say and return to our guys who want to know what's going on. I tell them. It looks like the affair of the heart has got Pullman tied up on the phone to the States. At least he got through, a little late for Easter, but he got through. A couple of the other guys still haven't had a chance to get to a phone where they can call home. We've been told we'll be staying in college-style dormitories with phones when we get to the Matsushita (National/Panasonic) Institute of Government and Management in Chigasaki. They should have some time to make some calls from there.

We're to be there for a three days. The schedule doesn't look too busy, mainly some Rotary meetings.

The Japanese are really getting uneasy now. We must be at least a half hour to 45 minutes behind schedule. That means the Kamakura bunch is late getting us on the road and the Chigasaki bunch will have to stand around and wait for us at the other end. It will be embarrassing for the Kamakura Rotarians to inconvenience the Chigasaki Rotarians, but there's not much we can do about it. Pullman should be coming any time.

It's at least another 20 minutes before Shimizu shows up with him. Pullman is in a tether.

"They kept pushing me to get off the phone," he says.

"Just get on the bus and shut up. I'm not all that pleased by the delay you have caused either," I tell him. He sulks aboard.

Shimizu is his usual calm self. We say our good-byes to the Kamakura Rotarians and board the bus. Finally we're on our way. Next stop the Matsushita (National/Panasonic) Institute of Government and Management in Chigasaki.

- Hai, so desu -

When the bus pulls up to the front gate of the Matsushita (National/Panasonic) Institute of Government and Management in Chigasaki I am reminded of an old European convent for some reason. It's not old, and it certainly isn't a religious institution, but the iron gates, tree-lined drive, and walled dormitories that apparently face in on some sort of a quadrangle or central campus remind me of a convent.

The Chigasaki Rotarians, several of whom I have already met, are waiting on us. They comment on the delay but don't seem all that upset about it. They even pitch in and help us lug our luggage into the building, down a long hall to what appears to be the main dining room for students at the institute. A sort of combination dining room and student lounge area in the best Western tradition.

The director of the institute, whom I met back in the States, comes in and gives us a briefing. He leads us up to the section of rooms we will occupy. With the exception of a Japanese – sit-on-the-tatami-mats – central room with a large television, the rooms we are to stay in are standard Western college dormitory style – steel bed and mattress, steel writing desk and table lamp, steel chair – all done in age-old college off-white.

I settle for a room to myself with a nice window that opens out over the rooftops of other buildings in the institute complex. There is no phone in the room, but I noticed there was one on the wall in the common area to this section of rooms. I assume that is the one we'll have to use for everything. It offers no privacy.

After we drop our bags in our rooms I ask the institute director where we can have our laundry done. It has been two weeks since we have had a chance to drop anything off at the laundry. Most of us are running out of clean clothes. He says he will show us and waits for the others to gather in the common area of the suite of rooms. Then he takes us back down stairs to the hallway that runs to the dining room except instead of turning into the dining room he turns the other way and takes us around a corner.

Smiling he walks us into a coin laundry and shows us the machines. He shows us where the soap for them is kept, and he even shows us where the irons are so we can iron our clothes once they are washed. Evidently this is the way his students do it. We explain to him that we don't want to do our own laundry, we want to send it out and have it done professionally.

He's not happy with that. Evidently people that stay in his institute do their own laundry in his institute laundromat and that is what we are supposed to do.

"No way," I tell him. "We will send our laundry out. Just tell us where the nearest laundry is."

"That is not on the schedule," he starts in.

"Wait a minute," I tell him. "We send our laundry out when we need laundry done. What's the schedule got to do with it?"

By now he is miffed. He turns and heads back to the dining room where the Chigasaki Rotarian hosts are drinking tea and coffee. Shimizu also has arrived. He's smiling as usual, but listens intently to whatever the institute director is telling him. Shimizu listens for a minute and then comes over to me.

"Do we have a problem?" He asks.

"A couple," I tell him. "We need to send our laundry out. They guys are tired and need some time off. And it doesn't look like we have any telephone privacy the way this is set up. I don't know if they've noticed that yet or not, but they will and they're not going to be happy with it."

"Come on over and sit down at the table with us," he says.

We join him and the other Japanese around a large square table to one end of the big dining room.

Apparently the laundry controversy has them stymied. I explain to them that all we want to do is send our laundry out. One mentions that it is expensive. I tell them that we don't mind. We have money for our laundry.

That was insult No. 1 for the day on my behalf, I believe. Apparently the Chigasaki Rotarians were told they were responsible for us and that means they are to take care of all our needs. If we want to send out laundry, they are going to take it for us, and they are going to pay for it. Some of them cannot see why we don't want to use the laundry facilities at the institute, so I simply tell them that we don't do our own laundry.

This attitude stymies most of the Japanese because they never have to worry about their own laundry. Their wives do not work. Clean clothes, including shined shoes, are laid out for them each morning when they arise. For us, two weeks without a stop long enough to send out our shirts and trousers, and get our blazers cleaned and pressed, means we are down to our least dirty dress shirts and are beginning to look a bit rumpled.

Besides that most of the team members on the trip came because they expected to meet with their counter parts in Japanese business and exchange ideas at least one full day a week. By the time we get to Chigasaki it is evident this is never going to happen.

Sitting around what turns out to be the negotiating table at the Panasonic Institute, we finally convince our Japanese hosts that we need to do laundry. But, somewhere in the translation the fact gets lost that we are willing to take our own dirty laundry to the nearest laundry and have it done. Once the Japanese concede to our laundry request then it becomes their responsibility to see that our laundry gets done, or so they believe. They tell us to go get our dirty laundry and bring it to the dining room. They will take it out for us. No matter of reasoning changes this so we all trot upstairs to drag our laundry down and send it out.

What has really happened, I discover, is that our schedule showed we had some open time for travel and settling in today – a much-needed rest stop for the team members – and the Japanese from Chigasaki have us on a different one.

When I bring my laundry down they tell me to have my people ready at 11 a.m. to load up and tour a newspaper printing plant and then travel to Atsugi Naval Air Station.

That was the limit.

I gather the team members in a library area of the institute. We agree that we will no longer be treated like livestock. That if the Japanese are not going to honor the Rotary Foundation vocational requirements, then we will not feel obliged to honor the Japanese Rotarians impossible schedules.

I tell one of the Japanese Group Study Exchange team members, who had been to Florida, to find the best interpreter they have and we will have a sit-down discussion with their Rotary leaders. We gather around a table in the library and I explain how we feel and express our need for a day off to Shimizu who in turn expresses it to his fellow Rotarians.

Negotiations begin.

Several of the Rotarians run back and forth to two nearby pay phones and relay the information to the Rotary governor's office in Fujisawa while we negotiate.

In exchange for a day off, I promise that we will attend all Rotary functions and that I personally will visit any factories or meet any obligations that had been made in our behalf if it means that local Rotarians will lose face by cancelling any appointments that have been made for us.

I again request the vocational days that we had been promised noting that I would not require any other team members to make a visit to any factory or other organization that was on the list simply because it had some vague relationship to some other team member's occupation or career.

I also ask that we be given the complete schedule for the day in advance, the same as the Japanese hosts were given – schedules which are timed down to the minute and never shown us.

In addition, I demand that when our schedule shows free time that we get that free time and when there is nothing on our evening schedule that we not be told at the last minute that we have to go to a two-hour Japanese banquet when it was not a regular Rotary Club meeting.

Then I wait.

The phone calls continue. The Japanese got back and forth between a meeting they are holding among themselves in the cafeteria.

The end result is that we can have a couple days off, the factory tours scheduled for the next two days will be cancelled, if we agree to meet the mayor of Chigasaki and attend the regular Rotary functions, which team members agree they enjoy.

The kicker is that I must sign a written contract for the Rotary governor's office saying I would assume all responsibility for the team members during their free time periods. I thought I was responsible for my team members, but by the Japanese interpretation of their role in our visit to their country they are responsible for everything.

Ah, so desu, The Japanese Way again – the paternal attitude. We are not old enough to be responsible for ourselves. Even me, as team leader, cannot be responsible once we are in the hands of our

Japanese hosts unless I sign a written contract stating that I will assume that responsibility.

I insist the contract be written in both Japanese and English, which it is. After about an hour's deliberation they come up with the appropriate wording.

I sign.

This is a tremendous step for the Japanese. They are responsible for us. To relinquish that responsibility to a foreigner is contrary to The Japanese Way. It is also a slap in the face to me and the Rotarians in Florida who chose me to lead this group.

Japanese pride themselves on their ability to operate on handshake agreements. It is impolite to require a written contract. But, since I have questioned their scheduling of our activities, they make a big deal of having me sign a contract that says I will be responsible for my team members during their free time. It is direct insult by the Japanese Rotarians.

Without being necessarily aware of it, the Japanese explain our situation to us in a handout they gave us when we arrived at the institute. It included excerpts from "An English Dictionary of Japanese Culture."

Under "*gaijin*" it reads: "...a foreigner in Japan. The term *gaijin* literally means all foreigners in Japan, but it actually refers to those of Caucasian backgrounds. The *gaijin* say that they often experience special treatment in Japan. They never fail to receive kind guidance and devoted assistance from people on the street. Their Japanese friends will invite them to the fanciest restaurants. When they visit a business office or an acquaintance's house, they may be flooded with expensive gifts and souvenirs. But many *gaijin* who are with Japanese companies deplore and protest that they are treated as permanent guests in their offices, excluded from important decision-making procedures. Their original proposals are likely to be politely rejected or silently ignored simply on the ground that they are not in accordance with Japanese customs.

"One of the reasons for these apparently contradictory attitudes seems to lie in the self-image that Japanese people have traditionally fostered. They are inclined to believe that they are culturally so unique that it is almost impossible for them to explain themselves or for other people to adapt themselves to Japanese ways of life. This psychological orientation, reinforced by their traditional *uchi-soto* (insider-outsider) mentality, has resulted in Japanese people's hesitation at cross-cultural communication at deep levels. They have formed an extremely exclusive society of their own."

Ah so desu, The Japanese Way

There in plain English – in a document the Japanese give us – is the explanation of that which is frustrating us. The Japanese Way is not going to let us experience the opportunities we had expected to enjoy on this trip, so by trial and error we have managed to work out a fairly good comprise with our hosts who, by the end of our second week here, are beginning to bend a bit and let us seek out our own opportunities – or so I
mistakenly think.

Some have been successful. For myself just the chance to roam around, visit with individual Japanese and consume all the English-language newspapers and magazines I can find allows me to pick up where I left off in 1981 in my studies of the Japanese economy. There are significant changes.

For Tim Wilson the opportunity to roam with his video camera gives him the chance to compile enough tape to produce a good television show or two on present-day Japan.

For Whitney Bain there has been an opportunity to visit one of the top resorts and spend a night. With the contacts he has made through a home visit and his stay at the resort, more will follow, so he has worked out an approach to his vocational studies.

For Rick Ramsay the going has not been as easy. The Japanese will only show him fire stations. Since he is a volunteer firefighter this hardly fulfills his desires to study the Japanese police system, which would be closer to his work as a full-time deputy sheriff. When we meet the mayor of Chigasaki I try an end run on this one by asking the mayor if he can arrange for Ramsay to work with the local police. We get the kiss-off.

Actually police in Japan are not local. They are part of a provincial/national police system. In fact, after World War II many of Japan's military officers and enlisted men were transferred to the police force. In many ways, the Japanese police operate like a national para-military organization.

Ramsay spending vocational exchange time with the Japanese police is not going to happen. He is adjusting, but rightfully disappointed in light of the fact that this was one of the great opportunities that was presented by the Rotary Foundation Group Study Exchange proposal.

Paul White is an anomaly because he has a degree in aerospace engineering but due to the lack of jobs in his field in the U.S. he now manages a Chinese restaurant. The Japanese, who are in a recession of their own, understand White's plight and enjoy a laugh when we explain it to them. But other than a visit to the Japanese Aerospace Center at Fuchinobe and a meal in a Chinese restaurant, White is left to his own devices to examine food handling and scientific advances in Japan.

Ron Pullman is probably the biggest oddity to the Japanese. They have no concept of what a financial strategist is, nor can they comprehend what he does by designing investment programs for major league baseball stars. In Japan, baseball stars do not get the huge salaries that American ball players do, so the Japanese do not understand the need for someone to plan their financial futures for them. Pullman's early meeting with an Japanese insurance company executive turned into a lecture on the evils of the American system. He learned quickly from that initial experience there was going to be no exchange of ideas or philosophies on investments as far as the Japanese were concerned.

Under our latest arrangement with our Japanese hosts, we start using our own time – when we can find it – to seek out vocational study opportunities. Sometimes the team members are successful, sometimes not. It doesn't seem to be a concern of the Japanese.

It's simply The Japanese Way to which we have adjusted – somewhat.

- Hai, so desu -

The confrontation is over. The team members have some time off and have headed for town. The Japanese Rotarians have left me alone at the Panasonic Institute.

I am drinking a cup of tea in the student dining room when the institute director, who came to the U.S. as part of Japan's Rotary Group Study Exchange, comes up to me with a paper in hand.

"Here is an article I have written about whaling," he says, handing it too me. "Why are you against the Japanese tradition of hunting and eating whale?"

I really am not sure I am against the Japanese hunting and eating whale, but from his opening gambit I really have no choice of what side of the argument I am on. The best I can do is agree to take his paper and study it, which I do. I return to my room with it.

The article makes no bones about the fact that as an American I have to be opposed to Japan hunting and eating whale. Guilt by association – by being an American. I realize there are plenty of whale huggers in the U.S., but I am not necessarily one of them.

A dozen years ago, when I visited Japan the last time, this same issue came up from another writer. I was lambasted for being an American and opposing Japan's taking and consuming of whales supposedly pushing the big seagoing mammals to the brink of extinction.

Two things make me want to avoid this argument, which is the kind that I don't believe anyone will win over the long run.

The first thing is that I know whale has been a traditional part of the Japanese diet forever. I see whale meat, and probably some porpoise meat as well, when I walk through the giant Japanese fish wholesale markets. Whale meat is an essential part, albeit a relatively small one, of the Japanese diet.

Secondly, I am aware that I am from a gene pool that creates people with the capabilities of destroying anything that gets in their way and is not to their particular liking. I am of white, Anglo-Saxon extraction, with a smidgen of some other cultural spices tossed in, that has produced a race of people who have felt so superior to others – Native Americans for one – that we did not hesitate to kill off the buffalo and destroy the entire culture of the Indians. I have no choice but to settle for being a descendant of those

who were capable of wiping out the buffalo-based Native American culture but, I don't have any desire to be a part of, or take a role in, wiping out the whale foundation of
Japanese diets.

I am sitting in my room, at my portable computer, working on notes from which this book will be written and have laid the whale article aside. I hear someone come through the door to our central meeting area down the hall a notch and around the corner from my room. I get up and go out to check who it might be since all the team members are off to town and I don't expect them back until late tonight.

As I round the corner, past the wall phone that only connects with other telephones within the institute grounds, I spot the institute director – the man who gave me the whale article – standing in the middle of our recreation area.

"That was a good article on whales you gave me," I say.

"*Ah so desu*, don't you agree with me?" He asks.

"It was a great article," I say.

"Are you getting rested up?" He asks. "Is it quiet enough for you here? Where have your team members gone?"

"I'm relaxing just fine. My team members are in town. Do you have any towels that we can use while we are here?"

"We do not have towels. You will have to find your own towels," he says and heads for the door.

I acknowledge the fact and go back to my room and start looking for my walking shoes. The team members are not going to be very happy when they get back from town tonight, want to take a shower and discover there are no towels. I'd better get cracking and go find some.

I leave the institute, walk up to the nearest train station and catch a train over to Fujisawa where one of the Saikaya Department Stores sits right near the train station. I have shopped in this store several times since we arrived and find prices to be fair and goods to be of high quality. Of course, I will later spend the night with the owner of the chain and his wife in Yokosuka and may be a little prejudiced as I write this in favor of
this chain of stores I suppose.

There is probably nothing more out of place in all of Japan than a working-age male shopping in a department store in the middle of a work-day afternoon. The store is overrun with women shoppers. I am the only male, other than some children with their mothers and an occasional store clerk, in the entire seven or eight stories of this Saikaya.

When I eventually find the towel section of the store it is packed with women digging through the piles and piles of designer towels.

I start looking for some standard bath towels and wash clothes that can be used by our crew for the rest of our trip. I don't need anything exceptional. Just some basic towels. Quickly I learn that basic is not a word that Japanese housewives understand. Their total focus is on bath towels that have one of several foreign designer logos embroidered on them.

There are piles and piles of these towels. I elbow my way through the women shoppers and check these designer towels out. I can't find any that are selling for less than $40-$50 apiece. I can't believe it. Who would pay that much money for a standard-sized bath towel when you can go by Towels By the Pound or some other such outlet and pick up a half dozen or more good cotton Cannon towels for the same amount of money.

That's back home, of course. Apparently the Japanese do not have access to such towel bargains.

These women are literally pawing through the expensive designer towels, apparently attempting to pick out that one particular towel they feel expresses them best. To me the towels all look the same. And their prices are all astronomical. I get some dirty looks from the Japanese female towel shoppers as I check the towels out. This is definitely not the place for a man.

Finally I locate one bin of non-designer towels. They are of lighter quality and of several different designs. They are selling for the modest price of $7 in exchange – less than 20 percent the price of the more popular designer towels that fill the department. I need at least a dozen towels and half a dozen wash clothes and decide to try and find enough of one single design in the pile to make up the order.

Occasionally as I am digging through the scattered loose towels in the pile a Japanese woman will come by and pick one of the less expensive towels up, examine it, and drop it back on the stack. Each one drops the towel with a snobbishness that I have rarely witnessed in the Japanese. Apparently the modern Japanese woman does not tolerate lower-quality, non-designer-label merchandise. Such things appear to be beneath the dignity of the modern Japanese housewife.

After about 20 minutes of digging I have my dozen matching towels and wash clothes. I am out of this department for just over $100, less than the Japanese housewives who have me surrounded will get out for if they buy just two bath towels and a matching designer wash cloth.

Now I have an arm load of towels stuffed in a paper bag that is probably not going to survive the train ride back to the Panasonic Institute. I have once again accumulated more junk than I have room in my luggage for – the constant addition of gifts from the Japanese is having a compounding impact on the amount of luggage we have to lug around. It's time to buy another duffle bag and since I'm in a department store a good time to do it.

It takes a while to find the luggage department. When I finally do, I find the same thing there I found in the towel department – expensive designer label luggage. There is a pile of small-to-medium-sized duffels with labels I have never before seen that are selling for I guess what the Japanese might consider a reasonable price – $50-$75 each. They are bags I can buy at home for less than half their price here. And, these have some weird labels.

I settle on a "Hot Dog" brand bag that costs me $60, stuff my arm load of towels in it, and retire from the shopping business.

- Hai, so desu -

I have a whole afternoon to myself here in Chigasaki. The rest of the team is off on junkets into town from the Panasonic Institute. I joined them for brunch at an International House of Pancakes across the street where we got a kick out of eating flat-tasting pancakes bathed in blueberry syrup with chopsticks – a quaint Japanese touch to a traditional American breakfast.

Earlier in the day I had checked what the students were eating for breakfast in the dining hall at the Panasonic Institute. The choices ranged from a bowl of traditional Japanese *misoshiro* breakfast soup and *nihon chato* – tea – to macaroni and cheese and what appeared to have been *to kouhi no nòmiso* – calf's brains – really nothing I was particularly interested in starting my day on. Instead I ate early in the morning a fine Japanese apple I had purchased for $5 in one of Shimizu's local grocery stores and had left to chill on the window sill in my room overnight.

After brunch with the gang at IHOP I spent most of the morning working on the computer, entering notes from which this book is being written. Then I decided to hike down the street behind the institute and over to the beach that curves around Sagami Bay and the Pacific Ocean.

To get to the beach I cross the main oceanfront highway and through cultivated windbreaks behind large picket fences on the sand dunes fronting the ocean. The dunes along the beach here are high. The sand is black, ancient volcanic ash. A paved walkway runs along the beach just below the dune line and fifty feet or more above the surf line. It leads westward about five miles to the fishing village just south of the city of Chigasaki.

I turn to the west and begin the long trek to the fishing village. The beach is deserted this afternoon except for one fishermen a mile or so away. He is sitting on a bucket at the surf line casting into the water that is sliding ashore in waves no more than six inches high. It is a relatively quiet surf. Off shore, over the reefs, I can see several fishing boats from the village to the west. Whether they are commercial or sports fishermen I cannot tell. I will check them out when I get to the village. With the long walk ahead we should both arrive at the small sheltered harbor there at about the same time.

This is a walk I have wanted to take for the past several years, ever since I read about the American plans to invade Japan in late 1945 and early 1946 had World War II not ended abruptly in August 1945 after the atomic bombs were dropped on Hiroshima and Nagasaki.

I remember flying down the coastal highway above me on a rented Japanese motorcycle back in the '50s, goofing off on a weekend run from Camp Fuchinobe south to the coast, along the coast to Odawara and back north to Mt. Fuji and home. I had no historical perspective in those days of what had been planned for this area. It was much less populated at the time. A quiet, undisturbed stretch of coast line, not the milling run-on of city after city that it is today.

As I walk the beach I realize that to me it is hallowed ground. Not for the battle that was fought here but rather for the battle that was avoided here by the end of the war.

Had the war not ended in August 1945 American forces were scheduled to invade the southern Japanese main island of Kyùshù in the area of Kagoshima, an invasion that in itself would have gone down as the bloodiest battle to date in history far surpassing the massive blood-letting that occurred on Okinawa.

Plans were for the Allied Forces to occupy Kyùshù from which they could fly sorties and employ other softening-up techniques against the main Japanese island of Honshu of which this stretch of beach is a part.

In March of 1946 American forces were scheduled to begin the invasion of Honshu, across this very beach along Sagami Bay, spearheading a drive northward into the Kanto Plain and the heart of Japan – Tokyo. Compared to the less than 100,000 Japanese troops involved in the bloody Okinawa campaign there would have been literally millions of Japanese troops on hand to repel this invasion. They would have been backed by tens of millions of Japanese citizens who had pledged to fight to the death in the name of their Emperor.

Walking along the beach today it is easy to see how defendable this stretch of land could have been. Foothills to the north connected by interlacing caves would have enabled the Japanese to mount artillery attacks that no amount of softening up could have negated their effectiveness.

Coupled with the highly probable possibility that the Japanese had perfected an atomic device that was to have been used against any force that attempted to invade the heart of their homeland, this would surely have gone down in history as the most costly, bloody battle of all times. There would surely have been a victor – most likely America because of its material superiority that was pitted against Japan's rapidly deteriorating productive capacity. But, there would have been no winners.

Knowing what I know today I have no regrets that the U.S. used the atomic bomb when it did. The lives lost to the introduction of the atomic age were miniscule in numbers compared to the millions of lives that would have been destroyed in an invasion of Japan over this very beach.

Indeed, it is to me hallowed ground simply because that final battle never took place. It basks in the peace I am enjoying as I walk along the seashore here today. I pray to God that it shall ever remain so.

I pass above the sole bucket-seated fisherman along the surf line and pause to watch him for a while. He has caught some fish. Small ones. They are piled on the sand alongside the bucket on which he is seated. He continues to fish oblivious to the world around him.

The offshore boats have headed for home port and our paths begin to vector towards the common point of the harbor ahead. I arrive at the small fishing village just as they begin to come into port. I tour a couple of the small tackle and bait stores along the docks inside the concrete-protected harbor of the village. They are not unlike our bait and tackle stores back in the Florida Keys. The main exception is in the style of fishing tackle they stock. The fiberglass rods they sell are not as well finished as those we buy. Instead of polished exteriors they have a rougher finish like no one wanted to take the time to buff out the fiberglass resins used in making them. And, the prices of these rods are two or three times as high as I can buy similar, but better finished ones, for back in the Keys.

One style of rod fascinates me. I never remember having seen it before. It is made of bamboo. Not split, but simply cut into lengths with appropriate metal ferrels to slide the lengths together. Line guides are wound to each section. They appear to be nothing more than solid bamboo shafts, some up to three-quarters of or an entire inch in diameter, simply varnished on the outside. They are not cheap – $40 to $70 per rod depending upon length and quality of finish.

The one thing lacking in these stores are any of the fine handmade bamboo rods that I found in Japan in the '50s. Two handsomely finished fly rod kits I purchased for my father and a friend back then set me back only about $30. I still have one complete set of those rods that I made by combining what was left of the two sets I had given Dad and Pop Wintermute after they both died. I fish it still today – both freshwater and salt water.

I inquire about hand-crafted split bamboo rods at one of the tackle shops. The proprietor tells me they are available by special order only. The cost: $4,000-$5,000 if I am interpreting the price he gives me correctly.

Passengers are unloading from one of the larger fishing boats that has docked. It is not unlike the head boats or party boats we run in the Keys. They take 30 or 40 people out fishing for a day, or a part of a day, for a minimum price furnishing both tackle and bait if the anglers don't prefer to bring their own. It appears the Japanese have developed a similar system to meet the demands of their fishing public.

Two men come off the boat carrying a large cooler between them. I ask them what they have caught and they proudly sit the cooler down, throw open the lid, and beamingly show me the literally hundreds of small – no more than three or four inches long – fish they have caught. It is the small fish Japanese traditionally serve with a bowl of *miso* for breakfast. I congratulate them on their catch. I notice they are carrying the bamboo sectional rods I saw in the store. I also notice they fish with a hook that is the size of ones we use only for catching live bait fish back in the Keys.

I make one more pass through the tackle shops and pick up a small top-water lure shaped like a beer can, complete with a Kirin Beer label. It becomes one of my favorite souvenirs of this trip.

I walk back to the highway and flag down a cab for the ride back to the Panasonic Institute.

- Hai, so desu -

There's a neat little restaurant tucked away down one of the streets winding out from the Chigasaki train station where Shimizu likes to go for lunch. It is called The Apple and is run by a Japanese couple, the wife of whom speaks perfect English and serves meals that span the border between east and west.

Today Whitney Bain and I have joined Shimizu there for lunch. I always order the special of the day that comes in a compartmentalized lacquer *bento* box. Some days it is a Japanese meal. Other days it is a American meal with the side touch of steamed rice garnished with a pickled vegetable.

We order lunch. Bain and I are talking about plans for the afternoon. All of a sudden Whitney stops talking and begins to stare at Shimizu. Shimizu-*san* is sitting rigidly straight, eyes unfocused, seemingly miles from where we actually are. I watch Bain watch Shimizu for several seconds.

"What is he doing?" Bain asks.

"It's a Buddhist practice of removing one's self from the immediate surroundings – enjoying the peace and quiet of one's own space," I say.

"Can he actually do that?" Whitney asks.

"Sure. I have seen Japanese people do it for some pretty long periods of time right in the middle of what would be a chaotic day for you and me," I say.

"Really?"

"Yep. Wait until he comes back and we'll ask him to explain it," I offer.

When Shimizu returns from his short trance and refocuses his eyes on us I explain to him that I have been trying to explain to Whitney what he was doing. He shrugs his shoulders, smiles, and says, "*Hai, so desu.*"

In a country so overrun with people and so short on space, this practice of Zenning-out, as I call it, is essential to maintaining one's sanity. I have never been able to master it to the extent that Shimizu and many of my other Japanese acquaintances have. Maybe some day.

- *Hai, so desu* -

I'm running short of yen and need to cash in several $100 U.S. bills and some traveler's checks I have left. Shimizu-*san* has agreed to meet me at a bank in Chigasaki and help me make the exchange.

At the bank it is obvious that this is where Shimizu does a lot of business. Everyone in the lobby knows him. He introduces me to the manager and several other people and tells them that I need to exchange some money.

I am led over to a chair in front of a seated teller behind a row of teller stations not unlike those in any American bank. Shimizu and one of the gentlemen we have been talking to take a seat on a couple of comfortable couches set in the middle of the bank lobby and engage in conversation.

The bank teller listens to what I want. Takes my traveler's checks and $100 U.S. bills, records several notes on a printed form, calls a clerk and hands it all over to her. She takes it across the platform area behind the tellers and into another room.

"It will be a few minutes," the teller says. "Please have a seat in the lobby and we will call you when your money is ready."

I join Shimizu and his friend on the couches. They continue their conversation and I study the many boards of current financial information on the wall – exchange rates, interest rates, etc., much the same as in any American bank.

On the table next to me I discover an application for a Visa card, written in
Japanese of course. I pick it up and study it, focusing on the arabic numbers that appear within the text. I locate a "13" and try to make sense of it.

Finally I ask Shimizu, "Is this the interest rate charged on this credit card?"

"*Hai, so desu,*" he replies.

Eureka, I have finally discovered what interest rate the Japanese charge on consumer credit cards – the rate that R. Okamoto, president of Saikaya Department Stores Co., Ltd., with whom I stayed in Yokosuka, does not know.

It has been about 15 minutes since I turned in my traveler's checks and $100 bills to the first teller. I know from experience that it doesn't take this long to exchange money in Japan when you are dealing simply with traveler's checks, so the delay must be in turning my $100 American into Japanese yen.

I can understand from a story I read the other day why $100 U.S. bills are suspect in Japan. It seems there is a brisk export business of older Japanese cars to Siberia where local residents claim the worst Japanese vehicle is better than a brand-new Russian-made car from which the steering wheel is liable to fall into your lap at any moment as you sail down an ice-covered, bumpy Siberian highway.

Recently Russian commercial fishermen visiting Japan have been buying up used Japanese cars, transporting them to Siberia, and selling them. The Ruskies have paid the Japanese for a lot of the cars with $100 U.S. bills. Many of the bills have turned out to be counterfeit. The Japanese are not taking any chances with my U.S. currency today. I don't blame them.

Eventually everything gets worked out. My name is called and I am directed to a different teller, seated behind the teller station on down the line from the previous one I had given my traveler's checks and money to earlier. I sit myself in the chair before her station. She counts out my yen, asks if there is anything else the bank can do for me to which I answer, "No, thank you," get up, and leave with Shimizu after saying goodbye
to his many friends in the bank.

Japanese banking is always a pleasant experience, albeit a much slower, labor-intensive process than any American banking experience I have ever had.

- Hai, so desu -

Tim Wilson is eating his third piece of cantaloupe for breakfast as I enter the hotel restaurant. I can usually tell when he is upset by the number of melon pieces he eats. Melon costs about $20 a slice. When Tim is upset with the Japanese, who pay for our meals, he indulges himself in melon for breakfast. The Japanese don't seem to realize the fine he imposes on them when they get to him.

"I've got a problem with sending faxes," Tim says.

"What's up?" I ask.

"When I go to the hotel desk to send a fax home, they make a copy of it, then fax from my original, return the original to me, and take the copy into the back room," he says. "They're keeping copies of our correspondence."

"Are you paying for it?"

"Sure. I pay them in cash. Whatever they ask. They still keep a copy of my faxes," he says.

"Has it happened before?" I ask.

"Yes."

"In other hotels?"

"Yes. Here and in a couple of others where we have stayed," he says.

"Once we figured out how to blind dial around their telephone systems with my computer, I've sent a couple of faxes direct from my room," I reply. "But in some hotels they break in to the transmission and tell me I can't fax from my room. In one, all I could get was a carrier wave like they were sending something on the same line, or trying to copy what I was sending. It's weird."

"Do you suppose they are spying on us?" Tim asks.

"I wouldn't doubt it. Nothing is private in Japan. To us they have a national paranoia about things. I noticed at one hotel we stayed in down in Hayama that they kept a log of all the telephone numbers we called from our rooms. The desk clerk gave it to me when I went to pay for a couple of calls I had made and then took it back after I paid and gave me the standard hotel receipt that didn't show the log of telephone numbers. Then I saw him give the list to the local Rotary leader. Yeah, they could be spying on us," I tell him.

"I don't like it. This is our private correspondence. What I am sending home to Nora has to do with our business. It isn't any business of theirs," Tim says. "Can't we do anything about it?"

"I'll see what I can find out," I reply.

Tim flags down the waiter and orders another slice of melon.

- Hai, so desu -

I keep picking up vague references in the Japanese press that there are problems in the Japanese banking system. It appears there are some difficulties similar to the savings and loan crisis that hit the U.S. a few years ago. But, you have to keep in mind that the Japanese banking system is a bit different than ours. The Japanese do not have a Federal Reserve System that acts as an intermediary between the government and the banking system. Japan has a government-owned and operated central bank.

Commercial banks are largely owned by the *zaibatsu* that own the major industries in Japan. Government and big business get along cozily in Japan, so no one is in any hurry to expose anyone else in this situation. Hence there is not much written about any banking crisis that might be looming.

My best guess is the Japanese lost more than a little on our S&L crisis. I was privy to one Eurodollar issue worth $300 million during a short banking career in the '80s. That issue never saw Europe. It was pre-sold to Japanese banks before it was launched. I'll guarantee when the S&L I had worked for went under, the Japanese never saw a penny of that money returned. I'm sure the S&L I handled public relations for was not a singular case. So, when I pick up on the fact there seems to be a minor banking crisis in Japan I don't view it as solely a Japanese phenomena.

On the other hand, since Japanese corporate-government culture is so closed I'm surprised I even pick up hints of the crisis in the Japanese press. I've asked a few questions, but no one is saying much about it. The standard answer from Japanese businessmen is: "The government is handling it."

Today Paul White came back from Tokyo with a copy of *Tokyo Journal*, more or less the *Rolling Stone* magazine of Japanese English-language publications. A short item in the magazine touched on the Japanese banking crisis. Acknowledging there was a crisis, the irreverent *Tokyo Journal* suggested the total of non-performing loans in the top 21 banks in Japan – that includes six or eight of the largest banks in the world – probably exceeds the total assets of those 21 banks.

Normally that would mean the banks are bankrupt, but Japan doesn't necessarily operate in ways to which we have become accustomed. Japanese banks keep writing-up the loans: Continually loaning more money to accounts that cannot repay so those accounts can pay the interest on the existing loans and make them look good. It's a viable practice here since the banks are owned by the same people who own the companies that borrow the money and can't repay it under present economic conditions. They are simply loaning themselves more money to make at least the interest payments on money they have borrowed from themselves and can't repay.

Can it go on forever? No, but the Japanese are innovative.

The best guess is they will merge several of their large banks that are having problems into a megabank – most certain to become the largest bank in the world – and work their way out of the hole by loaning more money to better customers thereby increasing their asset base and reducing their non-performing loans. It's a good bet the Japanese government is not going to stand in the way of such a merger plan.

- Hai, so desu -

There is one trick I have learned to make a little extra money while in Japan – bring along a German camera to sell. In spite of all the fine optics the Japanese have developed and sold to global markets they still have deep respect for the German optics that dominated the market before World War II even if those German optics are of current manufacture.

In 1981 I brought with me small Lieca 35-millimeter, rangefinder camera I had had for several years. It had once taken a water beating on a trip up the Niagara River to the whirlpool beneath the falls. I had always been skeptical about how long it would continue to operate even though I had sent the camera off and had it completely cleaned after the Niagara incident. I liked the camera, and had it with me on the '81 Japan trip when I walked into a camera store on the Ginza. The proprietor of the store spotted the Lieca and asked if I would be willing to sell it.

"What do you think it is worth?" I asked him.

He gave me a figure that was twice as much as I had in the camera. I sold it on the spot and used a Japanese Pentax camera I had with me for the rest of that trip.

This time I have brought with me another small Lieca my wife, Marie, and I had bought for her father for Christmas a few years ago. Something had gone wrong with the electronics in the camera and he had given it back to me replacing it with some other brand of photography equipment. I had let it set around for a year and finally decided to send it back to Lieca where they repaired it for less than $100 and returned it to me. I re-offered it to my father-in-law and he was not interested. He was more satisfied with the newer equipment he had purchased.

So, I brought it along this trip thinking that it would be a good backup if I needed cash.

Today some of the gang wants to visit the Ueno district of Tokyo. When I first saw Ueno in the '50s it was mainly Tokyo's black market area, hardly more than rows of tables set up under the elevated railroad tracks near Ueno Station where you could buy just about anything you wanted. It was an all-cash operation and you could bargain all day long with the vendors who bought and sold beneath the railroad tracks. Theoretically, in those days, the black market was off limits to U.S. military. In fact, some of the things we did in military intelligence included assisting the U. S. Army's Civilian Investigation Division in investigations of black market activities. Still that didn't prevent us from indulging in an occasional deal at Ueno.

The hottest item were $20 U.S. bills that sometimes we would receive from family and friends in the States. In the 1950s we were still using Military Script in Japan, script that we had to exchange for Japanese yen when we went to town. The official exchange rate was 360 yen to the dollar. I only made $108 a month in those days and that included my overseas military pay.

There were certain elements in Japan that were paying top yen for American greenbacks. A $20 U.S. bill in the mid-'50s would fetch you three bright, shiny Japanese ¥10,000 notes, plus an additional ¥5,000 note, if you were adept at bargaining with the black marketers of Ueno. That the greenbacks were being bought by the *Yakuza* – the Japanese mob – or the Communists deterred us not one iota when it came to getting a five-to-one return on our greenbacks.

Today Ueno stretches for blocks and blocks. It still retains some of its under-the-tracks flavor but is literally one walk-through shop after another. Feeding off it are streets lined with shop after shop selling everything under the rising sun. Ueno is probably more legitimate market today than black market but I have no doubts that you can still find anything here you ever wanted if you can come up with the price.

I try a couple of camera shops and show them my German camera. They inspect it and make me offers. They are decent offers but not as good as I think I can get. I try a third shop. There the shop owner inspects the camera more thoroughly. The first offer he makes me is double the price I originally paid for the camera. I hesitate, ask him plaintively if that is the best he can do. He examines the camera once more and makes me a higher offer. I take it.

Just as when I sold the camera to the man in the shop on the Ginza in 1981, this shopkeeper pulls out a form that he insists must be filled out stating that I sold the camera. I present him my passport from which he will take the information needed to complete the form. Just as the shop keeper did in 1981 he records the first name on my passport as my first name on the form, my middle name on the passport as my last name on the form, and slides it over to me for my signature. I scrawl my signature on the form, slide it back across the counter to him, hand him the camera, and he hands me my money. I take it and leave.

I've always wondered what kind of a file the Japanese have tucked away somewhere on a mysterious, camera-peddling American named David Cupp.

- Hai, so desu -

We spent the morning sightseeing in Hakone National Park, rode a bus up and down the mountain roads, took a cable car from one mountain peak to another, climbed at least two hundred steps up to a hot spring where we ate boiled-in-sulphur water pigeon eggs, and took a boat cruise across a big lake to where we scurried from a bus in the rain into a modern Western-style restaurant that looks out over the lake.

It has rained most of the day. Even though we are no more than 30 miles from Mt. Fuji, we haven't caught a glimpse of it.

Conversation over lunch turns to Japanese television. Some of the Japanese with us are curious about cable television. It is just coming to Japan. There are less than a half dozen cable channels available in selected urban areas, but it has been promised to the masses.

"From what I have seen on some of your commercial channels, you already have a lot of programs that are restricted to cable, or pay-for-view in our country," I comment.

"Like what?" One of the Japanese asks.

"Well I've seen a couple of shows on your commercial channels that wouldn't be permitted on commercial television in the United States. They would be restricted to cable or some other system where viewers could restrict access to them," I reply.

"What kind of shows?" I am asked.

"I saw one called TIT•TIT•TAK that was nothing but a bare breast show. I couldn't understand the Japanese in it because they spoke too fast for me, but I assume it was a regular game show. Then I saw another where a girl stood over the camera lens while the cameraman zoomed in on her crotch. Of course, she had panties on, but a little later the cameraman zoomed down her blouse and showed her breast and they weren't covered up. I don't know what that show was, but it was on one of your commercial channels."

"Those are not serious shows," one of the Japanese said.

"It's not whether they are serious or not, it is their content. Our Federal Communications Commission would not permit those shows to be shown on public channels in my country. There's is such a thing as obscenity that the FCC is pretty strict about. Maybe these are not obscene in Japan, but there certainly would be an outcry from some in America if they were shown on the public airways where everyone, including children, has access to them," I said.

"Even if the FCC didn't interfere we have a religious right that would raise hell with the station that broadcast the programs, and threaten to boycott the sponsors so no one would sponsor the shows. They could not get on the air without sponsors," I continue.

"But no one takes them that seriously here in Japan," the last man repeats.

"Someone must," I reply. "They have sponsors. I don't believe anyone, not even Japanese companies, sponsor programs if they don't have an audience. There must be quite a few people interested in these programs to attract the sponsorship they have. They must have an audience."

"The Americans brought these types of programs here," another Japanese chimes in.

"You've got to be kidding," I reply. "We don't even have these type of programs in America. These are strictly Japanese programs. There's nothing in American television that you can compare them to."

"It was the American influence after the war that brought this kind of thinking to Japan," the man adds.

"But this is Japanese television. It doesn't have that much of an American or foreign market. You can't blame this type of programming on the American occupation. I was here back in the '50s and I never saw anything like this. This is a new Japanese creation," I say.

"These are programs made by some Japanese young people. They are not the young people who represent true Japanese values," another Japanese says.

"Yes," I counter, "but the shows are shown on publicly broadcast commercial television. Anyone can see them. They are not restricted to just young people."

"Respectable people do not watch them," one of the men says. "I would never watch one of those programs."

"Would you want your daughter to watch one of them? Better yet, would you want your daughter to be on one of them?" I ask.

"She would never do such a thing," he replies.

"How do you know? Are you with her all the time? Do you control her television viewing directly?"

"I know my daughter. She would never do such a thing. These are programs that the lower class may indulge themselves in, but we do not watch them," he says.

- Hai, so desu -

Yokosuka has always been a different story. It is a military town, mostly Navy. First it was Japanese Navy, then American Navy and now both Japanese and American Navy.

From Yokosuka's dry-docks came the largest battleship ever built, the *Yamato* with her 18-inch guns, and the world's first super carrier, the *Shinano*. The *Yamato* was sunk at Okinawa, the *Shinano* on its first sea trails as it skirted around the southern shore of Japan from Yokosuka to the Inland Sea off Hiroshima.

The dry-docks in which these ships were built are still in use today.

In the '50s I came here for two reasons: The Navy Base Exchange had all the goodies in the world and the town of Yokosuka outside the Navy base had every type of entertainmentone could imagine. A trip to Yokosuka has always been a memorable adventure.

In the '80s I came here to interview the Japanese admiral in charge of the Japanese Naval Self-Defense Force and to tour a new Japanese destroyer that was more like a cruiser than a destroyer. It was the first destroyer I had ever seen with a flight deck and hangar. At the time I lived next to Mayport Naval Station in Atlantic Beach, Florida, outside Jacksonville.

Mayport, at the time, was the home of a couple U.S. destroyer squadrons and a big chunk of the carrier task forces based on the U.S. east coast. I had seen and been on plenty of destroyers before, but none to match the size, cleanliness, and modern technology of the Japanese ships of the 1980s.

Today we're riding into town to go to the *sumo* matches, do some home stays, attend a Rotary Club meeting tomorrow and then visit the Navy base. All of our luggage is piled in the back of the bus. We stop at a Japanese business hotel and are greeted by a group of local Rotarians who tell us to take our luggage up to the lobby of the hotel that is located on the third floor above street level. An escalator helps.

One of our hosts hands me a brief note written in English: "Have each bring just enough for home stay. Leave other luggage in hotel."

Once in the lobby of the hotel, I ask one of the Japanese who have been shepherding us what the note means. "We will leave your luggage here until you get back from home stays tomorrow," he says.

"Where?"

"In the hotel."

"Do we have rooms?"

"No you have home stays tonight."

"Where do we leave our luggage?"

"Here in the hotel."

"Do they have a security room?"

"The hotel will watch your luggage," the Japanese, a Yokosuka doctor, tells me. He is getting a little on edge from my questioning.

When I tell the team members, I am greeted with silent skepticism, but they break down some of their luggage on the floor in the middle of the hotel lobby and prepare small kits for their overnight stays. We pile our luggage in a corner by the front desk and are given some plastic tags with numbers that correspond to numbers the desk clerk has tagged to our luggage.

We return to the bus for the ride to the *sumo* matches. *Sumo* is to Japan what professional football is to the United States. It's the macho game in town. Ancient and steeped in tradition, much of which would take longer to translate than the average *sumo* match. Full historical translation would require a text that would weigh more than a *sumo* wrestler.

The big matches – the Super Bowl of *sumo* – are held in Tokyo in September. The matches we are going to attend today are regional matches held in various parts of the country to bring *sumo* to the grass roots and to give the wrestlers from the various stables a chance to work their way to the top. *Sumo* is as old as Japan.

We arrive at the matches in the midst of a carnival atmosphere and unload in front of the entrance to the local auditorium. Waiting in front of the entrance, I notice a black, four-door car drive up. The Japanese driver gets out and holds the door for two Caucasian males, one dressed in a business suit, the other in slacks, open shirt, and blazer. The one in the suit is the elder of the two. The younger man is blond and tall with a backbone as straight as an arrow. They are accompanied by a Japanese gentleman in the traditional Japanese, western-style, pin-striped suit.

I study them as they walk up the steps to the entrance to the auditorium. Are they businessmen on an outing for the day? Americans? Europeans? I wonder and then turn to examine the car in which they arrived. It has driven off. They disappear into the crowd and I return to watching the *sumo* wrestlers arrive from their nearby hotels. They walk to the auditorium, dressed in light *kimono*. Some have small entourages, others simply walk
down the street on their own. The single outstanding feature of all of them is their size. They are big.

One of our Japanese hosts arrives with my translator for the day. She is Japanese, works at Camp Zama in the Equal Opportunity Employment Office. Her English is perfect. I discover she was married to an American attorney who worked with the military in Japan for many years. He died several years ago.

We receive our tickets and enter the auditorium. When we pass through the gate, we are given flat, square cushions on which to sit during the matches. At first I think we are going to sit on the floor, as is the custom, around the *sumo* ring that is set up in the middle of the auditorium-gymnasium. Instead, we start up the stairs and are shown to balcony seats on the front row overlooking the gym floor and elevated *sumo* ring below.

Along with the *sumo* cushion we are given a bag that contains a small bottle of *sake* and a *bento* box lunch. The lunch leaves something to be desired, but given the choice of a cold *bento* or a Japanese hot-dog, I'll take the *bento*. Japanese hot dogs are bland and taste like they contain more sawdust than meat.

The *sumo* matches are fun to watch. The name of the game is to throw one's opponent off balance and out of the ring. This is done by crashing into the opponent, or by grasping him by his loin cloth and hoisting him out of the ring. Two bodies, each weighing in the neighborhood of 300 pounds, coming together at top speed, can make for some interesting situations.

The ritual before the clash is where the match is often won or lost. The wrestlers get hyped by throwing coarsely ground salt around their starting position. They squat and stare at each other, stand up, throw some more salt, and finally when one thinks he has the psychological advantage over the other, charge.

Sometimes the clash is like two football players in the shower trying to knock each other out. At other times, a quick mongoose-python sidestep and shove is enough to throw the opponent out of play. Whatever method is used, the matches last mere minutes – occasionally seconds. The lower-ranked wrestlers go first with each successive group being the next higher rank.

I like *sumo*. It is definitely Japanese. No other country can lay claim to it. It is a pure Japanese cultural delight. The final match is the highest ranking wrestlers participating in the match.

Today it is Akibono, actually an Hawaiian/American – not a Japanese – but one of only less than a hundred grand masters in the two-and-a-half millennia history of the game. It's one of the oddities, those little leaks you find occasionally in the great Japanese racial purity game.

Today my interpreter is as interesting as the *sumo* matches. Maybe it's because she is an older woman. Maybe it's because she works at an American-Japanese army base. Or maybe it's because she was married to an American for so long. I notice that she answers casual questions rather nonchalantly. Since she works in the EOO office at Zama, I ask her about the equal rights opportunities in Japan.

"How do they treat equal rights for women at Zama?" I ask.

"Women have equal opportunity. That's one of my jobs – to assure they do," she replies.

"Does Japanese law grant equal rights to women?" I ask.

"Oh, yes," she assures me.

"What is the punishment for not complying?"

"Oh, there is no punishment. Compliance is simply required," she says.

"Do you mean that if a woman lodges a complaint against her employer for discrimination based on sex, the employer is required to comply?"

"*Hai, so desu.*"

"And, if the employer does not stop the discrimination, there is really nothing you can do to him?"

"*Hai, so desu.*"

"So, you have the law, but no real means to enforce it?"

"*Hai, so desu,*" she replies.

- *Hai, so desu* -

After the sumo matches we climb back aboard the bus. The only schedule I had received for our group for today said we would attend the *sumo* matches, and then have home stays. But, after the little tiff over the luggage in the hotel this morning I got wind of a possible plant visit to NTT – Nippon Telephone and Telegraph, the Japanese AT&T – following the *sumo* matches and then dinner with some members of the local Rotary group before we were told with whom we would be spending our home visits. My interpreter was evasive about the subject when I broached it with her.

As we ride up the tree-lined avenue – cherry trees, but the blossoms have all fallen from them – we are not headed back towards downtown Yokosuka. We are headed out of town. I ask one of the Japanese hosts with us where we are headed. We are going to visit NTT.

The drive out of town takes us up a series of winding hill roads. We climb up into the low mountains that surround Yokosuka and Tokyo Bay. NTT's headquarters building is a big square, glass-faced building sitting on top of what I would call Signal Mountain. There are several outlying antenna fields. Satellite dishes dot the surrounding hills. My best guess is that NTT's headquarters did not end up here by accident. Its proximity to Yokosuka and Yokosuka's long-time association with the military tells me we are climbing a mountain from which many signals have been transmitted, including many that directed the Imperial Japanese Navy during World War II. It is a natural signal site.

We unload from the bus under a high square canopy at the entrance to the building. It is cold and windy here on the mountain top. We are led into the building, through a large, two-story lobby of polished wood and marble, up a staircase, down a wide hallway, and into a conference room, one wall of which overlooks the downhill side of the mountain and offers a view out over the bay towards the Pacific Ocean. If it were not for the permanent overcast and smog, I have the feeling I could see from here to the ocean a dozen miles away.

We are seated around a set of tables laid out in a "U" and receive packets of information on NTT. Included in the packets is a Japanese phone card, one of the unique features of Japan's telephone system. Instead of having to carry a large number of coins to use in pay phones in Japan, you buy phone cards. They are thin plastic, about the size of an American credit card.

Encoded into them is the amount you purchase. Most are in ¥1,000 denominations. You simply insert the card in a slot in Japanese pay phones, a small screens tells you what the balance is on the card. As you dial your call and carry on a conversation, the screen tells you how much you have left as the yen are ticked off to pay for the call. It's like a taxi meter built into a telephone. Instead of running up a bill, it deducts it from the amount left on the card.

The first one of these I saw was a "Hole-in-One" card one of the Zama Rotarians had. He told me a friend of his gave it to him after the friend had scored a hole-in-one in golf. Japanese golf tradition dictates that anyone who scores a hole-in-one must buy a gift commemorating the event for each of his friends. One-thousand yen phone cards, with an appropriate inscription are just the ticket. If you have a lot of friends, it could get rather expensive at about $10 a card. Today's Japanese seem to thrive on this type of ostentatiousness. They like being rich or appearing rich. Japanese pass up bargains that Americans are addicted to searching out. The Japanese seem to be willing to pay more for a label – the impression of wealth – than they pay for the product, or the usefulness of the product. Hole-in-One telephone cards at least give good value.

Our team members are rolling their eyes at another plant visit. They have had enough, but the Japanese persist on dragging us from factory to factory. The scenario rarely changes. Off the bus, "No cameras or pictures, please," march through the lobby of the executive offices and down a hall to be seated in a conference room. Within minutes young Japanese girls serve hot hand towels and cups of tea. Sip the tea for a few minutes and then comes the greeting by the managing director's first assistant. Most are male, but occasionally we have a female greeter.

When we are greeted by a female, you can bet she is the company's token female executive and she has been assigned to public relations. To a person, every female corporate greeter we have met this trip has been from the company's public relations section. We have not seen a female in any other executive slot in any of the Japanese companies we have visited. With the exception of the American female English language instructor we met at Johnson Wax, the only female – I guess you should call them *sararii-women* or *sararii-person* to be politically correct in the Japanese – we have come into contact with that could be vaguely associated with middle or upper management have been in public relations.

Today is no exception. The Japanese woman from public relations today is thorough. She explains the packet of material we have been given. Her English is excellent. Then she stacks some overlays next to the overhead projector and introduces her boss, a Japanese male executive who does not speak English. He welcomes us, and gives us a portion of the NTT spiel in Japanese. Then the woman from public relations places the appropriate overlay on the projector and repeats what he has said in English, reading off the overlay as if we were incapable of reading it to ourselves. It is a boring lecture that has put two of our team members to sleep. I've got to give them credit, though, they have learned – mainly by studying Japanese on trains – how to grab a nap sitting up. For the most part they never nod their heads. Occasionally a snore will slip out and then it becomes the responsibility of the team member sitting next to them to give them a poke, being careful not to knock them off their chair.

They're good at it. They're becoming professional lecture attendees – major league quality. With the schedules they have been keeping, they need the naps. As team leader, I'm not going to interfere with whatever opportunity they find to grab one.

Today's lecture is longer than usual. It's the standard "We are a high-tech company/we are a world leader in our field/we are big on research and development/we are a progressive company" pitch we have heard at every factory we have visited.

Today we are getting it in Japanese, then spoken English, then written English on the overhead projection screen. I'm having trouble staying awake myself during this one.

Just as it seems it will never end, the Japanese gentleman finishes his pitch, the Japanese woman finishes her translation, and there is a short pause to give us time to read it in English on the overhead. Then we are invited to follow the woman back down the hallway, down the stairs, across the lobby, to a tour of the company's public display of their modern technology.

Going through the lobby, I notice a single pay phone on one wall. I decide I will call our friend at Johnson Wax and see if she would like to have dinner tomorrow night. I'm aware that we are scheduled to have dinner at the Officer's Club on Yokosuka Navy Base, but I feel like playing AWOL for a change. I, too, need a break from the Japanese. It's my turn to take an evening off. The rest of the team can handle the Navy base dinner.

We are herded by our Japanese hosts into the display rooms where we are shown displays of microwave equipment, satellite technology, and fiber optics. None appear to be current generation. The fiber optic cables we are being shown, and told are the latest in Japanese electronics, have long been surpassed in transmission carrying capacity by fiber optic cable I have seen in the U.S. We're being told and shown a good story, but I'm sure it's not the whole story.

Alongside one of the displays I spot a Macintosh computer, the first I have seen in Japan. This is a 100-percent American-made piece of high-tech. I ask what it is doing in this display of Japanese high-tech. The answer I get from one of the male Japanese managers conducting the tour is nothing I understand in Japanese and the public relations woman doesn't seem to want to translate it into English.

As they move on, I sit down at the keyboard of the Mac and boot it up. The desktop appears but all the characters are in Japanese. I mouse the cursor over to the Apple pull-down menu, give it a click and it scrolls down. Since I don't read Japanese I am at a loss. I try clicking on what would be "About this Macintosh" on my computer back at the hotel. It prints out an information box on the screen. The writing is in Japanese, but the numbers are in Arabic. I discover this Mac is running System 6.0.7 software. Mine is already into System 7. If I'm going to get anywhere on this Mac I have to remember exactly where everything is located on the desktop pull-down menus on an English-language Mac. I've forgotten the layout for System 6.0.7. I'm sitting here trying to mentally recall a System 6.0.7 desktop layout to match with the Japanese desktop I'm facing.

One of the Japanese men from our group walks over and asks, "What are you doing?"

"Just playing around," I reply. "This is an American computer. One like the computer I use at home and the portable one I brought to Japan with me."

"We should go with the rest of the group," he says, motioning to the others who are standing in front of another aging technology display on the other side of the room.

"Okay," I reply.

Maybe it sounds like I am being unduly hard on the Japanese – Japan bashing – but I don't think that the case. This is the umpteenth "factory tour" our Rotary hosts have given us. We've seen many of the big-name, high-tech companies, listened to their canned talks, videos, public relations movies, been given the walking tour of a portion of their work floors, and had our pictures taken under the cherry blossoms with the managing directors.

But, our questions have usually fallen on deaf ears. I know that in Japan consortiums – a few to a few dozen companies, including NTT and its labs right here on this mountainside – are set up among various companies for R&D purposes. Since the 1980s the Japanese have been working on neural, or bio, computer systems and fuzzy logic – actually discovered by a scientist at Berkeley in the 1960s, pioneered by two Japanese scientists working for AT&T, and now among leading-edge development programs being pursued by the Japanese on their home soil.

But no one wants to talk about it.

Instead, we keep seeing computer and electronic equipment that is already doomed to obsolescence. It's ironic how many factory tours we have been on and have been told, "It's maintenance day," or "This is the traditional day off for the people in this department," when it's obvious that either the recession is forcing a cutback in production, or some type of retooling for new generations of high-tech equipment is taking place.

In the meantime, any hands-on experimenting we have been able to do has been with Intel 386, or pre-System 7 Macintosh equipment like the one I am sitting in front of right now.

I shut down the Mac and rejoin the group, then move away and walk down the hall towards a rest room. Our CIA-Man-of-the-Day follows me. "CIA-Man" is the code name we've used among ourselves to describe the one Japanese out of every group we have visited who seems to hang back and keep an eye on everything we do. One of the games the team plays involves being the first one to spot the CIA-Man every morning. Sometimes he is simply sitting in the hotel lobby reading a newspaper, keeping a watchful eye on us from the minute we step off the elevator.

Today's CIA-Man follows me into the rest room. He makes himself busy at a lavoratory while I patronize a urinal. I leave the rest room. He leaves right behind me. Instead of turning left to return to the display room, I turn right, walk into the lobby and over to the telephone. CIA-Man turns right, also. I stop at the phone. He walks past behind me and takes a seat along the wall within earshot.

I stick my telephone card in the machine, dial Johnson Wax in Oiso, ask for Tracy Ellingson, wait until she comes on the line, and start a conversation with her. We make a dinner date for the following night, and chat a moment about how the team members are getting along.

I hang up, retrieve my telephone card, and turn to walk back down the hall. CIA-Man follows and quickly catches up with me. "We have dinner with Rotary tonight and then you have home stays. Tomorrow we have dinner at the Navy base," he says.

"I know," I reply. "But I am taking tomorrow night off. I will skip dinner at the Navy base. I am going to spend the evening with a friend."

"But we have planned dinner for you at the Officer's Club at the Navy base," he insists.

"I know, but I am going to skip dinner. The rest of the team will be there for dinner. Wilson-*san* will be in charge," I tell CIA-Man.

"You are scheduled for dinner at the Navy base," he continues.

"*Hai, so desu*," is my final response.

Just as I arrive back in the display room, the rest of the team and our hosts start walking towards me. It is time to leave. We return to the big glass front doors. Once outside, in the cold wind on the mountain, we are lined up in front of the building for the obligatory pictures with the company's managing director. Then we load on the bus once again.

- Hai, so desu -

As our bus pulls up to the hotel we are told we have 20 minutes to make dinner at a Japanese restaurant across the street and down an alley. We decide to take the escalator up to the hotel lobby and sit down on one of the comfortable couches there for a brief rest.

In the lobby we find our luggage still piled out in the open. The team members are upset. I run down the Japanese doctor who has been acting as the senior member of the Japanese Rotary group all day and ask him why our luggage is still sitting in the hotel lobby.

"That is where they are going to keep it tonight," he says.

"Don't they have a luggage room?"

"It is not large enough. You have too much luggage," the doctor says.

"I can't let them leave our luggage sitting out in the lobby all night," I tell him.

"It will be safe. They will watch it," he says. "Japan is a safe place. Nothing will happen to it."

"I still cannot let my people's luggage sit out in a hotel lobby all night. We have a computer, video equipment, and many valuables. We lost a battery pack to the video camera at one stop earlier. I can't risk leaving our equipment out in public anymore. I cannot ask my people to leave their belongings in the middle of a hotel lobby all night," I tell the doctor.

"But you have to. That is what the hotel is going to do with it. They will watch the luggage. It will be safe," he says.

"This is a Navy town," I remind the doctor. "Yokosuka is not your typical Japanese town. I cannot guarantee my people that their belongings will be safe all night in a hotel lobby. They all know you lock your cars when you get out of them. They don't think you really believe that Japan is all that safe anymore. They do not want to leave their luggage in a hotel lobby all night."

"But that is the plan," he says.

"Then we have to change the plan. I will rent a room myself so they have somewhere to put their luggage. Somewhere where they will feel it is safe," I tell the doctor.

He walks over to the registration desk and has a conversation with the clerk on duty. When he returns he tells me, "They do not have a room. All their rooms are rented for the night. We must go to dinner now. They are waiting on us."

"*Hai, so desu*," I respond, trying to buy a little time to think this one through. The doctor is getting miffed. He is a proctologist. I am glad he is not my doctor.

"*Sumimasen* - I'm sorry," I begin to explain. "We cannot go to dinner until we get this straightened out. If this hotel has no rooms, then I am going down the street to another hotel, rent a room, and let my people put all their luggage in it for the night. Then we will go to dinner with you."

The doctor says nothing. The look he gives me convinces me I never want to show up in his medical office. He heads back over to the desk with a couple of his Japanese Rotarians. They talk among themselves on the way and they talk to the clerk again for a few moments. The doctor motions for me to join them.

I walk over to the registration desk. The clerk hands me a registration card and a pen. I fill it out, reach into my pocket and hand him a credit card. The doctor pushes the card away. "The hotel is giving you the room for the night. There is no charge."

"*Arigato* - thank you," I tell the clerk. Then I thank the doctor, walk across the lobby to the other team members and tell them what has transpired. We find some luggage carts, load up our luggage, and carry it off to our room where we lock it up.

We are late for dinner.

- *Hai, so desu* -

After the traditional Japanese style dinner of *sushi, sashimi, tempora* and beer, I make the customary introductory speeches. The local Rotary club president then tells each of us who we are to leave with for our home stays.

I am to go with the club president.

Rick Ramsay is assigned to the doctor.

The club president and I leave the restaurant, walk down an alley to the main street and hail a taxi. We get into the taxi and my Rotarian host gives the driver some directions.

"You are going to stay with the president of the Yokosuka Chamber of Commerce and Industry tonight," he says.

"I am not going to stay with you?"

"*Hai so desu*, you are going to stay with Mister Okamoto. He is president of the Yokosuka Chamber of Commerce and Industry."

The cab continues out of the business district and up into the hills around the bay area. The streets become smaller and smaller. Shops give way to homes. The higher we climb up the narrow streets, the larger the homes get. Finally the cab pulls through an iron gate, up a curbed brick driveway and stops in front of a Western-style home. A man and woman await us under the front portico.

The Rotary Club president introduces me to the Okamotos, then he turns to me and says: "I will be here to pick you up at eight in the morning."

"That's not necessary," Mr. Okamoto says in perfect English, "my car will bring Mr. Whitney back to his hotel."

The Rotary Club president says something to Mr. Okamoto in Japanese. Mr. Okamoto replies in his native tongue. The conversation is fast and I only catch glimpses of it. It concerns whether or not the Rotary Club president will pick me up in the morning or Mr. Okamoto's company car will deliver me to the hotel. I can't figure out how they resolve it, but eventually we all do our customary bows, the Rotary Club president leaves in the taxi in which we arrived, and I am shown into the Okamotos' house.

I take off my shoes and leave them on the terrazzo pit of the entrance hallway. Putting on the visitor's slippers I am offered I am shown by Mr. Okamoto into what appears to be the den of the house.

The room is large by Japanese standards. It is lined with books, and filled, but not crowded with Western-style furniture. One end of the room is a large round structure with floor-to-ceiling windows hidden behind lace drapery. The ceiling is hardwood over beams, just like my home in the Florida Keys.

The floors of the room, and what I have seen of the rest of the house, are solid oak. They are covered with Oriental rugs accenting the various use areas. On one side of the den is a Steinway grand piano. Next to it is a 1920's Victrola in a chest-high cabinet that is in mint condition. In front of me, across the room from where I am sitting on a couch, and behind the two easy chairs facing the glass and marble coffee table between Mr. Okamoto and myself, is an upright Player piano.

Mrs. Okamoto – Fusako is how her husband has introduced her to me – comes into the room, sits a crystal bowl of fruit on the coffee table, and asks if I would like to have a drink. Her English is as perfect as her husband's.

"Coffee would be fine if it is not an inconvenience," I respond.

"It will take just a moment," she replies and walks down a long dining table that sits in a wing off the den. She turns at a China cabinet, walks across the end of the table, which is surrounded by a dozen fine handmade hardwood chairs, and disappears through a doorway into what I assume is the kitchen.

Mr. Okamoto and I exchange pleasantries. He asks me about my work and I explain that I am general manager and editor of a weekly newspaper in the Florida Keys. It impresses Japanese more when I tell them I am president and chief executive officer of a publishing company, but the truth is that I founded the company, it bears my name, and I only sold outside interests in it when I needed money to keep the newspaper running in the early days. I have difficulty stretching the truth too far, especially when I head a company that grosses less than $1 million a year. In Japan, it takes billions to make an impression.

Besides, running a weekly newspaper of 20,000 circulation has no real counterpart in Japan. Weekly community newspapers are not a popular item. The only publisher I have met this trip who dabbled in community journalism was a young Japanese in Oiso who managed to publish four or eight pages a month in a format reminiscent of our old legal-size mimeographed newsletters of the 1950s and '60s.

Journalism in Japan is a closed arena. The daily newspapers dominate with circulations in the tens of millions. Their news comes from reporters who are members of various "clubs" sponsored by agencies of government. Like business and government in Japan, newspapers and government walk hand in hand on literally every thing they do. You will find an occasional questioning of certain elements of government, but rarely do you find an outright attack on government like we saw in the '70s with the Watergate scandal in the U.S.

In a setting like this trying to explain American-style community journalism where every town has some type of access to a local, or near-local, newspaper is impossible. On the other hand, Japanese don't seem to exhibit the same need to see their names and faces in the newspaper that we see daily in our local newspaper offices in the United States. An open society seems to need the access to free expression at all levels. An insular society, like Japan's, adapts well to nationalistic expression and doesn't seem to demonstrate the need for free expression at the local level.

Japanese are more impressed with the fact that I once worked for The Associated Press and that I have been nominated for a Pulitzer Prize than they are with the fact that I am the head of a successful small newspaper enterprise. It doesn't matter that I never won a Pulitzer, it's simply – like the AP – an internationally recognized activity of a large enough scale to be recognizable to the Japanese.

Mrs. Okamoto returns with coffee, served in a delicate, gold-trimmed China cup. She sits in the chair next to her husband, across the coffee table from me.

"What would you like for breakfast?" She asks.

"I had my driver stop and we picked out the best fruit," Mr Okamoto says pointing to the bowl of fruit on the coffee table.

"What would you like of it for breakfast?"

I look at the bowl. In it are two oranges, an apple, a grapefruit, and a banana.

"That is a fine grapefruit," I comment. "Is it pink inside?"

"*Hai*," Mrs. Okamoto smiles.

"That is an Indian River grapefruit from Florida, north of where I live in the Florida Keys. It is a very fine grapefruit, It makes excellent juice," I reply. "The oranges, though, are not from Florida.

Your government does not allow the import of Florida oranges. I do not know why, but Japan bans our oranges and apparently permits our grapefruit to come in."

"*Ah, so desu,*" says Mr. Okamoto.

"*Ah, so desu,*" says Mrs. Okamoto.

"The apple is also Japanese. Japan does not allow American apples to be imported. It has something to do with the pesticides we use. But I will admit, the Japanese apple is a very good apple. I have one for breakfast every morning I can find one. We do not have that variety of apple in the United States, as far as I know."

"The banana?" Mr. Okamoto asks.

"Probably from the Caribbean islands or Central America," I reply. "That's where we get most of ours from, also."

Mrs. Okamoto left the room, and I take the opportunity to ask Mr. Okamoto about his work with the Yokosuka Chamber of Commerce and Industry.

"It is not my full-time job," he smiles. "I am the chairman of a company that owns several department stores."

"May I ask what department stores?"

"*Hai*, the Saikaya Department Stores. They have been in my family for three generations. My son is now the president of them," he says proudly.

"You have one next to the station in Fujisawa, right."

"Yes, that is one of ours. Have you been in it?"

"Yes, I visited it my first day here to get some idea of how prices were in Japan now."

"What did you find?" Mr. Okamoto asks.

"Your prices are very high compared to those in the U.S. On things that I am familiar with – shirts, slacks, jackets, towels, and such – I found Japanese prices to be from five to ten times as high as for similar items at home."

"*Ah, so desu.* It is expensive to live in Japan now," Mr. Okamoto said. "The *yen* is very strong."

"It purchases only about one quarter of what it did when I was last here in 1981," I say.

"Do you notice a lot of changes?" He asks.

"Many. I noticed that now you accept credit cards. I do not recall that in department stores when I was here before. How much of your business is done on credit?"

"Not very much. About 80 percent of our business is still done in cash," he says, rising to go to the old Victrola. "Have you ever seen one of these?" He asked.

"Not as totally restored as the one you have. I have a cabinet a bit smaller than that in which I installed a stereo system for my wife. Mine does not play records. Does yours?"

He opens the cabinet doors and takes out a 78-rpm record, lifts the top of the cabinet, moves the megaphone and amplifier from the turntable, puts the record on the turntable, turns the crank on the side of the cabinet, places the needle on record and
it begins to play an old big band tune. Then he shows me the rest of the records in the cabinet. It is an extensive collection.

When the record finishes, he crosses the room to an upright piano not far from the couch and chairs on which we have been sitting.

"Have you ever seen a Player piano?" He asks.

"Yes, several."

Mr. Okamoto raises the lid on the keyboard, reaches up to an overhead shelf, turns on what looks like a compact disk player, and then takes a CD from a plastic sleeve and inserts it in the player. The piano starts to play, keys operating without anyone touching them, just like an old player piano, yet this one is driven by an electronic medium. We listen to another song.

"May I show you my garden?" He asks.

"Certainly," I answer.

Mr. Okamoto leads me to a door in the round, beamed ceiling end of the larger room in which we have been sitting. He opens the door and motions to a pair of slippers sitting outside the door.

"You may wear those."

I slip out of my house slippers and into the garden slippers. We step out into the backyard of the house. Pointing to a wing to our left, Mr. Okamoto says, "That is part of the old house. My mother still lives in that wing. Over here where the grass is is where our old house used to be. We built the new one, and then tore down the old one."

He walks me along a landscaped section of trees, flag stones, and rock garden along the rear of the property. It is evident that the garden is still very new. The trees are propped up with braces and many of the limbs are still wired into position and heavily wrapped with cloth as they are being trained. At the side of the house, Mr. Okamoto points to a large white, three-story building that looks much like an office building next door.

"That is my brother's home," he says.

There is no continuity to the two homes. They are a contrast of old and new. The Okamoto family has made efficient use of the plot of land that has apparently been in their family for several generations.

Back inside the house, Mr. Okamoto takes me over to the grand piano in the circular end of the big room in which we have been sitting. On the piano is a picture of a young Japanese woman in evening dress.

"My daughter," he says. "She studied piano and opera before she married."

Next to the picture is a music program from Paris. I see his daughter's name listed as one of the featured artists.

"Is your daughter a professional musician?" I ask.

"No, she is married and is raising a family," Mr Okamoto smiles proudly.

He leads me out into the hallway where he is joined by his wife. They ask me to sign the guest register. I do, and notice that I am the third to sign in English out of many guests. The other two are American Navy officers, who apparently have been in command of Yokosuka Navy Base.

The Okamotos show me my room. It is a western style room, quite elegantly furnished. Mr. Okamoto takes me into the bathroom adjacent. We change from our house slippers to bathroom slippers which are neatly placed just inside the bathroom door.

"This is your bathroom. It has a urinal and the toilet seat is heated," he says as he proudly shows them both to me. The urinal is a full-length one, much like the ones you find in schools in the U.S. I wonder what convenience they have for women guests, other than the heated toilet set, but I am too modest to ask.

Next the Okamotos show me their wing of the house – where they spend most of their time. They have a kitchen, small family dining area, and what we would call a Florida room in Florida. It has large glass sliding doors that open into the back yard. A giant screen television graces the cabinets on one wall. Mrs. Okamoto has a comfortable easy chair, and Mr. Okamoto a recliner. It is the most western room I have ever seen in a Japanese home.

Mr. Okamoto walks to the cabinet by the television and opens it. He holds out a microphone and smiles. Inside he has his own karaoke machine.

"The bath is off our bath room," he says, walking me across the hallway from the Florida room. It is equipped with a full shower room in which there is a large tub. Unlike other Japanese homes that I have stayed in, the tub in this one is empty. Mr. Okamoto shows me how easily it is to fill it with piping hot water.

"Would you like to take a hot bath?" He asks.

"I would really prefer a hot shower, if that is okay," I reply.

"That is fine," he says showing me where the towels are kept and walking me back to my room where Mrs. Okamoto has laid out a robe for me.

"Make yourself at home," he says, leaving me at my bedroom door.

With the exception of a Japanese writer I spent a night with in the '80s, I have always been amazed at the lack of books in most Japanese homes. The writer not only had books, he had filled one room of his family's pleasant, but compact, house with bookcases on rails that allowed him to pack a full room solid with books from floor to ceiling with the only open space in the room the distance between any two files. To access all the books in the room, you slid one floor-to-ceiling bookcase down the tracks against the next one revealing the books on the opposite side of the bookcase and those on one side of the next bookcase on the track. It was an ingenious system. I never lacked for something to read in his house. His two school-age children spent hours in the stacks doing research on their school work. A good portion of the library was in English, so I, too, had access to a lot of information on Japan, particularly Asian economics since that was the writer's specialty.

Before trundling down the hall in my slippers to take a shower I decide to check out the books in the Okamoto's parlor to see if I can find one to read after I go to bed. There are a few books, some in English, but mostly on classical music, not one of my favorite topics. On the coffee table I spot a large-format, hardbound book on using Japanese antiques to compliment décor in interior design. It intrigues me, so I take it back to the bedroom to read after I shower.

I head for the shower, located down the hallway between the new addition to the house and the old Okamoto home. To get to it, I have to pass the door to the Okamoto's den. They have switched to their evening, leisure *kimonos* and are sitting in their respective chairs watching the large-screen television on the opposite wall. I nod to them and turn into the bathroom across the hallway. What I have just witnessed, with the exception of the *kimonos* and the Japanese language on the television, could be a scene from thousands of Midwestern or Southern homes. It is so far removed from the Japanese homes I have visited over the years that it is impossible to draw a clear line of distinction.

I shower in the large bathroom, dry with two large white towels Mrs. Okamoto has laid out for me, dress in a large terry cloth *kimono* she has hung out for my use, slip back into my plastic slippers and return to my room, saying "good night" to the Okamotos as I pass their den door.

I stretch out in a large overstuffed easy chair with my feet propped up on the bed and begin reading the book on Japanese antiques. I am intrigued by what the Japanese refer to as antiques for use in interior decorating. For the most part, although they are often hundreds of years old, up through the '50s when I first visited Japan many of them were commonly used household items – braziers, storage trunks, *tatami* mats, etc.   Apparently as Japan has grown more Western – and much more affluent – over the past four decades, it also has acquired more of a Western attitude instead of a utilitarian attitude about many traditional household objects. Rather than using antiques, the Japanese seem to prefer to put them on display. For utility, if they want a more traditional look, they prefer today to have furniture manufactured in Early American, or Colonial, design and accent these custom-made arrangements with restored decorative Japanese antique pieces. A pleasant enough mix that begs the question: What is their real preference in furniture and style – Oriental or Occidental?

I climb into the large Western-style bed, pull the down-filled comforter up around my neck, and go to sleep pondering the question.

- Hai, so desu -

I am not sure what woke me up this morning. As I shuffle from the door of my room to the bathroom, I notice the Okamotos are up. Mr. Okamoto calls to me from down the hall, "Your breakfast will be ready in a few minutes."

I am still wondering if I woke up on my own, or if some movement in the house awoke me. Or if, like a lot of things you experience in Japan, the Okamotos awoke me very subtly.

It is chilly in the house this morning. The heated toilet seat is a nice touch. I shave, go back to my room and dress, and walk down the hardwood-floored hallway to the kitchen-breakfast nook area. Mr. Okamoto is seated at the table. Mrs. Okamoto is just placing my breakfast on the table at a seat that provides me a full view through sliding glass doors of the family's Japanese garden that I got a tour of last night.

Mrs. Okamoto listened to what I said last night very closely. This morning the *asahan* – breakfast – laid out before me consists of the traditional Japanese bowl of *miso shiro* – soybean soup with finely chopped green onions and other goodies. In front of me is a glass of freshly squeezed grapefruit juice, Indian River variety from Florida, of course, and thin slices of the Japanese apples I so highly praised. There is a noticeable absence of the oranges that were not from Florida. Toast and coffee round out the meal.

Mr. Okamoto and I engage in casual conversation over breakfast. Mr. Okamoto hovers in the background waiting on us. She never joins us at the table.

Mr. Okamoto asks, "Is there anything you need while you are here?"

"Maybe you could help me with one thing. I have had trouble finding an embroidered table cloth that my wife asked me to bring her. I have looked in several stores and watched shops, but it does not seem that embroidery – the real lace kind like you used to see on the back of Japanese taxi seats – is much in demand anymore. Do you know where I could find a good embroidered table cloth?"

He pulled a pen from his shirt pocket, took one of his business cards that he had placed on the table for me, and begin sketching a small map.

"We have some fine embroidery in the new part of our store in Yokosuka. It is not far from your hotel. Just walk down this street, turn here, and go in the entrance to the second store. You will find the embroidery on the fifth floor," Mr. Okamoto says.

"I appreciate that. I will try and get by the store before we leave. Thank you very much. My wife will appreciate it," I say, putting the card in my pocket. Since we are talking about his stores, I decide to revisit the business conversation Mr. Okamoto and I were engaged in last night when he broke it off to show me his music box and other collectibles.

"Last night we were talking about your department stores and credit cards," I venture.

"*Hai, so desu,*" he replies.

"I was going to ask you what interest rates are charged on credit cards in Japan, but we got off on something else," I say as I finish the last of my toast.

"I wouldn't know about that," Mr. Okamoto says. "My son would be the one to ask. He is now president of the company."

It is time to move on, so I don't question why the chairman, the head of the company, does not know the current interest rates on charge cards, but it seems curious to me. Remembering that the chairmanship of Japanese corporations is often more a ceremonial position than an operating position, although most chairmen sit in on major policy making decisions or their approval is sought before the decision is made, I allow to myself that Mr. Okamoto's apparent lack of knowledge of current charge card rates could be real.

Mr. Okamoto has arisen from the table and is giving me a quick tour of the kitchen, explaining to me how they have had it custom designed to accommodate the American appliances it incorporates. It is definitely a Western kitchen, albeit still small by our standards. His wife beams as he gives me the tour. He next suggests a morning walk.

At the *genkan* – the entrance to the house where you take off your shoes and leave them – I find my shoes lined up alongside his, both pairs highly shined. I have seen no servants in the house, so I assume his wife has shined my shoes as she customarily prepared his for the next day sometime the evening before, or this morning before I awoke.

Mr. Okamoto walks me down the brick driveway, through the gate, and then turns up the street which leads to a building on top the high hill on whose side his home is built. We walk up the brick street to the building and Mr. Okamoto points out that it is a building he and members of the neighborhood have helped build to house a library. It is a modern building, not yet open for the day. We tour the grounds, well laid out with brick and stone walkways with benches on which people can sit and enjoy the view out over the town below.

A couple of other men join us. Mr. Okamoto introduces them to me. It appears they all made a morning constitution of the walk to the top of the hill.

We spend about 15 minutes on the hilltop and then start back down the street. Coming up the street to meet us is the president of the Yokosuka Rotary Club who dropped me off the evening before. A cab has dropped him at the foot of the hill where the street turns off to go by the Okamotos and then up the hill to the small park.

Mr. Okamoto and he exchange a few words in Japanese, and then Mr. Okamoto turns to me: "Come, my car is ready to take us to your hotel. I hope you will excuse me. I have to go on to Kawasaki for a meeting today."

The chauffeur has parked the car, running, in front of the Okamoto house. As we walk to it, Mr. Okamoto motions me over to the small portico by the front door for pictures with he and his wife. The Rotary president snaps some with their camera, then his camera, and finally mine. We load into the black car – not quite a stretch limousine, but still a relatively large, black and comfortable automobile – for the trip downtown.

I sit in the back with Mr. Okamoto. The Rotary president sits up front with
the chauffeur.

- Hai, so desu -

Back at the hotel, the chauffeur lets me out of the car. Mr. Okamoto also gets out. We exchange pleasantries, bows, and good wishes for each of our respective futures. He excuses himself, reminding me of the meeting in Kawasaki he must make, climbs back into the car and his chauffeur whisks him off down the street towards the heart of Yokosuka.

The Rotary president and I ride the two flights of escalators up to the lobby of the hotel. In the lobby, Bain is talking to a couple of young Japanese women, White and Ramsay are seated on a couch not far away.

The Rotary president heads for the coffee shop across the lobby where CIA-man and a couple other Japanese are seated.

"How did it go last night," I ask White and Ramsay.

"You're in deep shit," Ramsay says.

"What for now?"

"The doctor was my home stay. He doesn't think much of you. Says you are just like most Americans – pushy, arrogant, demeaning. Says you're a *bakayaro* – stupid son-of-a-bitch," Ramsay says.

"Guess I disturbed the *wa* a bit yesterday over the luggage deal."

"You apparently disturbed more than the *wa*," White says.

"What's the schedule for today? Do we get some time off for shopping this morning before we have to go to the Rotary meeting?"

"I've got to work it out with the *honcho* over there," I reply.

"Have you heard anything about the rooms? Have they assigned them yet?"

"They haven't told us anything," White says. "We're only the peons, you know."

I walk over to the coffee shop, sit down in the middle of the Japanese Rotarians, order a cup of coffee, and ask the president, "My men want to do a little shopping. Do we have our room assignments for tonight yet? If they could take their things from my room to theirs, and have a couple hours for shopping, they would be happy."

"The rooms will be ready later," he says. "If you want to go shopping, we will take you."

"I think they want to go on their own. They all know where the stores are down the street, and won't get lost. They just want a couple of hours to do a little walking around and shopping by themselves."

"We will take them to the stores," he says, looking around the table at the other men who nod in agreement.

"*Dózo* – please – let me handle this," I say. "They have been with you and their hosts all day yesterday and all night last night, and they just want to spend a couple of hours on their own."

"*Chotto matte kudasai* – just a moment," the Rotary president says, getting up from the table. He is followed by the other Japanese. They huddle on the far side of the lobby toward the front of the building. I finish my coffee, get up, and walk back over to White and Ramsay who have been joined by Bain and Wilson.

"What's the deal? We going to get to go shopping?" One of them asks.

"You're going to get to go shopping. One way or another, I'll get us a couple hours off. They're over there talking about it now. They'll have to make a phone call to someone. Just watch. Give me a few minutes and I'll have you out of here. I've already earned the rank of Stupid SOB, so I might as well push it on through," I say, waiting for the Japanese group to give some indication they wanted to talk some more.

Finally the head man looks my way. I walk over to him. "We are going to go shopping. I have given my people two hours off to visit the shops downtown. They will be back here at eleven o'clock to get ready for your Rotary meeting. Will their rooms be ready by then?"

"*Chotto matte kudasai*," the leader said. "We will go with you."

I reach into my coat pocket and pull out the schedule the Japanese Rotarians had given us when we arrived. I pointed to the entry for that morning.

"*Gomen nasai* - I'm sorry. It says 'free' here on our schedule and that means free time to my men. They want their free time and I have given it to them. They will be back at eleven o'clock."

I bow, turn and cross the lobby to the team members. "Okay, you're off until eleven o'clock. Just make sure you are back here. They should have your rooms ready by then."

"Did they give you any trouble?" White asked.

"Don't ask. I've just given you until eleven o'clock to do whatever you like, so go do it."

When I leave the lobby on my own to head downtown, three of the Japanese were still huddling in their corner. Two are on the telephones. I wave and step on the down escalator.

- Hai, so desu -

The Saikaya Department Store, and its newer annex, is not difficult to find. Mr. Okamoto's map is flawless. I enter the store at its main entrance on the corner, a block off the main street behind the old store. I take about 10 steps into the building when a Japanese man approaches me.

"Mr. Whitney," he bows and introduces himself as the manager of the store. "I am to show you some embroidery. Please this way."

The man catches me totally off guard. I had not expected to run into anyone who knew my name. Mr. Okamoto apparently called ahead, on his way to Kawasaki, and told his store manager to make sure I was shown the finest embroidery in the store. I follow the man up the escalators to the floor on which linens and other items for the home and kitchen were sold. The manager takes me to a counter where a young Japanese man and woman are waiting with several embroidered table clothes to show me. I am absolutely taken aback by their attention to detail, their explanation in respectable English of the finer details of the embroidery work.

They show me a half dozen sets of fine table linens, each with price tags far more than I had expected to pay. Eventually I choose the most expensive – the Japanese custom – and they go to work folding each of the napkins that go with the table cloth into neat, cornered folds, packing each of them in a special box that holds the folded table cloth and napkins precisely as they have been folded. They then wrap the box and place it in a separate bag with handles on it. Thank God, I have a credit card with enough credit left on it to pay for the purchase. They process the transaction, and the young man hands me back the credit card saying, "We hope your wife enjoys it."

I thank them profusely, bow, and turn to walk away.

"Is there anything else you would like to see?" the manager asks.

There's certainly not much more I can afford, but since I have a hour or so left, I ask him if the store has a sporting goods department.

"*Hai*, please follow me," he says. We go down a couple of floors on the escalators and then through a skyway walk to the main store.

"This is not my store," the manager of the annex says. "Sporting goods are right here," he motions to a department just off the skywalk to our right. "I will get the manager of this store to help you."

"That is not necessary," I tell him. "I just want to look around and then I have to go back to my hotel."

"I will get someone to help you," he says.

"I will be all right by myself," I say.

He keeps looking back across the skyway as if he was not supposed to have crossed it. Yet he does not want to turn me loose on my own. It is evident that Mr. Okamoto has told him to take good care of me, to see that I find anything I want.

"Go ahead, I will be all right. I will tell Mr. Okamoto that you have treated me very well. I am most grateful to you. *Arigato* – thank you," I say bowing deeply to him.   He still hesitates. I bow again. "*Arigato*," I repeat.

"Will you be all right? Can you find what you want? I will get you some help," he repeats.

"I will be all right," I assure him again, bowing and extending my hand. "*Domo arigato gozaimasu.*" I try the more formal version of "thank you." He bows, shakes my hand, and finally leaves reluctantly.

I make a pass through the sporting goods department, checking out the golf clubs. I am astounded at the prices – $3,000 and $4,000 sets of golf clubs, two to three times the price for the same, or similar models, in the U.S. Now I know why I see Japanese men walking around in full golf dress carrying only a single golf club. They apparently are on their way to the neighborhood driving range. Most never play a round of golf, but they like, and dress, the look of a professional golfer, right down to the long-sleeve sweater tied around their necks, the arms crossed on their chest, the sweater covering their back – a look that went out in the U.S. several years ago but one that persists in Japanese sports equipment advertising photos.

This store is too rich for my blood, so I return to the street level, cross the main street and enter the street level mall that runs for a couple of blocks under the high-rise stores and office buildings along Yokosuka's main drag. There are hundreds of small shops along the covered mall. In one I find a "Rover Mini" duffel bag and buy it – the second duffel I have purchased on this trip to hold all the gifts the various groups have given us along the way.

The Mini Rover is my favorite car in Japan. If I lived here, I would own one if I owned a car. I am a small car fan although I have owned some big ones, including a near-classic Lincoln Continental with the rear suicide doors. At home I drive Volkswagens and I have seen some VWs in great shape here in Japan, especially a Karmann Ghia that drives around Fujisawa.

Still the Rover Mini seems to me to be the car best suited to Japan traffic and limited parking. It is a small, boxy little car built by the British to withstand that country's intemperate climate. It is perfect for Japan. The Rover Mini bag lifts my spirits.

- Hai, so desu -

Back at the hotel the room assignments for the night have been made. The rest of the guys are anxious to get their things out of my room and into their own. They're all waiting for me in the lobby. We make the shift, take time to freshen up a bit, and then meet in front of the hotel where the bus is waiting to take us to our Rotary meeting.

The meeting is not that far away. Once we get there we are ushered into a room that appears to be a security center for the building we are in, and asked to stay put. The Japanese go about their business. Finally we are told they are ready for us in the meeting. Our hosts line us up and lead us to the door. When we enter, we are welcomed by a standing ovation from the gathered Rotarians. This has happened several times before, but I never quite get used to it. Rotary where I come from is a more loosely organized breakfast, luncheon or dinner meeting. Few groups sing songs. Fewer still seat their guests by age from front to rear as many groups in Japan seem to do.

Women, conspicuously absent, except for a secretary who takes information at the door and possibly her assistant, at Japanese Rotary meetings, are common place at most meetings I attend in the U.S.

- Hai, so desu -

After the Rotary meeting we are loaded back on the bus and head down the street to Yokosuka Naval Station, the afternoon stop on our itinerary. The bus rumbles down the street, and just before we get to the main gate at Yokosuka, it pulls over to the side of the street. I look at my watch. It is five minutes to one. We are not due to be at the base until one o'clock, so the bus sits outside the gate for five minutes. At precisely one o'clock, it pulls up to the gate where a white-haired Japanese gentleman boards and is introduced as a local chamber of commerce official who will be our host and tour guide for the afternoon.

Before we begin our tour of the base, we are taken to the base headquarters building to meet the base commander. The headquarters building is the same one used by the Japanese Imperial Navy up through the end of World War II. Along its walls are many black and white photographs depicting the history of Yokosuka, first as the heart of Japanese Imperial Navy operations, then as the United States' main navy base during the Occupation, and now as a joint Japan-U.S. naval center.

I have been told the base commander's name is Capt. Rice and quietly wonder whether he drew the assignment because of his particular talents, or because of his name. We are led into his office. I realize Capt. Rice – now in Navy blue dress uniform instead of civvies – was the tall, blond American I watched arrive, with an older Caucasian and a Japanese gentleman, and enter the *sumo* matches yesterday.

When I am introduced to him, I say: "We saw you sitting on the front row at the matches yesterday."

"Ah, yes," he smiles. "I accompanied the admirals to the matches. Did you enjoy them?"

It turns out Capt. Rice came up through the ranks to become an officer, and eventually a captain and base commander. He views his job more as a city manager than a base commander.

"Like running a city of 30,000 people," is how he describes his job. The admirals run the fleet, the base commander manages the base physical facilities and those sailors assigned to the base in support of fleet activities. Today only about 9,000 of the people on Yokosuka are Americans, or employees of the American navy. The remainder are Japanese naval personnel and their support forces.

As we leave his office, the captain reminds us that we are invited to dinner for some "good-old American cooking" at the Officers Club once we complete our tour of the base. On the way out the door, I turn to him out of earshot of our Japanese hosts, and say, "If you won't be offended, I have another dinner date tonight and would like to leave the Officers Club before dinner is served. It's my night to go AWOL."

The captain smiles, "That's fine. I need to cut it a little short, also. I may just drop in for a few minutes before dinner."

- Hai, so desu -

Tours of Yokosuka Navy base have always been interesting. It was one Japan's busiest bases during World War II, and was never bombed because Allied forces believed they would need to capture the base early in any invasion of Japan and use the base, and its super dry-docks, in the eventual defeat of Japan.

It has been Japan's Annapolis in the past, and its history is a history of the old Imperial Japanese Navy and the newer Japan Maritime Self Defense Force. The latter has grown to be the third largest navy in the world, although its mission – by constitutional decree – is strictly defensive.

My first visits to Yokosuka were in the 1950s when many of its buildings were simply old Japanese Navy facilities that had been converted to American use. Any Japanese on the base at that time were mostly shipyard helpers and base laborers. The base is surrounded by high hills that are part of its physical facilities. The first time I saw the base, most of the tunnels cut into the hills were still open and being used for storage and other purposes.

When I returned to the base in the early '80s, some of the caves had been blocked off, there were more American-built structures, and some of the base had been returned to the Japanese who had built some sleek modern, state-of-the-art destroyers that were to become the nucleus of their new navy.

One of the hush-hush topics – too sensitive to speak of in public, or question American or Japanese naval officials about – was the presence, or absence, of nuclear weapons at Yokosuka. Again, by constitution, the Japanese had sworn off nukes and it was a silent understanding that no nukes arrive in Yokosuka aboard American vessels. The Japanese navy would never have a nuke aboard, of course.

Over the years I discovered an interesting story that might explain where all the nukes went. American ships certainly left U.S. ports with nukes on board, but where did they go when the ships pulled into Yokosuka and other Japanese ports? I suspect many of them found a place to roost in the Bonin Islands, 500 miles south of Tokyo. The Bonins play a unique role in Japanese history. They were originally settled by Caucasian mariners, but eventually ended up in Japanese hands. The white settlers who had by then built homes and families on the Bonins were forced to declare themselves either in or out of Japan. Many of them chose to become Japanese citizens, the first *gaijin* to have the foreigner label removed, and the first Japanese citizens to become non-Japanese Japanese.

The Bonin Islanders got along pretty well on their own, exchanging commerce with the many ships of many countries that came their way, but always with allegiance to Japan, which they now considered they motherland. Then along came the big war in the Pacific. The Bonin Islanders were forced to back their Japanese citizenship by conforming to the conscription laws and supporting the war in which their motherland was supposedly attempting to free Asia from the yoke of white imperialism. Of course, the Japanese navy invested heavily in the islands, and particularly in some of the large caves on some of those islands.

At least one huge cave was reportedly lined with copper, and maybe lead, and set up as a sort of last-ditch archive for Japan's imperial papers and paraphernalia should the war take a desperate turn in the wrong direction. Since the caves were not needed for archival purposes during the war, they became munitions stores. At the war's end, American forces were quick to seize the islands, the caves, and make the Japanese-Japanese disappear. The Caucasian Japanese were allowed to remain and restore their lost farms and businesses.

For the most part, under American occupation, the Bonin Islands were more or less invisible. They remained occupied by the U.S. for a quarter of a century and then, during the big turnover period in the 1970s when Okinawa along with other American holdings that had been wrestled from the Japanese during the war, the Bonins were returned to Japan.

Once I learned the Bonin story, I pretty well understood where American nukes went in the early years to avoid coming into Japanese ports. But, following the turnover, no one wants to talk about whether or not the Japanese might be letting Americans keep a few nukes nearby in the Bonins, a violation of the Japanese Constitution denouncing war and nuclear devices.

My best guess is there is still a diplomatic slight-of-hand going on over nukes in Japan. It is buried in silence.

On today's tour of Yokosuka, more and more of the local caves have been sealed. There appear to be few new buildings on the American sector of the base. The giant dry-docks are in full use. One of the biggest surprises to me comes when our bus turns a corner as it weaves its away around the dry-docks and there before us are three submarines tied up, all flying the old Japanese battle flag. For some reason I just wasn't ready for that, but then I guess any navy as large as Japan's is certainly going to have submarines in active service.

The bus pulls up at the foot of the gangway to the *U.S.S. Blue Ridge*, a signal-communications ship tied up today in Yokosuka's basin. When all else fails, the *Blue Ridge* is America's link with the world outside Japan. Its mission is providing communications for the military, and I assume the diplomatic corps, with U.S. elements in the rest of the world – should the need arise. We are to get a tour of the ship, which resembles a large, grey floating porcupine – antennas of every size and shape sticking up from its clean-shaven deck and mounted around all edges of the superstructure and bridge. We make our way to the ward room on the *Blue Ridge*. The ship is getting a little long of tooth. Compared to the ultra-modern Japanese destroyer I visited on my last trip to Yokosuka, the *Blue Ridge* looks like it is only a couple leagues from the cutting torch.

On deck I look across the basin and see the American aircraft carrier *Midway* tied up for repairs. Is there some cruel irony in the fact the U.S. bases the *Midway* in Japan? Is it a reminder to the Japanese that the Battle of Midway was the beginning of the end for the air and naval supremacy the Imperial Japanese Navy enjoyed for the first hundred days of the Pacific War? I ask a couple of our navy guides. They chuckle.

- Hai, so desu -

Our tour of the Navy base wraps up at the Officers Club. They've done some remodeling since I was here the last time, but it's basically the same Yokosuka Officers Club I have visited in the past.

After a few leisure minutes we are shown a private dining room where a service bar has been set up. Before I finish my first Diet Coke, Capt. Rice arrives. We exchange pleasantries, and I excuse myself and head for the door.

CIA-man of the day asks where I am going. "Out on my own for the evening," I tell him.

"You are scheduled to eat dinner with the captain," he says.

"I have already made my apologies to the captain. He understands. Wilson-*san* will be in charge of the team for the rest of the evening." I walk out of the room into the hallway.

CIA-man says, "Wait, please."

I stop in the hallway while he goes and gets the Japanese man from the chamber of commerce. They both approach me.

"You are scheduled to have dinner with the captain," Chamber of Commerce says.

"I know, but I cleared it with the captain this afternoon. I am finished for the day, and am leaving the base."

"Where are you going?" Chamber of Commerce asks.

"Out for the evening. I have a personnel visit to make."

"You are scheduled to be here."

"I know, but I have been excused by the captain, so I am leaving."

The two Japanese huddle for a minute. I turn and start down the hall towards the front entrance to the Officers Club.

"*Chotto matte kudasai* – just a minute, please," Chamber of Commerce yells softly to me. I turn and wait for him to catch up.

"How are you going to leave?"

"I'm going out the front door, catch a base taxi to the front gate, and walk off the base," I say.

"You cannot do that. I have to check you off the base," Chamber of Commerce says.

"*Daijóobu* - certainly," I reply.

Chamber of Commerce walks with me out the front door, then asks me to wait a minute while he crosses the parking lot to the bus we arrived in. He speaks to the bus driver who, after a couple of minutes of conversation, starts the bus. Chamber of Commerce motions for me to come to the bus. We board and head out of the parking lot to the road that leads back to the main entrance to the base. The bus driver stops in a parking lot a couple of hundred yards up the hill from the main gate. Chamber of Commerce motions for me to follow him. We walk to the main gate area where he tells me to stand by while he talks to the guards.

There is a steady flow of Japanese leaving through the front gate, an occasional American. I watch as Chamber of Commerce talks to the guards in the office with an open window adjacent to the gates. An American Marine looks over towards me. I catch his eye and make a slow motion with my head towards the gate. He nods in the affirmative.

Chamber of Commerce tells me I can now leave. I bow to him, "*Arigato -*
thank you," and am on my way.

On the way through the gate, I wave at the Marine. He nods back with a smile. I am finally out of here. I need the break.

Visits to Yokosuka have always been exhausting.

- Hai, so desu -

I'm down to the last English-language, Chamber of Commerce-
type publication left in the news rack and wondering what I'm going
to read next. I'm sitting in the center of the lobby of a resort hotel on
the edge of Hakone National Park playing a sort of Japanese version
of the Mexican standoff with the governor of the local Rotary
district.

We're doing the seniority thing in Japanese: "I'm your
superior so I'll make you wait 10 to 20 minutes." Dinner with the
governor was to have been at 6 p.m. It is now 6:45 p.m. He and his
entourage sit in one corner of the lobby trying to figure me out. I am
sitting in a big chair in the center of the sunken lobby leisurely
reading all the newspapers.

For two days one of my team members, Paul White, has been
sick. Yesterday he began getting a sore throat. It all started when we
snuck in a couple hours of shopping in Yokosuka before being
herded off to a Rotary club meeting, where we made our
presentations in Japanese before heading for Yokosuka Naval Base
where Paul began to notice he was getting a sore throat.

We spent the afternoon climbing up and down ladders on the
American admiral's flagship in Yokosuka Naval Base, dined with
the base commander, and then tried to grab a good night's sleep in a
local hotel after having spent the previous night at the homes of
various Japanese Rotarians. By this morning Paul's throat was really
giving him fits.

The local Rotarians, who were already upset with me because
two days ago I refused to let them leave our luggage stacked in the
lobby of a hotel in the old Navy town Yokosuka overnight while we
went on home stays, gathered us up early this morning, loaded us on
a bus and shipped us off for Odawara where we toured an old castle
and made a presentation to another Rotary Club.

The bus ride took all morning. By the time we got to the
Rotary luncheon, Paul could barely speak. As soon as lunch was
over we were loaded back on the bus and whisked off to see other
sites in the area. I asked the Japanese if we could stop by a pharmacy
and get Paul some cough medicine.

But, we had "the schedule" to keep. Every time I reminded
the translator that we needed to stop and get some throat medicine

for Paul, he countered with "we are behind schedule" and needed to keep pushing. Japanese Rotarians don't get behind schedule.

So when Paul couldn't swallow enough to taste the green tea at a late afternoon tea ceremony I reminded them that it was essential that we stop and get him some medicine. Again, they reminded me we were behind schedule, that we had to get back to the hotel, that they would take care of him when we got caught up.

Back on the bus, up the road past at least a couple of pharmacies, and on to the hotel we went. We unloaded in the rain at the front door, walked inside and our Japanese hosts stopped us in the lobby as the team members started to head for their rooms.

It was 5:30 p.m. We had been going solid since 8:30 a.m.

"The governor will be here for dinner shortly. We will have dinner at six o'clock," one of the Japanese Rotarians said to me.

"Look, I've got a problem with that," I said. "First of all I've got a sick team member and your people have refused to stop and get him medicine. I'm going to take care of him. Besides that, I asked you early today for a full schedule so I could tell my people what we were going to do and I have yet to see it. You did not tell me until less than an hour ago that there was a dinner with the governor scheduled for tonight."

"We have to wait for the governor," the Rotarian said, just as the governor's car drove up and all the Japanese lined up and bowed like a string of shooting gallery ducks that were being mowed down by Annie Oakley.

The governor, whom I had already met a few times and who had attended an earlier tea ceremony with his wife, entered the lobby and was brought over to where I was standing. We went through the same formal introductions we did every time we met.

"I have to go to Hokkaido tomorrow," the governor said. "I have moved dinner up to six o'clock, because I have to catch an early plane."

"Fine," I replied. "But, I have a sick man and I want him taken care of. Your people have been putting us off all day."

At that point the Japanese who was working as our interpreter that day stepped in along with the second in rank from the local Rotary group. They did not like what I had said to the governor.

"What do you want us to do?" The interpreter asked.

"Get Paul to a pharmacy right now. Do you understand NOW?"

They grabbed Paul and hustled him off.

"I've given the rest of my team members the night off since we had no advance notice of this dinner. They are tired and need the break. I'm going to my room and freshen up," I told the governor. "I'll be back down to have dinner with you at six o'clock."

I was back in the lobby five minutes early. Paul was no where to be seen. The governor and his herd of underlings were seated off in a corner of the lobby. I grabbed all the English language publications in the news rack and headed for a big easy chair smack-dab in the middle of the lobby.

The seniority wait set in. At about 15 minutes past six one of the Japanese from the governor's entourage came over to suggest they were ready for supper.

"What did you do with White-*san*?" I asked.

"They took him to a hospital."

"Is he that bad?"

"I'll check," the man said and went back to the governor's group where they went into conference, one leaving the crowd for a few minutes.

Five minutes later the man came back to where I was sitting and said, "Mr. White has a temperature of 39.7 and they are going to give him some medicine."

"That's a pretty good fever," I replied. "Are they going to keep him in the hospital?"

The Japanese looked at me like I had asked an inappropriate question.

"I want to know what you plan to do with Paul. I'll wait right here until you find out," I said and turned back to the last thing I had to read, a Chamber of Commerce tabloid.

There is another conference going on around the governor over in the corner. People are coming and going, some towards the phone. I read on, watching them out of the corner of my eye. A little before seven, the governor stands up and starts my way. I wait until he reaches the center of the lobby and stand up.

"I'm sorry, but I have to catch an early plane. I'll have to miss dinner," he says.

"I'm sorry, too," I replied. "I'm concerned about Paul, so I'll just wait here until someone lets me know what is going on."

The governor extended his hand and bowed. I returned the gestures and he was off trailed by a group of local Rotarians who bowed him into his car.

It was a little after seven when the group returned with Paul. He had been given a shot and medication for his fever and sore throat. All he wanted to do was go to bed. As soon as he walked into the elevator I turned to the group of eight Japanese still hanging around in the lobby and said,

"Okay fellows, let's go to dinner."

Walking across the lobby of the hotel to the restaurant one of the Japanese looked at me and said, "Maybe White-*san* gets sick because he is so fat." Paul is on the stout side. The remark was uncalled for.

Mustering my best Japanese I looked at the man and gave him my interpretation of: "Maybe you're so rude, because you're so short."

It was a strange evening.

- Hai, so desu -

Asking someone how much money they make is simply not a Japanese trait. At least that's what I thought until it happened to me at dinner tonight. Maybe I was set up, but it was something I wasn't prepared for when it came.

The team members have the evening off. They are tired and want some space. They have been herded around by our hosts for several days without a break and just want to get off by themselves where they don't have to make an effort to keep up with the Japanese.

I am honoring the daily request that we eat dinner with a group of local Rotarians. Dinner is in a French restaurant in an upscale tourist hotel. It is a first-class layout. The menu is in French with one item – the nightly special – in Japanese clipped into the upper right hand corner of the inside of the oversized two-page menu. My French is nothing to rave about but it is better than that of the Japanese, including one whom I have worked with before as an interpreter.

There are eight of us. The *honcho*, or senior man, in the group of seven Japanese is seated across the table from me. We're seated at a long table in the middle of the restaurant. The Japanese are debating over the items on the menu. The interpreter turns to me and asks if I know what an item – the dinner course – means.

"That's what comes with the *entreé* – a soup, a salad, and coffee or tea," I explain.

"Does that mean you have to order the meat separately?" He asks.

"Yes," I explain showing him an *entreé* that offers a small fillet of beef for $37. "Add this to the dinner course and you have the same meal, with the exception of an extra salad, that is on the special. This way the same basic meal costs a total of $57 instead of $85 for the special."

"Are you sure?" He questions.

"*Hontoo*, for sure," I reply.

The interpreter turns to the No. 1 Japanese at the table and begins to explain in Japanese what I have told him. The rest of the table is listening to the explanation but *honcho*-san doesn't seem to be impressed. No one else at the table is going to order until they see what the senior member of their group orders. He listens for a minute and then waves his hand across the top righthand side of the menu.

"We'll have this," he says in Japanese. Everyone else at the table nods in agreement. I am not asked what I want. I am going to get what the senior Japanese orders, just the same as those who are his juniors. He has ordered the most expensive item on the menu. In Japanese that means it is the best. No one with him will dare question his decision. They, too, are going to eat the best. I have no choice. I would be quite happy with a fish *entreé* that would cost only about $40, or the less expensive version of the fillet of beef.

Once the routine of ordering dinner is out of the way and a dozen large bottles of beer are set on the table, I order my orange juice so we can *kanpai* our way into dinner. I pour the glass of beer in friendship for my senior host. The interpreter seated to my right pours my glass of orange juice. The No. 2 Japanese, seated to the left of No. 1, proposes a toast to our health, we touch glasses and get down to the serious drinking and conversation.

"Can I ask you something personal?" The interpreter asks.

I notice that No. 2 Japanese, seated directly across the table from the interpreter, is tuned into what the interpreter is saying to me. "*Daijóobu*, sure," I reply.

"How much money do you make?" The interpreter asks.

I didn't expect the question so I pause a minute.

"I'm sorry," the interpreter continues. "I know that is a personal question, but could you tell me. Some of the others are curious."

"*Daijóobu*, but it is not an easy question to answer in Japanese because what I earn each year is determined by how good a job I do and not by how long I have worked for my company or in my job," I explain.

"Can you give me some idea?" He asks. He's getting a little antsy. Apparently he is under some pressure to get this information out of me. No. 2, while trying not to be obvious, is listening intently to the conversation between us. He understands English.

"Okay, let me put it this way," I begin. "In the worst of my last 10 years I made only $20,000. In the best I think I made $107,000. In any year, my income could fall into that range depending upon how well my business does."

The interpreter picks up a napkin and hands it to me with a pen. "Can you show me that? Write it down."

I write the range of income on the napkin. He studies it for a while, then turns to the other Japanese and, translating the figures to their *yen* equivalents, tells them.

"How do you live?" One of the Japanese asks me.

"Quite well, *domo* – thank you," I reply.

"You can live on that small an income?" Another Japanese asks.

"*Hai*, yes, my wife also works."

"Outside your home?" One of the Japanese asks. "What does she do?" Another chimes in. "How much does she make?" A third asks.

"She's a certified post-anathesiology nurse. She wakes the patient up and helps him recover from surgery when the doctors are done operating. She makes between ¥2.5 million and ¥5 million a year depending on how busy her hospital is." This time I do the translating to Japanese monetary terms.

There is a small discussion between three of the lower ranking Japanese at the end of the table.

"And you live well on this?" One finally asks.

"*Hai, so desu*. We live well. We own our own home. We own three cars. We own two boats. We live in one of the most expensive areas of Florida and really do not feel that we are lacking anything."

"You own a home?" One of the lower-ranking Japanese asks.

"*Hai*, we own our own home. It has a mortgage but that is the only money we owe personally. My business owes money and as long as it does I choose not to take much salary from it. But between the two of us my wife and I feel we live very well."

"How much of a mortgage do you have on your house?" One of the Japanese asks.

"About $70,000 - ¥7.5 million."

"How long do you have to pay it off? Five, seven years?"

"Right now it is an interest-only mortgage because I needed money to build my company. The payments are about $800 a month because the interest rate is high. I am thinking about refinancing it on a 15 or 30-year mortgage."

"Thirty years?" One of the Japanese asks.

"*Hai*, 30 years. That is a common mortgage repayment schedule in my country. I understand you now have 100-year mortgages in Japan."

"They are something new," the Japanese replies. "No one I know has one." He probably wouldn't know if his best friend had one. Japanese just do not discuss their personal finances but they seem to be having a good time prying into mine tonight.

"How much is your house worth?"

"About $150,000 – maybe ¥16 million or ¥17 million."

"Do you own the land it sits on?"

"*Hai*."

"For that small amount of money?"

"*Hai*. The land and the house are one unit in my country."

"How much land?"

"A little more than 600 square meters."

"*Aa sóo*," one of the Japanese seems to be taken back by the figure. "How big is your house?" he asks.

"About 150 square meters."

"*Aa sóo*, that is not a small house," one of the Japanese remarks.

"It is modest in my country," I explain.

"But the price is very low and you get much land with it," another Japanese says.

"Not really. The average cost of a home in the United States is between $100,000 and $120,000. In some areas of the country you can buy a 200-square meter house on a quarter acre lot for less than ¥10 million. Land values are much different than in Japan."

The soup arrives. I have been watching No. 2 out of the corner of my eye. He has been relatively quiet but has listened intently to everything that has been said. In most crowds one would not notice that he is Japanese. He is wearing a $1,000 dark silk suit. His hair is white and combed to hide a balding spot on the top. He wears heavy framed-in-black glasses that disguise any surgery marks that might show from a cosmetic overhaul he might have had to make his eyes rounder. I got a look at them up close earlier in the day when he had to take his glasses off to read a note someone handed him. I'll swear he's had eye surgery. He'll spend that kind of money to look more Occidental but he won't spring for bifocals. He's doing his best to look younger and more Western. He is definitely vain.

After a couple of slurps of soup he finally looks across the table at me. "I net $55,000 a month," he says.

I finish a spoon of my soup, look through the tops of my glasses at him and reply, "But I don't need $55,000 a month. If I netted that kind of money I could invest $52,000 or $53,000 of it. We live quite well on what we make. The cost of living in my country is not nearly as high as it is in yours."

"I don't think so..," he begins.

"Let me give you two examples. Your cameras and cars. We buy Japanese cameras and Japanese cars in the United States for half the price you pay for them here in Japan."

"Our taxes are high," he replies.

"Our taxes are high, too," I counter. "But high taxes can't account for the high price you pay domestically for products you sell us at much lower prices. Your country is dumping products on our markets to keep your export business alive. You are being charged the difference."

"That cannot be," the interpreter injects into the conversation. "If that were true we would read about it in our newspapers."

"Your government agencies control the economic information your newspapers get. You don't have a free press like we do," I reply, "You're not going to read about the high price you are paying at home to support exports that sell for much less in my country. It's not going to happen."

I finally get bailed out by the second course – the extra salad listed on the nightly special. It includes a slice of raw tuna, a slice of raw snapper, a small piece of smoked eel, and a few slices of raw vegetables. It's pretty, but hardly worth the extra $27 we're paying for it unless, of course, we're trying to impress someone with our wealth.

- Hai, so desu -

It four o'clock in the morning and the phone is ringing in my hotel room at the Oiso Prince Hotel down on the southern coast of Japan. I answer it. It is Wilkie Wilkerson from the Rotary district governor's office from our district in south Florida. They have had a call from Ron Pullman's family. His father is seriously ill – "May not make it." They want Ron to come home immediately.

It is either three or five in the afternoon in Florida. My mind does not work that fast at this time of morning here in Japan. I do, however, promise the Florida office that Pullman will be on a plane headed for the States before today is over.

Then I turn over and go back to sleep. For two reasons actually: (1) If I recall correctly Pullman once told me his father died two or three years ago so this is simply another chapter in his affairs of the heart, and (2) Shimizu will call me at eight in the morning and we will work this out. Shimizu calls me every other other morning at eight a.m. wherever we are. This is his morning to call. He's more dependable than clock work.

The phone rings me awake again. I look at the clock. It is 8:10 a.m. It is Shimizu. He tells me his Rotary district governor's office also received a call concerning Pullman's father's illness. We discuss how to best get Pullman home. Shimizu will check flights and make reservations. I will round up Pullman and his gear and take him to Tokyo Narita Airport.

No sooner does Shimizu hang up than the phone rings again. It is Pullman. He has gotten a call from his family and is in a rush to get home. I assure him that as soon as he can pack his bag I'll be ready to take him to the airport. It's a long train ride of something like a hundred miles to the airport with a change of trains in Yokohama.

But, it's Saturday and a good day for a ride. The rest of the crew has some slack time today – a visit to a local Shinto Shrine and "spring cleaning" parade in which they will wear the traditional robes of the shrine and help carry its portable shrine on their shoulders with one of the local Rotarians whom they have learned to enjoy this past month. After the shrine airing parade they have been invited to his house for a lobster cookout.

They'll be okay.

Shimizu calls back and has made reservations on a flight back to the States for Pullman. It leaves in early afternoon, so we have sufficient time to make it to Narita. I call Pullman, tell him to meet me in the lobby with his luggage and we will leave immediately for Narita.

The trip starts with a cab ride from the Oiso Prince to the local train station. There we board the line to Yokohama where we will change to the line to Narita. Pullman is anxious to get on his way. He isn't as upset about the news of his father's ill health as one would imagine under the circumstances. He is hyped about getting on a plane for home. I offer him my condolences concerning his father's condition. He puts on his most serious face and accepts them. I am convinced this is an affair of the heart, not a heart attack, but we play it out right down to Pullman's departure from Narita. He does 'fess up a couple of years later. The whole ploy was so he could get home to see the woman who would eventually become his wife.

With Pullman on the plane headed east I have the rest of the day to myself. I'm on my own again in Japan. There are a few things I would like to do. No. 1 is to return to Tokyo and see if I can locate a group of Americans that used to get together in the Roppongi area every Saturday after work.

I pull a Green Car ticket from the vending machine at the Narita train station and ride in style – one of only three occupants of the plush swivel seats in the Green Car; the other, a young woman and her paramour apparently returning from a honeymoon, occupying a single swivel easy chair with her in his lap and him freely exploring various parts of her body as she giggles her way toward Tokyo.

The ride from Narita to Tokyo takes nearly an hour, even on the express train. It is a pleasant ride, through open countryside that resembles the Japan that I saw in the 1950s. There is more modern farm machinery, but the open rice paddies and wood, thatched-roof farm houses are reminiscent of a Japan that is slowly disappearing. I swivel my Green Car easy chair around and watch Japan whiz by my window.

Nothing fascinates me quite as much as Tokyo Station. Especially its depth – layer upon layer of train tracks, subways, and connecting rail lines. Every train in Japan seems to come together here. When we arrive, I take the time to ride escalators up and down exploring the various levels of the station. There are at least a dozen. Tokyo has not only grown up, it has grown deeper over the years.

In front of the grand old Victorian station I catch a cab for Roppongi. We loop up around the Diet Building, jump on the freeway for a short run, and then back down to the major intersection of the international settlement. I stop in the Florida Cafe and ask directions to International House. They point me up the street away from Tokyo Tower. I begin walking. A couple blocks up the street I find myself walking along a high concrete wall. Another block or so and I find myself standing in front of a gate guarded by Japanese Ground Self- Defense Force personnel. I stop at the guard's box to ask them to give me directions to International House and discover that I am standing at a point where I used to check in to visit the Third Operations Group, a military intelligence outfit that I worked with nearly 40 years ago.

This has to be the old Hardy Barracks, the heart of the American occupation forces in Tokyo in the '40s and '50s. While talking to the Japanese guards I look up the tree-lined driveway and discover the old Third Ops building still stands just like it was when I used to report there. I had wondered what had happened to this former U.S. camp. Now I know. Instead of being open to the street it is hidden behind a concrete wall. The rest of Tokyo has grown up around it. Today it is headquarters for Japan's Defense Forces.

The directions I get for International House send me on down the street to the corner of the concrete wall and then around the corner deep into the heart of the area. The street begins winding down hill, around a corner, then back up another hill. Eventually I run into what I believe should be International House. There is a Mercedes parked out front with the motor running. An Occidental man comes out of the large stone building that I had assumed was International House. He heads for the Mercedes and I ask him if this is International House. It is not. Apparently it is a private school operated by the Catholic Church. He does not know where International House is.

By now I have become fascinated by the growth in layers of Japan. If I find International House, okay. If not, I am having a good time just walking the streets of the area and exploring how the Japanese have built one layer of their major city on top of another. Where there used to be rolling hills of mostly residential areas today there are layers of buildings, mostly businesses or high-rent apartment complexes where many of the international community live. They are literally stacked one on top of the other. Streets span valleys on concrete-arched bridges. More buildings are stuffed beneath the bridges and above them on land that is apparently man-made.

It reminds me of a visit with a Japanese writer and his family during my 1981 trip to Japan. We were out walking along the street that ran by his family's compound an hour's train ride out of Tokyo. We came to an intersection of a long-winding road that ran through the village. It was packed with relatively new homes. My Japanese host pointed up the street and said, "This used to be a quiet stream that ran by our property, but it was filled and made into a street."

The Japanese have a knack for doing that. They fill in rivers and streams or cover them over with highways and create new layers of land alongside them as they build ever upward. It is fascinating, reminding one of the man-made planets of Star Wars.

I walk up hills, down hills, up stairs, down stairs for couple of hours. In three weeks in Japan, walking constantly, my legs have strengthened tremendously. Even my fused right ankle is giving me less pain. My weak left knee that enables me to walk on my fused ankle without a limp most of the time seems to have strengthened. It has not given out involuntarily over the past couple of weeks. The Japanese, with all their walking, have a built-in conditioning program that far surpasses anything we have devised for maintaining physical fitness in the U.S.

I find myself standing at the corner of Akasaka Palace Grounds, more of the Imperial Household holdings a few miles west of the main Imperial Palace Grounds in the heart of Tokyo. Nearby I spot a subway station that I remember from my visit here in 1981. It was where I met a fellow American writer for a night on the town back then. I decide to grab a train back to Tokyo Central and tour the Ginza.

Back in Miami I have an old friend, George Butler, who is my personal accountant. I have known George since I returned from Japan and moved to Florida in 1958. We met working together at American Heritage in Jacksonville. George, back then, told me stories of how he was part of the first occupation forces in Japan.

I have looked for something for George since I arrived in Japan this time, but have not found anything that jumps out at me as a "George Thing." We have bags of gifts that have been showered on us by the Japanese. They will be taken back to the States and distributed to members of our Rotary club. Things like a knit Japanese baby's suit that will go to Scott Marr whose wife has just had their first child, a fine Japanese silk scarf that is tailor made for the classic looks of Gretchen Holland, lacquer ware, carvings, statues, books, prints and photos that will delight our Rotary members. We have so many gifts that I have two extra duffle bags I have purchased to transport them. Since they are gifts I won't have any trouble getting them through customs, but the airlines are going to soak me a couple hundred dollars per bag for the excess luggage. Nothing in any of this stuff seems appropriate for George.

If any one thing that George has ever told me about his time in Japan struck me as symbolic of the quick change made by the Japanese at the end of the war, it was of the march his outfit made into Tokyo – particularly down the Ginza. Along part of the march, to prevent any demonstrations by Japanese residents, Japanese troops stood along the parade route, their backs to the arriving American troops, facing their own people as a means of assuring order. It must have been a horrifying experience to be confronted by legions of foreign troops marching into your city as you stood in defeat.

Likewise, the American troops in that first occupying force knew they were walking a fine line. As always when the first troops arrive in a situation like this there are not enough to suppress any instant uprising of any magnitude. They are outnumbered from the start – cannon fodder to say the least – should all hell break loose.

Top that with the fact the Japanese had been taught by their military that American troops were barbarians who would rape their wives and daughters, loot their homes and carry off their livestock, and it wasn't a very pleasant situation to march into.

But somehow George and his fellow soldiers did, all remained relatively quiet, and the occupation of Japan got under way without any major incidents.

I wonder what it would be like to retrace George's steps.

Could I find part of the parade route through Tokyo he told me about? It took in the Ginza and Tokyo Station where the Japanese soldiers stacked their arms, boarded trains, and returned home as the American troops moved in to occupy the city. Both are still here.

My train pulls into Tokyo Station. I walk up eight flights of steps to the street level, emerging from the front of the grand old station just as the sun is preparing to set behind the towering buildings of downtown Tokyo. I walk across the street to the Post Office and turn down one of the major streets of the Marunouchi District, Tokyo's major financial district, home to the country's major banks and home to the "long-bond" traders, many of whose careers in recent years have been spent investing vast sums of Japanese capital in American government securities. A tremor or two here could eventually cause major shock waves in American financial markets.

It's not a long walk to the Ginza, a half dozen blocks at the most. I emerge in an area of Tokyo that has always seemed to me to be the center of the Japanese world. I think we used to refer to it as "Ginza and Z" back in the '50s. We Americans had difficulty with Japanese names so we redubbed the major streets in Tokyo with letter designations to help us find our way around the town. Ginza and Z Street was one of our landmarks.

Today this is the most expensive real estate in the world. Prices are astronomical. Japan is about the size of California yet all the real estate in Japan is currently valued at about three times that of all the real estate in the United States. Such high valuations are used to collateralize many of the massive nonperforming loans being held, and written up, by Japanese banks that appear to be teetering on the brink of financial disaster similar to the recent savings and loan debacle that cost American taxpayers $200-$300 billion to clean up.

Here, at this intersection, in the midst of the most expensive property in the world, lies 2,500 years of Japanese history inexplicably bound to whatever future this country has. It is forever intricately woven into the future of the rest of Asia, the U.S. and the entire world. This is the center of what has been and what is to come. All the readings of all the tea leaves in Japan have not yet revealed what the outcome will be. But just as unsure as George and his fellow soldiers were that day they trooped by this point before a local population that was equally as unsure of what was to come, out of this mixture of culture, high finance, and a growing global economy must come the understanding that will forge a peaceful and relatively prosperous future for all involved.

It ain't going to be easy.

In many ways we're still at opposite poles. Still in many ways we are walking hand in hand, albeit those hands often do not rub one another in any terms of endearment.

As I turn down Ginza police are just setting up barricades blocking off the street. They are carrying park benches out into the center of the street. At 7 p.m. on Saturday nights the heart of the Ginza is turned into a parkway where people can stroll in the street, sit on park benches amidst the towering office buildings and department stores, and revel in the prosperity that the bubble economy of the '80s brought them.

The bubble has not yet completely burst, but it is leaking badly and will get worse before it gets better, but tonight the people on the Ginza appear oblivious to it all. They are enjoying the fruit of their labors that have taken this country from ruin at the end of World War II and made it the world's second largest player in the global economy.

It is a grand sight to see. I walk right down the middle of the street retracing the steps that George and his friends took 48 years ago. Oh, how it has all changed, even from my first stroll down the Ginza 37 years ago. Other than the old clock building, everything else is new. The buildings, some with glass reflective fronts, could be the heart of London, New York, Paris, Berlin or any other major city of the world. The people, dressed in the latest Western fashions, could be any nationality. But, of course, underneath the facades they are pure Japanese.

I duck into a Burger King for a pure American meal – hamburger, french fries and a Coke. I sit at a table that looks out onto the Ginza and watch the Japanese stroll along the street and sit for spells on the park benches in the middle of it. Two young Japanese women sit down at the table next to me. They are dressed in the latest New York and Paris fashions – designer logos delicately woven into the fabrics of their dresses, cigarettes in hand, hamburgers on their tray. They are too busily engaged in conversation to eat. Their hamburgers remain unwrapped as they smoke their cigarettes and carry on a conversation that is too fast for me to follow. I do, however, pick up snippets about men as they chatter on endlessly. It is a conversation that could be taking place, and probably is, in a cafe in The Village in New York or along Newport Beach in California. How homogenized our younger generations have become. How distant they are from the past that has shaped us. How lucky they are to have been spared the horrors and agonies of war.

Can they make the peace last?

Can they keep the economic ball rolling that has brought Japan and other countries into the most prosperous of all times? The answer is in their hands, not ours.

Back on the street I find an empty bench sitting at an angle across the center line in the street and take a seat. The lights of the Ginza are beautiful tonight. There is no sign of the devastation that once existed. There is no sign of the pain and suffering that went on far too long in far too many lives on this very spot. There is no sign of the occupation forces that once marched down this street, nor no legacy that has been left by them. This is modern Japan, a world power, a significant and vital trading partner of the U.S. – the key link in east-west relations, more Western than any country in the East, more Eastern than any country in the West. Our futures, like it or not, are inexplicably interwoven.

A Japanese couple, enjoying their late middle age, strolls down the middle of the street apparently looking for an empty bench on which to spend a few enjoyable moments. I stand, bow to them, extend an arm towards the bench on which I have been setting and offer it to them. They bow in thanks and take the seat. We exchange not a word, but I notice we both smile. It is the subtlest of exchanges between two divergent cultures that have clashed in the past and undoubtedly will clash again in the future, but for a fleeting moment some magical harmony has existed between us.

I stand for a moment on the center line of the street, bow my head, and say a prayer of thanksgiving for what exists here today out of the chaos that was such a large part of my early life, for George and his friends who survived and for those on all sides who didn't. I ask the God of My Understanding to nurture the peace that exists between our two countries and to recognize and nurture the differences that exist between our cultures. Amen! So be it! That's the best I can find in Japan for my old friend George.

No visit on a Saturday night to this part of Japan would be complete without a stroll through Shimbashi, more particularly Shimbashi Alley – the heart of more partying by Americans in the two decades that followed World War II than probably any other single spot in the world. Shimbashi and "R&R" were synonymous to GIs. I leave the Ginza and stroll down to Shimbashi Station. It's another half dozen blocks away. The station, like all the railroad and subway stations in Tokyo, has grown tremendously over the years. I take a leisurely walk through it and exit on the side where the infamous Shimbashi Alley used to lure us into the pleasures of the night.

Shimbashi Alley is still there, the main street lit by a neon gateway. I have no idea where the old Club Bacchus was. No more idea than where my old six-foot-tall Japanese stripper friend, who for a ration book a month took care of all my needs when I was in town, might be today. I have no desire to reopen those doors of my past. They live best in memories hued by the passage of time. But, I would like one more look at Shimbashi Alley.

Actually the Alley is more than one street. It is three or four blocks wide and a half dozen or more long. Today it no longer caters to GIs, or even Americans for that matter. Foreigners in Tokyo spent their time in Roppongi, a far cry from the crude, unsophisticated clubs that made up Shimbashi Alley after World War II and Korea. But still today the Alley is packed with nightclubs. Barkers in dark suits, fedoras and sunglasses stand at the doors to the clubs doing their best to lure passing Japanese men into their establishments. Pictures of near-naked Oriental women – Phillipino ones seem to be the big lure – are plastered on placards around the doorways.

It is obvious the barkers don't want me to bother them. They make not one move towards me in an effort to solicit my business. Likewise, I have no truck to make with them. I recognize the sunglasses, the occasional missing tip from a little finger and tattoos exposed briefly from a shirt sleeve beneath the jackets of their dark business suites. These are the *Yakuza* – the Japanese mob, Mafia, La Cosa Nostra. The soldiers of which, by ancient tradition, garb themselves in full body tattoos and cut off the ends of their little fingers to show loyalty to their chieftains.

The *Yakuza* control much of the entertainment in Japan, guns – yes, despite a nationwide ban on personal firearms guns do exist in Japan – drugs, gambling and much of the black market. They are organized into families or clans much as our La Cosa Nostra, but instead of denying their existence they are accepted as part of the culture. They buy and sell politicians, control a huge army, literally hundreds of thousands, of soldiers that can be employed – both combatantly and non-combatantly – in the name of any cause they support at a minute's notice. They are accepted by the Japanese. All they do is not bad. Often, because they are more flexible, better organized and controlled, they are the first to respond with aid for the common citizen in natural disasters. They extract dearly from the local citizenry, yet they are the first to give back when it is needed. They operate with lightning speed in a culture that is slowed to a painful crawl by its massive bureaucracy.

One trick the *Yakuza* have that is uniquely Japanese and, to the best of my knowledge has never surfaced as a major role of American gangsters, is blackmailing corporate Japan. In exchange for promises from the various *Yakuza* leaders, Japanese corporations pay the mob vast sums not to disrupt their annual stockholder meetings. Not to pay such duty extracted by the *Yakuza* is tantamount to dismantling the corporation. It is an accepted cost of doing business by Japanese companies.

Today it is apparent the *Yakuza* control Shimbashi Alley.

They don't want me. I don't have any need for them. It is time to walk back to the station and catch a series of trains for the long ride back to Oiso. I have trampled the past enough for today. It has been a pleasant day by myself in Japan.

- Hai, so desu -

I have been to dinner with my friend Tracy Ellingson from Johnson Wax and am catching a late train from Hiratsuka back to our hotel on the coast in Oiso. When the train I am waiting on pulls into the station I see the rest of the team members riding in one of the cars. I join them.

They have been out on the town for an evening with a young Japanese man their age they have met and begun to share some of their spare time with.

"You know, Onishi-*san* is a frustrated person," Paul White says.

"Really," I reply. "Why?"

"He is stuck in the company he works for and can't decide whether or not to move on."

"What seems to be the problem?" I ask.

"He's got nearly a dozen years in and no where to go. If he moves to another company he has to start all over again – pay and all – under the Japanese hiring and seniority system," White says.

"What other options does he have?" I ask knowing the answer before Tim Wilson spits it out.

"He could go into business for himself, but that is not The Japanese Way. They have few entrepreneurs here and he is scared to take the first step," Tim offers.

"Just like England," I say, relating to an experience I had a dozen years ago in the United Kingdom.

I had once told a friend of mine, who was a director of Pan American World Airways back in its heyday, that my idea of a delightfully enjoyable weekend escape would be to fly to London, catch a train from Victoria Station out to Windsor, buy a *London Sunday Times* and set on a park bench and read it enjoying fish and chips from a local pub for dinner.

The friend apparently never forgot the remark. He called me one Monday in February 1981 and asked what I was doing the following Thursday.

"Nothing once I get the Sunday pages put together," I said. I was at the time Business and Economics Editor of the *Florida Times-Union* in Jacksonville. "What's up?" I asked.

"Pack your bags. You can go to Windsor Sunday and read the *Times*. I've got to take 40 travel agents over and back on a familiarization trip. Come on and join me," he said.

I took him up on it and caught hell from my editor when I got back for taking a trip that cost me less than the average consumer had to pay. I think I spent $140 on it out of my own pocket. My editor had no sense of humor when it came to things between old friends. I suppose I would have been all right had I not written a column about what I discovered in England, the same story I related to my friends on the train between Hiratsuka and Oiso.

After high tea at Grovesner Place, a trip to Harrod's where the travel agents on the fam trip picked up shopping bags with the Harrod's crest on them and later filled them with cheaper goodies from a nearby discount store, a tour through Hyde Park, and a Saturday night dinner complete with Beefeaters serving the courses at long tables in a dockside warehouse alongside the Thames River down beneath the Towers of London, I was ready to shag out of town.

My PanAm director friend waved me on. I rode the train up to Windsor and bought the *Sunday Times* just as I had promised myself. I sat on a park bench along the road outside the castle wall and spent the better part of the morning reading the *Times*. When I got hungry I walked across the street to a pub and ordered fish and chips, expecting the air to be filled with the smell of frying oil. Instead, the pub tender threw some fish and chips in a tray, stuck them in an overhead microwave oven, pushed the button, waited for the buzzer to go off, poured them onto a newspaper, rolled them up and handed them to me collecting a quid or two in the exchange.

I took my fish and chips to a table near the front window of the pub where I could watch the people stroll up and down the street in front of Windsor Castle and enjoyed my not-too-fresh meal of non-authentic English fish and chips.

At the table next to me were three men, about my age, having their daily lager. They were talking about the possibility of moving to Canada, or maybe the U.S. I couldn't help but butt in.

They were intrigued by what I did for a living and the fact that I had worked for several different newspapers and wire services in my career. They were more than willing to talk about the current economic conditions in England. More the economic stalemate they found themselves in than the overall economic conditions of the country, which to them from their perspective never seemed to change.

One was an accountant, another a dentist, and the third an engineer. All three, in their early 30s felt they had reached the peaks of their careers under England's rigid, albeit it faultingly denied today, class system and paternal employment attitudes. They were simply, under the British system, as far as they were ever going to go in their careers and were looking for a way out to better themselves.

The only way out for them was to leave the country, to find employment in a free market system not governed by class distinction or seniority employment rules. They had even considered becoming entrepreneurs and we discussed that at length. The more they talked about the possibilities of becoming their own bosses and guiding their own destinies, risks and all, the more enthusiastic they became.

"What's holding back Onishi-*san* from taking such a plunge, or leaving Japan to pursue his career elsewhere?" I ask the team members on the train between Hiratsuka and Oiso.

"He's just afraid to take the first step," was the reply.

Not taking the first step is being afraid of risking. Risking on the part of individuals is not something fostered by socialistic democracies whose economies are more controlled than the free market-based - countries like England and Japan. Taking individual risks smacks of non-conformity or lack of control by the governing entities, of the son being disrespectful of the father.

It probably is never going to happen in Onishi-*san's* life. It might in the lives of the three Englishmen I met in the pub back in Windsor, but the odds are probably that it will not happen to more than one out of the three. Cultural limitations seem to be the most subtle mental ball and chains we wear in life.

- Hai, so desu -

We're riding to another meeting aboard another fine Japanese bus with another group of Japanese Rotarians and my mind keeps drifting back to an article I read the other day in one of the Japanese English-language newspapers. It had to do with the chairman of a large Japanese company retiring and turning the reins of the business over to a "younger" man.

The retiring chairman was in his mid-80s. The "younger" man he turned the reins over to was only 67.

- Hai, so desu -

We're standing on a railway platform waiting for a train to Tokyo where the team is going to spend a rare evening off visiting the old black market area of Ueno, visiting the electronics district in Akihabara, and cruising the Ginza.

When I walk up to Tim he says, "They're doing it again. They're keeping copies of my faxes home."

"What happened?"

"I went to the desk and gave them a fax to send to the States. The clerk gave me a price. I gave her the money. Then she made a copy of the fax, faxed the original, gave it back to me and kept the copy. They're doing something with these. They're spying on us," Wilson said.

All I can do is shrug and think about how much it's going to cost our Japanese hosts tomorrow morning when Tim starts ordering melon slices for breakfast.

In Japan the school year starts in April, just when the Cherry blossoms are in full bloom.

This morning I was reading an article in one of the English language newspapers about how some children, whose mothers had decided to deviate from the norm, were being shunned by their classmates because they showed up for school with book bag-backpacks in bright colors. Black has always been the tradition. It goes well with the student's black school uniform.

Conformity is built in to the Japanese from Day One. Black school bags are what Japanese children have always carried to school. You don't just go out and buy a yellow or red one and expect to be accepted by your peers.

I'm looking out my hotel room, up the street towards an overpass that leads to the local railway station. A group of young school children – my guess is they are about the age of our fourth or fifth graders – is hiking up the stairs to the overhead entrance to the station. They have finished their traditional school day, had lunch, and are now headed for their *juku* – school after school – classes. They all carry black book bags.

- Hai, so desu -

Tracy Ellingson from Johnson Wax is a wonderful discovery. Not only is she a beautiful American woman who is fluent in both the Japanese language and Japanese culture far beyond where I can ever hope to get, she is a delightful person to be out on the town with when you have been immersed in the Japanese culture for nearly a month.

We are due to go to dinner together tonight. I take a train to Hiratsuka where she lives in the Lions Mansion apartments just a couple of blocks from the train station. We will eat in a local restaurant where she is friends with the master.

I arrive at her apartment and she lets me in. It is three rooms – a living/sleeping room, a kitchen/general purpose room, and a dressing/storage room off of which is a Western-style bathroom.

Altogether it is about 700-800 square feet, not small by Japanese standards. Although laid out in the Western tradition, the floors are covered with *tatami* mats and shoes are removed at the door.

Instead of sitting on a couch or in a chair in the main living/sleeping room, we sit on the floor and visit.

Tracy pays $750 a month for the apartment with her employer paying an equal amount. That helps explain why many large companies like Johnson Wax are locating their national headquarters in Japan farther and farther from the extremely high-rent districts of Tokyo and the Kanto Plain.

When I was in Japan in 1981 I spent some time with an American who worked in Tokyo for an international high-tech conglomerate. One of the things they had promised him if he would do a tour of duty in Japan was that they would provide him and his family with living space equal to that they enjoyed in California.

The result was that his company paid more than $7,000 a month for his apartment in Tokyo. With *yen* costing almost twice as much to buy today than in 1981 my house in Florida would rent for something like $14,000-$15,000 a month in Tokyo. For what Tracy is paying for her small apartment in Hiratsuka, not counting her employer's contribution, I could find her a small two- or three-bedroom, two-bath house in the Florida Keys. Not on the water at that price, of course, but within a couple hundred feet of it.

While I don't always agree with her interpretations, Tracy gives me great insights into the Japanese culture, why it is like it is. She lived here in her younger years when her father was stationed in the American military at Camp Zama. She has me fax to him in Madison, Wisconsin, a copy of the section in this book I wrote about my visit this trip to Zama. He enjoys it.

She also helps me with my limited Japanese. She is fun to be with. She knows the masters of the restaurants we visit and the shopkeepers along the way. She is brilliant and well read and shares her books with me.

She has been in Japan three years this time as an interpreter and English instructor for Johnson Wax. She is due to go back to the states in about a month and is feeling the upcoming losses of leaving behind the many friends she has made among the Japanese.

Tracy's sense of the Japanese culture, language and customs is impeccable. Spending an evening with her expanding my own knowledge of Japan is like taking a graduate course in Japanese sociology. It is one of the highlights of this trip. I learn a lot from her.

One thing that we are never able to connect on has to do with my search for people who might have been connected in some way to Japan's atomic programs during World War II. One of the things that drew us together was an early discussion I had with her on this topic. She knows a man who was, in some way, connected to those programs. A Japanese man.

At my begging, Tracy talked to the man about being privately interviewed by me in a way that would protect his identity. He initially agreed to the interview, but every time we attempt to set up a meeting he has some excuse to not follow through. I will leave Japan without ever talking to the man. I can't blame that on Tracy, she went out of her away, and against her adopted second culture, to try and set it up for me. It just didn't work out.

- Hai, so desu -

It's near the end of the trip. I'm sitting in an imitation Japanese *yakitori* shop in the basement of a Western-style hotel that's half way up the side of a mountain near Lake Hakone. I've just had a five-course steak dinner with the team (and our interpreter) in the hotel's restaurant where the bill for dinner looked like a down payment on Trump Center.

The interpreter isn't ready to turn in yet, so he asked me to stop for a drink with him. He orders a batch of *yakitori* – tasty barbecue chicken pieces on skewers – and a whiskey and water. I order a Coke.

He is working me for English slang lessons, reminding me that I know more Japanese than I let on. Halfway through his second whiskey and water and an explanation of "Put it where the sun don't shine," he changes the conversation.

"The director we had dinner with last night is frustrated with you," he says.

"Why this time?" I ask.

"Two of your people don't want to go to Hiroshima, and that is a trip you specifically asked for."

"*Hai, so desu.*"

"Why they no want to go? Why they not honor your contract with us to take them?"

"What contract?"

"In Japan when a man agrees to do something for another man it is like a contract," he says. "We do not have to sign a paper. We trust – what do you call it – a gentlemen's agreement."

"*Hai. so desu.* Do you really want to know why they don't feel they need to honor this agreement? Why I don't think they are required to honor this agreement?"

"Sure I want to know. We take it serious when we make an agreement with you," he said, draining the last drop from his drink.

I ordered another whiskey and water for him and a Coke for me.

"Before we came to Japan we sent the information about each of our team members to your people so they could set up the vocational exchange days that the Rotary Foundation suggested we get each week.

"Your people agreed that Wilson-*san* could visit a television studio, that Ramsay-*san* could work with the police, Bain-*san* could work with some food and beverage managers in Japanese hotels and resorts. But here it is almost four weeks into the trip and we haven't been given one vocational day like the plan for the trip said we would get each week.

"Some of my people got time off from their jobs because their bosses thought they would be learning something about the work they do by visiting Japan. But so far all we have had are factory tours and a couple of stops at fire stations. Anything we have done vocationally we have had to do on our own when we could find some free time.

"We haven't even gotten the day or so a week of free time the Rotary Foundation plan suggested we should be given. Only when I signed a contract to be responsible for my team members one day did we finally get a day off. You know that I know that making me sign a written contract was an intended insult. That's not The Japanese Way as you like to put it. You know that, and I know that."

"*Hai, so desu*. Why did you sign contract?"

I picked up a stick of *yakitori*. "You know *gaman*?" I asked.

"Yes, of course I know *gaman*. It is Japanese. It means to – how do you say it – endure," he said rolling the "r" in endure into an "l."

"My people had been on factory tours and 12 to 14-hour days for nearly two weeks with only one day off. They needed another day off. I signed the contract to get them a day off even though I knew it was an insult to me because I had disturbed the *wa* – made a wave – when I insisted they be given a day off. That's my *gaman*. I endured the insult."

I waved the *yakitori* stick at him. "You see this stick. If you had put a turd on it and told me if I ate it you would give my team members a day off, I would have eaten it. That's my *gaman*. I'll endure whatever shit you want to hand out to give my team members a chance to enjoy this trip. I've been here before. I know a little bit about Japan. I don't understand it always, but I know some of it."

"I think you know a lot more about Japan than you show. I know you can understand a lot more of our language than you speak. Sometimes you answer questions in Japanese before I interpret them.

But why are your team members upset if you know this is The Japanese Way?"

"Because they are not Japanese. They do not want to be Japanese. They do not like being treated like prisoners, like children, watched all the time. They don't like being lied to and spied on."

"What you mean lied to and spied on?"

"Remember the first two days when we were together, and some of my team members wanted the telephone and fax numbers of the hotels we would be staying at so they could give them to their people in America?"

"*Hai, so desu.*"

"Do you remember how hard it was for us to get those telephone numbers? How we were told at first it was too difficult?"

"*Hai, so desu.*"

"Do you know that I now know that you had those numbers all along, that every interpreter we have had, every hotel we have stayed at, every Rotary group that has hosted us, has had those numbers?"

His face reddened. "I don't know..." he started to say and then hesitated.

"The numbers were available from the start. But, they were all written in Japanese characters, not Roman, and we couldn't read them. We discovered them a couple of days ago when someone saw one of the Rotarians use the list to make a phone call. We're rarely allowed to see our daily schedule. They just herd us on a bus like cattle early in the morning and keep us going until after dinner. Sometimes they tell us what the schedule is. Sometimes our hosts just say, 'Let's go, *dozo*,' and point to the bus. But the schedule in Japanese and the piece of paper with all our names and pictures and all the phone numbers is always with someone who is with us."

"Yes, I believe, maybe..."

"So, my team members were lied to about the telephone numbers and they know they were lied to."

"*Hai, so desu.*"

"You want to hear the rest?"

"*Hai, so desu.*"

"Do you know that copies are made of our faxes and saved for someone and apparently a copy of the telephone numbers we call are kept for some reason?"

"What you mean?" His eyebrows arched.

We paused and lit our umpteenth cigarettes.

"My team members started telling me the first week that when they went to the hotel desk and sent a fax a copy was made of it, the fax was sent, and when they paid for it the original was returned to them but the copy was taken into the back room."

"What that mean?"

"It means that someone is keeping a copy of our private correspondence for some reason even when we are paying for it. The team members don't like that."

"I don't know...." he said.

"I don't know, either. At first I just thought like you. It is The Japanese Way. The team members don't like The Japanese Way. They think they are being spied on. They think Japanese treat them like children. They are frustrated, too."

"What can we do?"

"Not much now. The trip is almost over. We just do the Japanese thing and keep smiling. But if the Rotary Foundation ever asked me what I thought of the Group Study Exchange program with Japan I'd be inclined to tell them to forget about it. I don't think we should be wasting the money when the Japanese won't honor the program proposal Rotary made."

"You want I should tell the Japanese Rotary members?"

"You have to tell them. It's The Japanese Way. That's your job. You know, and I know that. But I'll make it easy for you if you want. I have not said anything to you here tonight that I wouldn't tell your Rotary governor. I'll write it down in my report of the trip, and maybe he will read it."

"Hai, *so desu*. Is that why your team members don't want to go to Hiroshima?"

"Part of it. But mostly they are just tired. The trip has worn them out. They want a couple of days to rest. I'm tired, too. I'm going to bed. You want me to pay the bill?"

"No. I sign. Rotary will pay."

- Hai, so desu -

Today is Sunday, April 18, and Shimizu is meeting us in Tokyo and taking us to a baseball game. Today we get our first look at the new Tokyo Dome – The Egg. The Egg is the city's ultra-modern domed baseball stadium, a far cry from the old park where I watched the Giants – Japan's national team and almost-annual national champions a la the New York Yankees – play in 1981.

We are to meet Shimizu at the corner of the Imperial Palace grounds in downtown Tokyo, not far from the massive Tokyo Central train station.

Outside the station we walk past the main Japanese Post Office, down the street, through the heart of the Tokyo financial district, to the Imperial Palace. Shimizu is waiting for us on the corner not far from the famous twin bridges that lead into the palace, the same bridges across which Emperor Hirohito passed on his way to the Daiichi Insurance Building across the street to denounce his deification to Gen. Douglas MacArthur shortly after the American occupation of Japan began in 1945.

Shimizu and I exchange pleasantries as he points out the Imperial Palace entrance. I mention that this is the spot where many Japanese officers came to commit ritual suicide when the war ended. He acknowledges the fact as we wave down a couple of taxis to head for the stadium.

April 18 has been a traumatic day in Japanese-American relations. Hopefully the game between the Nippon Ham Fighters and the Swallows that we are going to see today will be more pleasant.

As we stop in front of an American-style restaurant near the stadium for a pre-game lunch – we're not going to enjoy the traditional bento box lunch that we used to pick up on the way into the old stadium and eat in our seats as the game progressed - I mention to Shimizu that today is the 50th anniversary of the death of Admiral Isoroku Yamamoto, the great Japanese admiral who warned the Japanese early on that a prolonged war against the U.S. would not be a winning situation but still planned and carried out the bold strike against Pearl Harbor and later the calamity that occurred at Midway.

Shimizu acknowledges the fact and relates that Yamamoto is a great hero in Japan. I know. For the past two weeks the newspapers have been full of tributes to the admiral. In fact, there is a group of

people in his home province who have traveled to Bougainville and found a piece of the plane he was riding in when shot down and killed by American P-38s. They want to build a shrine-museum to the admiral whose spirit, like
all Japanese warriors who died in battle, is enshrined at Yakasuni Shrine not far from the Imperial Palace.

Yakasuni today has been downgraded – for public consumption – to a museum, but still to the Japanese it remains the most sacred spot in the country honoring their war dead all of whom are considered heros for having given their lives in the name of the Emperor.

What I don't mention to Shimizu, or any of the others, is that April 18 is also the day that Jimmy Doolittle and his raiders flew off the deck of the aircraft carrier *Hornet* 650 miles from Tokyo and delivered the first bombs dropped by Americans on the Japanese capital that up until that time was considered invincible by the Japanese military. The year was 1942 – 51 years ago.

The Doolittle Raid caused Yamamoto to change his plans and prepare the Imperial Fleet for a massive attack on Midway and later a possible invasion of Hawaii. The Midway attack resulted in the loss of four Japanese aircraft carriers, hundreds of pilots and planes, and gutted the punch of the Japanese Imperial Fleet, especially its air wings that Yamamoto had been first to realize were the trend in modern military power.

Both the Japanese disaster at Midway and Yamamoto's death were the result of American code breaking. Although the story was never told during the war and for many years afterward, American codebreakers and traffic analysts had unlocked the Japanese Navy codes early on and the results of their work tipped the American forces to the upcoming Midway attack and to Yamamoto's inspection tour of the southern Pacific
Japanese naval facilities.

The Japanese, including Yamamoto, never believed their codes could be broken. Even after several unexplainable incidents like Midway and Yamamoto's death, they arrogantly believed that a combination of their unique language and then-complicated encryption systems made their codes unbreakable. America's ability to read the Japanese most secret mail helped create a balance of power in the Pacific that was impossible to achieve materially in the early years of the war.

The third incident that occurred on April 18 is closer to home for me. It occurred in 1945 on the island of Ie Shima off Okinawa. Ernie Pyle, my favorite writer of all times, was killed by a Japanese sniper. Pyle, whose column appeared in the newspapers I carried during the war, was the subject of the first book I ever wrote, a small one for the American Legion on Okinawa back in the '50s. I traveled to the site where he was killed on Ie Shima and later to his grave in the Punch Bowl in Hawaii.

Later I read every one of the columns Pyle wrote during the war from microfiche files of the Ocala, Florida, *Star-Banner* when I was news editor there in the late 1960s. Still later I wrote a long feature story for the Associated Press on the 25th anniversary of Pyle's death in 1970. He is still the finest writer that ever graced the pages of an American newspaper in my estimation.

I order an American lunch of hamburger and french fries sitting at a table that gives me a view of the door in the corner of the building and the street beyond. If there were not a single sign in Japanese that I can see from where I sit the street scene outside could be any American suburban shopping area on a Sunday afternoon. If you don't dwell on the Oriental facial characteristics of the people going up and down the street outside nothing else betrays the fact they are not middle class Americans out for a Sunday afternoon shopping stroll.

After lunch we head for the stadium – The Egg. It is a beautiful structure. We have seats behind home plate on the second level. The Japanese cheering sections – actually people who arrive well before the game and practice their choreographed cheers while waving large vertical banners bearing good tidings for their team – are about to wrap up their practice.

This is Japanese baseball, not American baseball. There is a difference. Although Japanese baseball has its roots in American baseball and borrows the English words of the game to supplement the Japanese language, it is still Japanese baseball, not American baseball. It has evolved out of the Japanese culture, inheriting a public politeness not necessarily found in the American game. Its fans are polite. Its players are polite. Even its officials are polite.

At the beginning of each game the two teams take the field, line up opposite each other stretching out in a line from home plate to the pitcher's mound and bow politely to their opponents.

Japanese enjoy the art of the game as much, or more, than the competition. No slouching here. No jeering. No spitting tobacco juice on the umpire.

It always amazes me the pitchers can throw a complete game after the warm-up they go through. Often they pitch a 100 fast balls in preparation for a game, nearly a whole game worth of pitches. It's not particularly that they are trying to grove their fast ball, it's more that they are trying to grove their style. Perfection is the game. Not making a mistake and embarrassing one's self and one's teammates is paramount.

Winning is important in the league and eventually the national standings but not so much so that the Japanese for years played to a tie and went home if a night game went beyond the time that its spectators would have had to miss the last train home. I think they have changed that in recent years. Maybe the Japanese have built enough capsule hotels in their major cities to accommodate all the fans that miss the last train home on nights when baseball games go into extra innings.

Japanese baseball has its heroes, of course, but none like the great Yomiuri Giant Sadaharu Oh who smashed a career total of 868 homers – besting both Babe Ruth's and Hank Aaron's home-run records in U.S. baseball. Oh-*san*, whom I interviewed at a ball game in Tokyo's Korakuen Stadium in 1981, the year after he quit playing, will forever be a legend in Japanese baseball. Oh-*san* is so revered in Japan that no other Japanese player would consider besting his records. It is doubtful if any of them could since Oh-san batted with a compressed wood bat, something that is no longer used in Japanese baseball.

It's for certain that no American playing in the Japanese leagues – each Japanese team is allowed to have two American players on its roster – will ever break Oh-*san's* records or any other prominent Japanese baseball player's high marks. Japanese pitchers simply won't pitch to them when they get near a record.

I have even heard that Japanese baseball managers simply will not let them play if they are in a position to threaten an existing Japanese record.

The game is well under way. There are nearly 30 hits so far and only a half dozen runs. The third-base coach keeps holding up runners from second. Unlike American ball, where if there was even a slim chance to make it home the third-base coach would be waving the players by, in Japanese baseball the third base coach is always ultra conservative. He is not going to be blamed, nor is he going to let his players be blamed – both bringing great embarrassment to their team – by waving a player home unless there is an absolute chance the player can make it safely.

Japanese baseball is both beautiful and boring to watch. Even crowd watching wears thin. The spectators are all stamped out of the same mold – generally. Today there is an exception and he is sitting behind us a little drunk, I presume, jeering the umpires, the teams, the crowd and everyone else except the Emperor. The Japanese with us, without realizing that this is pretty normal behavior in an American baseball stadium, spend the better part of the afternoon apologizing for the man.

I get up and go up to the top level of the stadium behind where we are seated and get a hot dog and orange soda from the food booth. The tastelessness of the hot dog is a dead giveaway that this is Japan, but nothing else is any different than what I would find in Joe Robbie stadium at a Florida Marlins game in Miami.

Nature calls. I need to go to the rest room. Too many orange sodas. I locate one a short distance from the food booth and walk into the men's room where the urinals are lined up with the first few in view of the open rest room door just like in Tokyo Station.

I am standing at a urinal doing my thing when a woman walks in. She starts at the first urinal, steps up beside the man who is occupying it, looks down at his penis and says, "*Konnichiwa.*" After she takes a good look, she backs off and moves on to No. 2 and repeats the exercise. I am No. 4 in line.

Some things never change in Japan.
- Hai, so desu -

At dinner tonight with a group of Japanese Rotarians one of them asked me what I was most interested in concerning Japan.

My reply was current economics and the history of Japan's atomic program.

An older Japanese, down towards the end of the table – meaning he was towards the lower end of the pecking order in seniority among the group – asked me: "Do you know who Dr. Nishina was?"

Dr. Yoshio Nishina was an internationally recognized physicist who developed U-237, the uranium isotope that made nuclear fission easier. He headed up the Japanese atomic program during World War II.

"Yes," I replied. "Did you know him?"

"*Hai*," the man replied. "I knew him. I worked with him."

Several other Japanese jumped into the conversation at this point. The older man who knew Dr. Nishina was pushed aside conversationally. We talked about economics the rest of the evening.

After dinner I tried to work my way around to the older man, but others kept me occupied in conversation. The last time I saw him, he was walking out the door with a couple of the local Rotarians on each arm. I never ran across him again.

- Hai, so desu -

We're checking into a new hotel to visit a new group of Rotarians in a new city.

We have an interpreter who has been with us before. He's been to the States. He handles the language fairly well. We're standing in the lobby getting the usual check-in instructions.

"Rotary will pay for your rooms, laundry and meals. You will pay for your telephone and fax messages, okay?" The interpreter asks.

Tim Wilson has the video running so I decide maybe it's time to put some of this on his video tape. Few will believe it.

The conversation goes like this.

"Sure," I say, "but can we ask that they not make copies of our faxes to keep."

"What?" The interpreter asks.

"The hotels have been making copies of our faxes and keeping them for someone. They are our personal correspondence, and we don't think they are anyone else's business. Can we be assured they are not going to be copied?"

I know this is not going to get translated. The interpreter stands there smiling – The Japanese Way when the *wa* gets disturbed.

He turns and says something in Japanese. It has something to do with paying the telephone bills. I don't hear anything about making copies of our faxes.

The interpreter turns back to me. "We'll pay for your telephone calls and faxes, okay?"

"No, that's not the point. We've always paid for our telephone bills and faxes. We just want you to stop copying them, okay?"

"*Hai, so desu.*"

We finish checking in and then head for the elevator. The five of us on the team and the interpreter, who is spending the night at the hotel with us, are on the elevator.

"Hey, I'm sorry about the fuss over the telephone bills," I say to the interpreter, adding, "but just where do those copies of our faxes go?"

"Governor's office," he replies.

We're walking down the hall to our rooms. Tim Wilson looks at me and says, "I couldn't get the camera up fast enough in the crowded elevator. I'm sorry I missed recording that last conversation in the elevator."

- Hai, so desu -

It's our 25th day. Whitney Bain, Paul White, myself and three Japanese Rotarians are on the 7:03 a.m. local train winding its way from the mountain town of Hadano to Odawara where we will catch the 8:07 a.m. *Shinkansen* bullet train for Hiroshima. We're traveling light. I've brought only my portable computer and a light backpack with a change of clothes and have them tucked away at my feet as I sit on one of the bench-style
upholstered seats next to one of the train car doors.

"Hey, *honcho-san*," Bain yells from a seat a door down the car. "There's Fuji-*san*."

I look up from the spot I was staring at on the floor trying to grab a short nap – The Japanese Way on trains – across the car and out through one of the vertical glass windows on the door on the opposite side of the train. Sure enough, there was Mt. Fuji.

Just the peak of the 11,000-foot ancient volcanic mountain showed behind the nearby peaks of a 5,000-foot mountain range. But still, it was Fuji-*san* snow-covered and brilliant in the morning sun. My first full glance of Mt. Fuji after nearly a month in Japan.

Maybe things were beginning to look up for us. Fuji-*san* had always been a good sign. Legend is that if you don't catch a glimpse of Mt. Fuji while you're in Japan you will never return.

"Thanks, Whitney," I said, and then leaned back and stared at the mountain until the train shot into a tunnel and Fuji-*san* disappeared from view.

- Hai, so desu -

I woke up early this morning. Mainly because I went to bed early last night. After dinner at a Korean restaurant and a walk across town to our hotel near Hiroshima Station there was nothing left to do but read a two-week-old copy of Business Week – dated April 12 but containing stories announcing events that were going to happen April 3-5. I paid $6.25 for the magazine at the desk in the hotel lobby.

The first thing I noticed when I awoke was a sign on a building a hundred yards from my hotel window. It read in English "More To Few." I can't read the Japanese writing beneath the sign, nor do I recognize the company logo emblazoned above it. From outward appearances the 10-story building appears to be an office building. I have no idea what business takes place inside. I wonder if maybe it is not symbolic of Japan's "Winning is Everything" philosophy.

Yesterday after we toured the Hiroshima Peace Memorial Museum, I walked outside and found Shimizu-*san* sitting on a railing among the hundreds of pigeons in the park. As is often the case with him, it appeared that he was deep in thought.

As I approached him, Shimizu said, "It is good that you asked that your people could visit Hiroshima."

I thought for a moment I was going to get some comment from him similar to the one I got from a Japanese friend I was traveling with the last time I visited Hiroshima in 1981. That friend, who had written three books on Asian economics and with whom I had traveled across Japan for a couple of weeks, had said to me as we walked out of the museum, "How could you have done this to us?"

"Come to Hawaii with me next week, and I'll show you Pearl Harbor where you sent us the invitation," I had countered.

I knew Shimizu viewed World War II – The Great Pacific Conflict to Japanese – from a different perspective than my author friend. Instead of having been a child who survived the fire bombings of Tokyo and was moved to the country for the remainder of the war as the author had been, Shimizu, then 16 years old, had been a cadet at the Japanese Army's equivalent to West Point in the closing days of the war.

"Why do you say that?" I sat down beside him on the polished chrome railing of the short fence surrounding the green common area of the Peace Memorial Park. "I have neutral feelings about what took place here. How about you?"

"It is war, that is all," he said. "But it is good that younger people see what war can do."

"What did you think when you first heard about the bomb?" I asked.

"A professor at our school told us about it. And then he said under his breath, 'The war will end.'"

"Had you not been trained to fight on regardless? Were you not looking forward being graduated from the military academy and getting into the war? Wasn't that what your life was all about back then?"

"War is not good for anyone," Shimizu replied. "I was glad that the war ended."

What a change in attitude from the last time I visited the park. Then I had gotten up early one morning and gone for a walk from my hotel. As I walked across the park towards the monument that contains the names of all the Hiroshima victims who perished in the blast on Aug. 6, 1945, an elderly Japanese man sitting on a park bench 20 or 30 yards away looked at me and raised his right hand. He shot me a bird – gave me the finger, a genuine American gesture (the Japanese equivalent is rubbing the tip of one's thumb between the first and second finger on the same hand). I returned the remark in kind and bowed. The old man stood, placed his hands rigidly at his sides and returned the
bow. We smiled at each other quietly, turned and walked off in separate directions.

In my trips to Hiroshima I have never come here to celebrate the war or the use of the atomic bomb. I was 9 years old when the war ended. I had a paper route. I delivered the news of the bombing. I remember clearly the great celebration we had when the war ended. Then it was good news to us, but over the years, and after much study, I have grown to realize that the real news was not that an atomic bomb had been dropped on
Hiroshima and that the war might be coming to a close. The real news was that the world had been drastically changed. All lives had

been altered by the atomic age. The old ways – for everyone – were dead.

Over the years I have been a student of the history of the war. Documents more recently discovered and histories written in recent years say the atomic bombing of Hiroshima had little effect on the generals. They had a stranglehold on Japanese government and had pursued a dream of putting the four corners of the world under Japanese control for more than a decade; and they were hardly upset by the bombing of Hiroshima. The generals reasoned that the fire bombings of Tokyo had claimed far more lives than the atomic bombing of Hiroshima. They reasoned they had sustained the bigger losses from the fire bombings, and they could tolerate the smaller loss of life from the A-bomb as they prepared to defend the home islands. They reasoned, and probably rightfully so, that the U.S. had only a limited number of the big bombs. They had more than 70 million residents armed and ready to defend the mountainous and easily fortified homeland. The generals wanted to continue the war.

It took the entrance of Russia into the war in its final days and the intervention of Emperor Hirohito to end World War II. The emperor – the supreme power in Japan during the war – could have intervened earlier and stopped the devastation, but he did not. Despite the fact that his 63-year reign was called Showa – Enlightened Peace – Hirohito didn't object to the deification of his office that his generals had promoted in their effort to conquer the world. He had left his castle in Tokyo and toured the fire-bombed areas of Tokyo before we bombed Hiroshima. He certainly knew about his own country's atomic project and the Japanese military's plan to use the A-bomb on the American fleet when it moved in to invade the Japanese home islands.

Hirohito was no prince of peace. He was no god. He was a warlord. He survived war crime prosecution only because the U.S. wanted a swift end to hostilities. Emperor Hirohito had subscribed to the "More To Few" – winning is everything – philosophy of Japan.

As we arrive back at our hotel, Shimizu suggests a cup of coffee in the hotel restaurant. We talk about the changes in the city since our last visits to Hiroshima, mine 12 years ago, Shimizu's 20 years ago. The city has grown, modernized, and is at least twice the size it was when I last saw it.

Suddenly he raises his cup in a *kanpai*. "No more Hiroshimas."

I raise mine. "No more Pearl Harbors."

- Hai, so desu -

Emperor Akahito performed like a true Japanese today.

On Okinawa he turned the duty shovel of dirt to plant a symbolic tree and then offered his "condolences" to the Okinawans for the suffering they endured as a result of World War II.

No apology for the Japanese atrocities inflicted on Okinawans. No hint of guilt on behalf of the Japanese for the role they played in helping destroy Okinawa and Okinawans during the war. No apology for hoodwinking the U.S. into aiding Japan in subjugating the once-proud Ryukyuans to eternal Japanese domination.

Only condolences.

- Hai, so desu -

If I had to pick out the most beautiful incident of our whole trip it would be one that occurred near the end of our visit as we met for a farewell party with a group of Rotary clubs from the western reaches of the Kanagawa District in an inn in Hakone.

We gather in a large western-style meeting room. Aroundthe walls are tables of food of every description. As is the custom in all such meetings we stand in a circle around the room to raise our glasses in a *kanpai*. The leaders of the Japanese Rotary groups open the meeting by first singing the Japanese national anthem and then the American national anthem.

Once again, they overlook our man from the Bahamas, Whitney Bain. For some reason the Japanese cannot grasp that our group represents two countries – the U.S. and the Bahamas. The concept of a country that is made up of hundreds of islandsand a population of less than a quarter of a million people –fewer people than live in most Japanese small cities – does not seem to compute in the Japanese mind.

As the Japanese finish singing the U.S. national anthem I look over at Bain and ask if he can sing the Bahamian national anthem. He assures me he can. I thank our Japanese hosts for honoring us with their songs and tell them that we have one other country with us that we shall all pay tribute to. Then I ask Whitney to step into the center of the circle and sing the Bahamian national anthem.

He steps forward and, in a fine baritone voice, booms forth the Bahamian national anthem. It is absolutely beautiful – a black man with a fine *a cappello* voice standing in the middle of a circle of Orientals dotted with four white men from America – singing "God Save the Queen."

I realize when it was over that the Japanese probably still do not catch on. The Bahamas, though an independent nation now, have keep the British national song from their colonial days as their national anthem. The Japanese following the opening of their country by Commodore Perry and his black ships a century and a half ago had sent many a mission to England, including the young crown prince Hirohito, to study English ways. The Japanese patterned their once mighty Imperial Navy after the British model. They have probably heard "God Save the Queen" before and recognize it purely as a British anthem. They really have no frame of reference to understand that it, too, is the anthem of the now-independent Bahamian nation.

Oh well, we tried. Bain's rendition was absolutely beautiful.

- Hai, so desu -

Theories abound about the final outcome of the enormous balance of trade deficit being piled up by the United States as Japan continues to flood our markets with its goods and services.

Most are just that – theories. But once in a while one comes along that really rings a bell. That's the case with Michael Lewis's "How a Tokyo Earthquake Could Devastate Wall Street" reported initially in Manhattan, Inc. magazine in June 1989 and repeated in his 1991 book "The Money Culture."

We're on our way home. We have an hour or so to kill in Narita Airport after a six-hour bus ride covering the 75 miles of bumper-to-bumper freeway traffic from Fujisawa. I'm cruising the upstairs smoking lounge looking for something to read when I spot Lewis's book in a newsstand. It's the paperback version marked $6.99 on the cover. The book shop manager charges me ¥1240, or $11.59 for it at today's exchange rate, the lowest we've seen. The dollar has declined 5 percent against the yen since we arrived in Japan a month ago.

I find a seat and am reading the Table of Contents when I spot Lewis's "How a Tokyo Earthquake Could Devastate Wall Street" article. I go right to it.

From the first paragraph I am hooked. Lewis talked Manhattan, Inc. in to sending him to Japan to investigate the impact of earthquakes on the Japanese, and hence the world, economy. He ran into many of the same difficulties we have had in getting information from Japanese sources, but scored a couple of key interviews that produced sufficient information to write a topical article.

The substance of it is that there will be another big earthquake in Japan one of these days. For the past four centuries – in 1633, 1703, 1782, 1853, and 1923 – they have come with regularity on a 70-year cycle. The last one on Sept. 1, 1923 was totally devastating to the Tokyo area. It recorded 7.9 on the Richter Scale, swept the water out of Tokyo Bay and sent tidal waves back in that destroyed the entire coastline. Sixty thousand people died in one fire cyclone created by the quake as they sought refuge in a city park. The stock market collapsed, the banks failed, and only government intervention saved the insurance companies.

Today 30 million people live in Tokyo's earthquake zone. No one talks much about another giant earthquake, but they suffer endlessly through nearly a hundred tremors annually, most of which do not register more than a miserly 4 on the Richter Scale.

But, Lewis reports there are some among the Japanese who know the big one will hit once again. The disaster will be more awesome this time due to the millions more who live in the area and the concentration in Tokyo of the nation's government and financial centers.

When the next one hits, the stock markets will again be destroyed, communications with the outside world will be severed, banks will be closed, and the world will wait in silence. Investors will begin selling stocks they hold in Japanese companies, or companies doing business with the Japanese, because they fear the worse. Internationally markets will begin to slide.

A couple of weeks after the earthquake, when communications with the outside world have been re-established, brokers in New York, London and other world money centers will begin to get calls from Japanese who have invested billions upon billions in the *gaijin* markets. "What is the sell price of my XYZ stocks (bonds, Treasuries, etc.)?" will be the main question. The Japanese will start selling their foreign holdings to refinance the rebuilding of their country. The effect will be a torpedoing of international markets.

When the Japanese get their rebuilding under way, they will reopen their banks and stock markets. Since they have not suffered the internal losses that they have wrought on foreign markets, they will reopen at the levels near where they closed when the earthquake hit. Backed with that strength there will be a run of money from declining markets in the rest of the world to the climbing markets in Japan. Japan will have scored a major world economic victory.

Sound far fetched?

Lewis reports: "When foreign journalists stumble into MITI (Ministry of International Trade and Industry) and demand to know what will be done about Japan's trade surpluses, they sometimes get this strange answer: 'When the earthquake comes, the trade surplus will go away.'"

(Maybe there is something to this theory: A minor quake hit the Tokyo/Kanagawa area three weeks after we left, a major quake struck 500 miles to the northeast of Tokyo a month later, and five months after our visit a quake measuring over 8 on the Richter scale devastated Guam, six months later a major earthquake killed more than 20,000 people in India. And then there was the great Kobe earthquake. Could it have been the major one that was due on the 70-year cycle?)

- Hai, so desu -

A tarpon, the largest I have seen this morning, just rolled behind my bait. Will he take it? The only pull on the line is the live mullet bait swimming cross current in the shadows of Channel 5 Bridge connecting Craig Key with Long Key. I wait for the strike.

It's a beautiful sunny morning in the Florida Keys. I'm fishing a morning session of an invitational tarpon tournament sponsored by the Boy Scouts of America National High Adventure Sea Base on Lower Matecumbe Key. My guide is Capt. Matt Pribyl of Long Key. My fishing partner is Dr. Norman Baker, a retired heart surgeon from Columbus, Ohio, and director of this year's tournament that will raise about
$25,000 to support the Sea Base.

My inner clock is still struggling with the 13-hour time differential between the Florida Keys and Japan. It's 10 a.m. here, 11 p.m. in Japan. I'm five days home and still sleeping in strange stretches, still having that mid-afternoon sinking spell that comes with the jet lag accumulated between Tokyo and Miami.

But it's good to be home, good to be sitting on the poling platform of Matt's Hewe's Bonefisher trying to tempt a tarpon with a live mullet bait. I can't help but think how the Japanese wouldn't hesitate a minute to eat my bait, probably raw. They'd make a banquet out of the tarpon that we catch and release.

Sportfishing doesn't fit easily into their culture. The tarpon isn't going to take the bait this time. My mind isn't going to concentrate on my fishing. It wants to wander back over the past few weeks. What did I see, what did I learn in Japan this trip?

The Japanese remain secretive and deceitful by the standards of our society. Their culture is different, of course. Their society is closed. They do not understand us any better than we understand them. They play their cards close to the vest. Their ethnocentric attitude does not translate into anything we easily comprehend. They have never declared war and then attacked. They have always attacked and then declared war. Whether a military dictatorship as in the '30s and '40s or an economic dictatorship as now, the Japanese are not likely to change this inherent characteristic.

Tim Wilson turned out to be the team member who seemed to grasp most quickly the intricacies of Japanese-American relations. For a first-time visitor to Japan, his observations were astute. In a summary of the trip he prepared for Rotary International Wilson wrote:

"Japan and the United States are at war. A cold war, perhaps, but, where business is concerned, a war nonetheless.

"Americans tend to think of our first significant contact with Japan as coming 50 years ago at Pearl Harbor. The Japanese, however, see the war as beginning 140 years ago when American ships cruised into their harbors and demanded that the Japanese open their markets. They apparently acquiesced, but I don't see that the relationship has changed dramatically since then. They still see us as belligerent, and we still want them to open their markets.

"As early as that first contact, Japanese political philosophers observed that direct military confrontation with the United States would likely end in Japan's defeat, but that Japan would surely be victorious in a stealthily fought economic war. All of which is to say that the Japanese view the state of their entire economy as a matter of national security. They would no more allow American business people to see the inner workings
of their economy than an American arms contractor would have shown his Soviet counterpart how we made arms during the height of the Cold War."

Hai, so desu!

In March 2011 the much-dreaded big earthquake hit Japan. Not in Tokyo as many feared but farther north along the country's east coast. It was the mother of all earthquakes and tsunamis. It claimed tens of thousands of lives, reduced Japan's productive capacity by several fold and left a country already short of natural resources even more so. The following is a column I wrote for www.suddenlysenior.com pointing out another of the major problems to be faced in dealing with Japan's latest disaster.

Japan's Other Disaster – Seniors
By Dave Whitney

I don't know whether it was my second or third trip driving through Sendai, Japan, in the 1950s that I noticed two old Nipponese women sitting on a bench outside one of the local train stations.

I was an analyst for an Army Intelligence operation in Japan that had a detachment near the harbor in Sendai and visited the area from 1956 to 1958.

Sometimes only one of the old Japanese women, both always clad in cone-shaped straw hats, dark work shirts, black pants and black shoes, or boots, with a split between the big toe and the others, would be there in front of the station and sometimes she would be joined by the other.

I asked a young Japanese who worked for us about them one day and he told me this was not an uncommon sight in many areas of Japan. When elderly women were no longer capable of producing and became a burden on their family they often found a place like the local train station to spend their last days. There were no social safety nets to protect them. Many even went to their temple and received a blessing that was to insure them of a comfortable death even if it included suicide.

The suicide rate among seniors in Japan was extraordinarily high for many, many years until the Japanese government undertook several social programs to provide proper care for the elderly 20-25 years ago.

For most of its 2,500-year existence Japan had only about 5 percent of its population that was over 60-65 years old. Living conditions and wars had managed to keep the elderly population down. As late as the 1950s the life expectancy in Japan barely exceeded 50 years. In the last half-century it has risen to around 80 and the number of elderly in the Japan population has grown to between 20 and 25 percent of the total population.

Things were just getting comfortable for seniors in Japan, although the Japanese government was facing a financial disaster in funding its elderly programs, when the "Big One" hit – an earthquake like none ever seen before in this earthquake-prone country, followed by a tsunami that inundated and totally destroyed much of Nippon's northeast coast.

None of the area in which we had operations and worked around Sendai in the 1950s was left intact by the 9.0 quake that hit Japan. Top that off with a looming nuclear disaster in the region and nothing bodes well for the local population, especially the elderly.

One of the first photos to hit the Internet and news programs the morning the quake hit was one of several private planes trashed in the rubble of what had been the Sendai airport. I immediately recognized them as belonging to a friend of mine and shot an e-mail message off to him.

Luckily he and his wife, who is a flight attendant for a major airline that flies back and forth between Atlanta, Ga., and Tokyo, were in Atlanta at the time. But their daughter was on spring break visiting her aunt and grandmother in Sendai.

By the end of the first day the daughter was able to get a text message out to her parents in Atlanta that she was fine but her aunt and grandmother were missing. She was able the next day to find her aunt, who had made it to high ground before the tsunami hit, but the family spent a suspense-filled three more days before the grandmother was located. She, and a dozen of her friends, had made it to a nursing home and climbed above the floodwaters. When the tsunami waters subsided it was the only building left standing in the area. They spent three days in the building without food, water or heat in the freezing winter weather before they were discovered.

Not many were that lucky. The death toll from the quake and tsunami will reach the tens of thousands before they are done counting and many; many of them will be seniors.

An estimated half-million Japanese are existing in shelters, millions more in the streets as the Japanese struggle to get a new recovery going. There is a paucity of food and water plus deplorable sanitary conditions but in these beginning phases of the recovery things remain relatively orderly. There is no looting, the Japanese queue up in polite lines for what few supplies they can obtain.

Over the longer run, if roads and rails cannot be quickly repaired to get basic necessities to the people, there is no telling what will happen. It will be a test of whether or not cultural politeness can trump starvation and disease, notwithstanding whatever added burden the teetering nuclear disaster foists upon the quake survivors.

The Japanese are a very resourceful. I watched them recover from the disaster of World War II, but it was not without pain.

In the same Sendai area, at Camp Weir, and U.S. Army base in 1957, the high number of elderly women scavenging expended ammunition brass from the rifle range resulted in one being shot and killed by an American soldier, Spec. 3rd Class William Girard. Girard was convicted of the killing in a compromise settlement between the U.S. Army and the Japanese civilian government, a compromise not necessarily satisfactory to either party, but one that kicked off an international incident that held the headlines in both countries for many weeks.

On the day of the shooting there were upwards of 150 elderly Japanese scrounging for a living on the Camp Weir rifle range.

Japan has come a long way in providing better living conditions for its elderly since 1957, but at a cost that has severely crippled its economy a decade into a national economic stalemate.

Some estimates show that if the cost of providing for the elderly in Japan – on a par with the benefits those of us in the U.S. enjoy – cannot be brought down it could mean rising the retirement age in Japan to 77 providing only a three-year social safety net on the average for the elderly.

It's unimaginable. Japan's birthrate is not high enough to replace those in the work force who pay the taxes needed to support the elderly as more and more reach retirement age.

It's a disaster piled now upon three more disasters – a historic earthquake, followed by a historic tsunami over which hangs a major nuclear disaster.

The photos I am seeing of people huddling around open fires, cooking in the streets, and huddling together in makeshift shelters reminds me of that part of the Japanese recovery I witnessed in the 1950s.

The *Sankei Shimbun* is a daily newspaper in Japan published by the Sankei Shimbun Co., Ltd. It has the sixth highest circulation for a newspaper in Japan, and is considered as one of the five "national" newspapers. *Sankei Shimbun's* name literally means "Industrial and Economic Newspaper."

The close ties between the U.S. and Japan, regardless of their cultural differences, remain intact as witnessed by this commentary from the *Sankei Shimbun:*

SANKEI SHIMBUN COMMENTARY JUNE 11, 2011

On March 11, 2011, our country experienced an unprecedented national catastrophe. Japan was simultaneously hit by the biggest earthquake in our recorded history, the Great East Japan Earthquake, the subsequent giant tsunami, and multiple incidents related to the nuclear power plant. The number of victims and people unaccounted for are in the tens of thousands. This is the most serious state of emergency for Japan since the end of World War II sixty-six years ago. More than 130 countries and regions, many international organizations and NGOs have extended help in this gravest hour. Of all the governments offering aid, the United States of America provided Japan the most effective and extensive assistance on the ground.

Operation *Tomodachi* (Friend) in particular, a joint operation led by the U.S. forces stationed in Japan, began the day after the earthquake. Nineteen warships, including the nuclear-powered aircraft carrier *USS Ronald Reagan*, 140 aircraft, and approximately 18,000 troops were mobilized to aid Japan to lead the remarkable efforts of the recovery of Sendai airport, which became crucial to subsequent relief efforts, delivery of goods to the disaster victims, and search and rescue operations for the residents of the devastated areas. This joint operation took advantage of the bases in Okinawa, Yokosuka, Yokota, Misawa and other areas, and the members of the U.S. Army, Navy, Air Force and Marines stationed there. Coordination and cooperation with the Japan Self-Defense Forces (SDF) has also been successful. The relationship between the SDF and the U.S. Forces has never been closer before.

In addition, America has provided assistance and advice, such as sending special units trained in managing nuclear crises and

USAID rescue workers. These actions immensely fortified us with newfound strength and resolve, together with your messages of "We stand by the people of Japan," and "Japan is not alone." As we express our sincere gratitude to President Obama, the United States government and military, and the American people for their friendship and sense of solidarity, having so genuinely manifested the proverb of "a friend in need is a friend indeed," we take into our hearts the importance of the two nations' alliance. Thank you America.

Will the Japanese survive this latest disaster as they have the many in their past? Undoubtedly. Mainly due to the *gaman* that is unique to their ethnocentric culture.

-- Dave Whitney

www.ingramcontent.com/pod-product-compliance
Lightning Source LLC
Chambersburg PA
CBHW072130170526
45158CB00004BA/1314